Leonard Bernstein

AMERICAN ORIGINAL

Also by Burton Bernstein

The Grove (fiction)
The Lost Art (fiction)
The Sticks: A Profile of Essex County, New York
Thurber: A Biography
Look, Ma, I am Kool! And Other Casuals (fiction)
Sinai: The Great and Terrible Wilderness
Plane Crazy: A Celebration of Flying
Family Matters: Sam, Jennie, and the Kids

BURTON BERNSTEIN AND BARBARA B. HAWS

Leonard Bernstein

AMERICAN ORIGINAL

How a Modern Renaissance Man Transformed Music and the

World During His New York Philharmonic Years, 1943-1976

An Imprint of HarperCollinsPublishers

92
BERNSTEIN
c. 1

"Leonard Bernstein's Separate Peace With Berlin" originally appeared, in different form, in *Esquire* Magazine, October, 1961. Afterword originally appeared in *Family Matters: Sam, Jennie, and the Kids* © 1982, 2000 by Burton Bernstein.

Manuscript of "Something's Coming,"from *West Side Story* by Leonard Bernstein and Stephen Sondheim, from the Leonard Bernstein Collection in the Music Division of the Library of Congress. Reproduced by permission of Leonard Bernstein Music Publishing Company LLC.

"The Leonard Bernstein Score Collection/New York Philharmonic Archives," Bernstein's markings reproduced by permission of The Leonard Bernstein Office, Inc.

First edition

Madeline Rogers and Barbara B. Haws, Editors
Rebecca Winzenried, Ann Stedman and Nan Wakefield, Assistant Editors
Barbara B. Haws and Richard Wandel, Photo Editors with the assistance of Elizabeth Goetz

Designed by Carole Erger-Fass, BugDesign

This publication has been supported by **Furthermore: a program of the J.M. Kaplan Fund**

Library of Congress Cataloging-in-Publication Data

Bernstein, Burton.
Leonard Bernstein/Burton Bernstein and Barbara B. Haws. —1st ed.
p. cm.
Includes index.
ISBN 978-0-06-153786-8
1. Bernstein, Leonard, 1918-1990. 2. Musicians—United States—Biography.
I. Haws, Barbara B. II. Title.

ML410.B566B47 2008
780.92–dc22
[B]

2008013702

08 09 10 11 12   /QW 10 9 8 7 6 5 4 3 2 1

For Lenny, of course, and Shirley and Felicia, too.
—*B.B.*

For Eliot and Bill
—*B.B.H.*

contents

ix   **Introduction** *by Barbara B. Haws*

3   **Foreword** *by Burton Bernstein*

11   **Helluva Town: My New York 1943 to 1976** *by Alan Rich*
16   A Brother's Recollection: On the Town

35   **Leonard Bernstein: Humanitarian and Social Activist** *by Paul Boyer*
54   A Brother's Recollection: Paying the Price

59   **Bernstein's Musicals: Reflections of Their Time** *by Carol J. Oja*
76   A Brother's Recollection: Easy Laughter of a Grand Wit

85   **Leonard Bernstein and Television: Envisioning a Higher Purpose** *by Tim Page*
92   A Brother's Recollection: The Maestro's New Medium

102   **Leonard Bernstein's Separate Peace with Berlin** *by Burton Bernstein*

117   **An Idealist Abroad** *by Jonathan Rosenberg*

135   **As Music Director: A Quest for Meaning and Identity** *by Joseph Horowitz*
152   A Brother's Recollection: Charismatic Teacher, Consummate Performer

157   **On the Podium: Intellect and Ecstasy** *by Bill McGlaughlin*

173   **Bernstein and Mahler: Channeling a Prophet** *by James M. Keller*
178   A Brother's Recollection: Mahler's Muse Tempts Another

193   **An American Voice** *by John Adams*

207   **Afterword** *by Burton Bernstein*

210   **Chronology**

214   **Contributors' Bios**

216   **Illustration Credits, Acknowledgements**

218   **Index**

Reconsidering Leonard Bernstein

BY BARBARA B. HAWS

another book on Leonard Bernstein?
Aren't there enough already? After all, Lenny was the most photographed, televised, documented, scrutinized, analyzed, criticized, and finally lionized and celebrated artist of the second half of the twentieth century. What more could there be to say?

Ninety years have passed since Bernstein was born, nearly twenty years since he died, and fifty years since he was appointed Music Director of America's oldest symphony orchestra, the New York Philharmonic. Time and cultural distance provide the opportunity to explore not only the unseen connections within Bernstein's own life and work, but between him and the time and place in which he lived.

The intent of the book is not simply to provide another telling of the Bernstein story but to place him in a particular context and to explore the synergies that arose between the person and that context. And to reinforce or contrast that outsider's view, Burton, Lenny's brother, provides the personal, firsthand accounts. For the most part, the context here is New York City between 1943 and 1976 and to a certain and crucial degree the groundbreaking social movements and political actions in the world at large during that time.

Why These Years? Why New York City?

The year 1943 marks Bernstein's well-known conducting debut with the New York Philharmonic, a concert that was heard live, coast-to-coast, which put him on the front page of *The New York Times*. Although the concert was a truly impressive career start, no one would have predicted that fifteen years later a forty-year-old American would be appointed Music Director of the New York Philharmonic—

*Just another New Yorker…
Leonard Bernstein on
Seventh Avenue outside
Carnegie Hall, 1956.*

which up to that time had been held by Europeans, most of a fairly advanced age.

At around this time, Bernstein burst onto the Broadway scene with a spectacularly successful show, *On the Town*. Thus began a long association with that unique American institution, the musical, and with a group of collaborators that included writers Betty Comden and Adolph Greene and choreographer Jerome Robbins; that eventually led to his teaming up with others that included Stephen Sondheim and Arthur Laurents and *West Side Story* in 1957.

In 1943, one could begin to see the end of World War II and discern the political, economic, and military factors that would make the United States a world power and New York City the cultural Capital of the World—the center of wealth, entertainment, television, recording, art, baseball—the most exciting place where anyone could hope to live, the place everyone outside looked to. I would argue that it was due to New York as the cultural capital that Bernstein became a household name even to people who only dreamed of visiting the city, who never set foot in a concert hall or went to a production on the Great White Way.

Being the New Yorker. On location for a photo shoot on a Manhattan roof with the Empire State Building as a backdrop.

The end point of our story, 1976, marks the nadir of the city; its breathtaking fall from grace—a time of white flight, subways filled with graffiti and muggers, beautiful parks fallen into decrepitude, tourists too afraid to visit, politicians booed just for being politicians, and the elimination of arts education in the public schools. As a practical matter New York City went bankrupt, because Wall Street stopped financing the city's deficits. The *Daily News* captured Washington's antipathy for the city's crisis in its now-famous 1975 headline, "Ford to City: Drop Dead." Reflecting not only the city's malaise but the nation's, under Nixon and Agnew, Bernstein wrote his last politically relevant musical theater piece, *1600 Pennsylvania Avenue*, which quickly succumbed under its own weight and the critics' brutal objections. Finally in 1976, as the United States celebrated its 200th birthday, Bernstein took his Philharmonic on tour to Europe for the last time, also in celebration of his country's Bicentennial, with music exclusively by American composers.

The coming together of Bernstein and New York City, with the Philharmonic serving as his primary vehicle of expression, gave rise to extraordinary public scrutiny. And even though he invited the scrutiny and most of the time seemed to relish it, New York was the place that rendered his smallest utterances newsworthy, his grandest gestures second-guessed, and all of his activities, larger than life.

A Multi-Faceted Interpretation

We invited nine writers to take on specific topics. None of them had particularly close or personal relationships with Bernstein, which provided the "distance" that is

Finding his way backstage at the Herodus Atticus *amphitheater, Athens, Greece, 1959.*

useful in hindsight analysis.

The chapters take us from the general to the specific and back to the general, revealing intriguing connections through varied interpretations of the same events and activities. These different viewpoints create a rich and provocative picture of the man and his time.

What was it like to live in the city during Bernstein's time? Remarkably, no comprehensive history of New York City for these years exists. So we view the transforming metropolis through something of an "Everyman" history. To paraphrase the well-known tagline of a 1950s television show, "There are eight million stories in the *Naked City* and this is one of them." Our Everyman is music critic Alan Rich, who provides his own personal account of arriving, finding that place to live, getting that dream job, recounting favorite eateries, encountering the famous, living through history-making events, and becoming one of the city's stories. Of course,

*Making friends.
Russian maids at
Bernstein's Moscow
hotel wish him a
Happy Birthday.*

Rich is more than an "Everyman." He rose to be chief music critic of the *Herald Tribune* and later a writer for the early issues of *New York* magazine, which became a significant antagonist in the Bernstein Story. But his experience does have a universal quality, since few who arrive in New York are exempt from the extreme challenges or exhilarating pleasures posed by becoming one with the city.

If there was a single universal idea that informed all of Bernstein's work and actions, it was his hope and vision that the world could be a better place. This made him a lightning rod for a diversity of opinions: that he was naïve and out of touch; that he was a threatening figure on the radical fringe; that, with his prominence, he could have done much more to right social wrongs. The American historian Paul Boyer weaves together a remarkable account of Bernstein's lifelong social and political involvements, overlaying them on the broader cultural movements of the time: growing up in Roosevelt's America; barely escaping the "red scares" and McCarthy witch hunts; attempting to enlarge the opportunities of race and gender through the Philharmonic; participating tirelessly in the anti-Vietnam War movement; and becoming disillusioned with the Presidential administrations and the Military

Industrial Complex. That he was both an agent of change and a person trapped by his own beliefs was made painfully clear when, within a five-month period in the winter of 1969, he defended his leadership before a Human Rights Commission against charges of racial discrimination at the Philharmonic and in January 1970 had to fend off virulent criticism from influential New Yorkers for raising money for the radical Black Panthers' legal-defense fund. At his core, whether he got it right or not, Bernstein's heartfelt belief that the world could be a better place animated nearly all of his actions.

That credo showed in his compositions—particularly his Broadway shows. As musicologist Carol Oja points out, Bernstein's early musical-theater works (1940s and 1950s) capture the dichotomy of an era whose veneer of optimism and prosperity covered over simmering issues of war, subterfuge, cynicism, urban decay, and racism, which would explode and dominate the cultural and political landscape of the 1960s. Revealing how small a divide existed between the world of Broadway and the "serious" music world at this time—how artists, choreographers, and dancers then easily "crossed over"—makes the appointment of Bernstein, the star of Broadway, as Music Director of the Philharmonic, less surprising than one might think.

Bernstein's embrace of television catapulted him onto the largest stage ever enjoyed by a classical musician. Even though he had appeared several times on national television during the early 1950s in the award-winning *Omnibus* programs—deconstructing Beethoven's Fifth Symphony and celebrating the music of J.S. Bach, for instance—the lion's share of Bernstein's television work at this time was with the Philharmonic. Music critic Tim Page demonstrates how Bernstein and television were a perfect match. He had the message that the medium desperately needed to fulfill its promise as a provider of quality cultural programming. With the new industry headquartered in New York City, Bernstein was in the right place at the right time to make a difference—not only to teach music but to convey his particular world view of universal understanding through music.

Feeding a circus elephant while visiting Kiev with the Philharmonic. Bernstein could never resist making friends with nearly any animal that crossed his path.

Bernstein put that belief in music as a universal language into action with an active—even hyperactive—schedule of international touring. American historian Jonathan Rosenberg, who has been working on a broad study of international politics and classical music, focuses on three groundbreaking Philharmonic tours, to Latin America, the Soviet Union, and Berlin. As an "Idealist Abroad," Bernstein used music, television, and the Orchestra to convey again his own hope for a better world. The irony, of course, is that even as the U.S. State Department was anointing him as its representative for American culture abroad, J. Edgar Hoover and the FBI had Bernstein under surveillance for possible anti-government or Communist associations.

In an extensive piece, Burton Bernstein recounts how he accompanied the Philharmonic on its landmark 1960 tour to Berlin. His delightful personal account captures the many details of life on the road with a big band, but more importantly, he reveals a very personal side of Lenny that only a brother knows.

Of course, this multi-faceted man was best known and celebrated as a musician. In three essays, his unique qualities as a conductor, musical thinker, and champion are explored. The music historian Joseph Horowitz demonstrates what a necessary corrective Leonard Bernstein was in the Philharmonic's history by examining the music he programmed with the Orchestra. He uncovers a fascinating thread in Bernstein's Philharmonic programs, revealing the conductor's search for his own identity; what it meant to be an American and, in particular, an American musician. Coincidently, as the chaos and confusion of the radical sixties seem to overwhelm, we see a change in Bernstein's programming—a turning away from the new and contemporary toward a deeper exploration of the classics. Opportunities in Europe were not to be missed, but life in New York City had become harsh and Bernstein found himself out of step with the contemporary American music scene.

Bernstein's passion on the podium is perhaps the most indelible image he has left us. By evaluating Bernstein's marked conducting scores in the Philharmonic Archives and analyzing his televised performances, conductor, composer, and radio personality Bill McGlaughlin brings together the ephemeral with the workaday to understand better Bernstein's hold over the popular imagination and his remarkable rapport with musicians. Melding the flamboyant public display with the private meticulousness seen in the scores provides new insights, and confirms long-held assumptions about what Bernstein was hoping to achieve.

Bernstein's relationship to the music of Gustav Mahler flowered during his Philharmonic years, so much so that, to this day, no conductor is more closely identified with Mahler. As feature writer and program annotator James Keller rightfully asserts, only part of this association can be attributed to Bernstein's numerous performances and recordings. His true distinction was to take Mahler beyond the music-loving public, making the composer an indelible part of the culturally defining tragedies of the 1960s through the performance of Mahler's Second Symphony on the nationally televised JFK memorial program. Keller shows that the enduring connection between Bernstein and Mahler in the American consciousness was created by the convergence of television, new recording technology, New York City, inspirational interpretations, and relevance—

articulated by Bernstein—of a long dead composer to current events of the time.

American composer John Adams writes about coming of age with a new type of musical inspiration, an unabashed, vividly flamboyant personality who could do everything from play jazz to baseball—the quintessential American. The sheer volume of Bernstein's activities were impressive, yet predictable since Americans expected their cultural heroes to be proficient in both high and low culture. But the "serious" music scene outpaced Bernstein, and with the composing world turning to atonality and minimalism his natural lyrical and romantic inclinations were considered not up to the times. The group of American composers he was so fond of championing in the 1950s and 1960s was hardly added to in later years, and his later composing never found the success of his earlier works.

Throughout, essential connective tissue is supplied by Burton Bernstein, Lenny's brother and retired long-time staff writer for *The New Yorker*. While the other authors provide distance and perspective, Burton takes us in close and supplies insightful personal stories that reflect on many of the topics in the book:

With his family, Nina, Jamie, Felicia, and Alex on their Park Avenue balcony, 1970.

Lenny's encounters with Herbert von Karajan and Alma Mahler; a visit to Puerto Rico that inspired a famous riff from *West Side Story*; the already mentioned Berlin junket; the painful aftermath of the Black Panther episode; and simply what it was like to be Leonard Bernstein's brother.

What the Archives Tell Us

For nearly 25 years I have had the remarkable privilege to work with the Philharmonic's archival collections. They are packed with Leonard Bernsteiniana: his photos, writings, memos, scripts, reviews, clippings, programs, jottings, poems, batons, concerts, interviews, films and his conducting scores, which came to us only after his death. Leonard Bernstein conducted the New York Philharmonic 1,247 times, more than any other conductor before or since. No matter what other orchestra he was conducting and no matter who was conducting the Philharmonic, Bernstein always thought of the New Yorkers as his own personal orchestra. He was possessive about it, and without a doubt they were his second family. That deep and significant relationship and the ways he used it to carry out his personal mission inspired this book. Not just the magnitude and depth, but the sheer joy, thoughtfulness, and, at times, despair—all captured in the Philharmonic's archival collections—are what suggested the topics covered in these pages.

As a historian working in a music institution, I have been particularly interested in how the world at large, with all its complexities, issues, politics, and controversies, are played out on the stage of the Orchestra. But, of course, the Orchestra represents the city, and its people use it as a place of solace in times of despair or to rally the troops in times of war. Whether it was Arturo Toscanini at the old Madison Square Garden leading the Philharmonic in a rousing Wagner concert to raise money for World War II war bonds or Kurt Masur's unforgettable Brahms *Ein Deutsches Requiem* just days after 9/11, or Lorin Maazel leading a contemplative performance of John Adams' *On The Transmigration of Souls* commissioned in memory of victims of the World Trade Center disaster, the American symphony orchestra time and time again has played an important defining role in American society simply by its sheer size, genius, and ability to inspire. More than most, Leonard Bernstein understood this—the power of the symphony orchestra and its music to be a relevant player in society. What I hope you will find here are some new insights into how Bernstein, his music-making, and his world merged and collided. It's hardly comprehensive. What's particularly interesting when attempting to understand a complicated and intriguing figure like Leonard Bernstein is that when you start to scratch the surface, more questions and unrealized possibilities keep rising to the top.

Part of New York City's pride is its resiliency; its ability to self-destruct, bounce back, and reach ever new heights. Lenny was like the city; his star rose to amazing heights only to experience a painful dimming, and yet, he persevered, becoming one of music's most beloved and revered statesman. The city goes on, reinventing itself; although Lenny was mortal his remarkable transformation of America's music scene is unquestioned and forever.

With members of his "second family," from the New York Philharmonic's brass section, (from left) Aubrey Facenda, Ranier De Intinis, John Carabella, and Jerome Ashby.

To the
New York Philharmonic-
Symphony Society
in deepest
gratitude & for
giving me my
great opportunity —

Sincerely,
Leonard Bernstein
NYC- 2/4/44

foreword

BY BURTON BERNSTEIN

t the tender age of eleven summers,
I found myself sitting uncomfortably in the plush, velvety conductor's box high
above the stage of Carnegie Hall between my far more uncomfortable parents,
Samuel and Jennie Bernstein, formerly of Ukrainian shtetls and currently of
Sharon, Massachusetts. It was the Sunday afternoon of November 14, 1943,
and—incredibly, against all odds—Sam's and Jennie's first-born son, twenty-five-
year-old Lenny, was about to conduct the New York Philharmonic in an entire concert before a packed house of sophisticated concert-goers and to be radio-broadcast
all over the war-ravaged world. None of us had ever set foot in Carnegie Hall
before. The only one missing to share our nervous excitement was my parents'
middle child, Shirley, who couldn't make the trip to New York City on such short
notice from Mount Holyoke College.

The reason we had found ourselves in this most unlikely place and situation has long since become a signal part of American cultural legend:
to wit, Bruno Walter, the renowned German-born maestro, was much
too ill with influenza to take the podium that Sunday, and our Lenny,
just recently appointed assistant conductor of the Philharmonic (ordi-
narily a glorified gofer job back then), had to fill in with practically
no warning. To make matters even more difficult for poor Lenny and
the disconcerted musicians, the Sunday's program was a rather knot-
ty one—Schumann's *Manfred Overture*, a modern piece by Miklós
Rózsa, Strauss' *Don Quixote,* and Wagner's *Die Meistersinger*
Prelude. Tough going for even a healthy Bruno Walter; nigh-
impossible going, it would seem, for young Lenny Bernstein,
freshly out of Harvard, the Curtis Institute of Music, and some
discouraging musicianly jobs in Boston and New York.

THE PHILHARMONIC-SYMPHONY SOCIETY
OF NEW YORK
1842   1878
CONSOLIDATED 1928
ARTUR RODZINSKI, Musical Director
1943   ONE HUNDRED SECOND SEASON   1944

CARNEGIE HALL
SUNDAY AFTERNOON, NOVEMBER 14, 1943, AT 3:00
Broadcast over the Coast-to-coast Network
of the Columbia Broadcasting System
4025th Concert

Under the Direction of
BRUNO WALTER
LEONARD BERNSTEIN

PROGRAM

SCHUMANN   Overture to "Manfred," Op. 115

MIKLOS ROZSA   Theme, Variations and Finale, Op. 13

INTERMISSION

STRAUSS   "Don Quixote" (Introduction, Theme with
Variations and Finale) ; Fantastic Variations on
a Theme of Knightly Character, Op. 35
Solo 'Cello: JOSEPH SCHUSTER
Solo Viola: WILLIAM

ARTHUR JUDSON

Lenny with his mother, Jennie, and father, Sam, shortly after his Philharmonic debut.

My parents and I were in New York that weekend for an entirely different Lenny event—a song cycle he had written was to be premiered by the mezzo-soprano Jennie Tourel at a recital in Town Hall the night before, a pretty big deal for a budding composer. Lenny's folks and kid brother were due to leave for Sharon the next day. Obviously, when Lenny told us the momentous news, we stayed for another day and night in order to witness this impossible Hollywood fiction in Carnegie Hall at three o'clock Sunday afternoon.

In the cavernous hall, once the orchestra had done its cacophonous tuning and settled down along with the audience, a hulking bear-like man walked out on the stage and an awful silence fell. Who died? everyone seemed to be thinking. The Philharmonic's Associate Manager, Bruno Zirato, announced in his gruff Italian accent that Maestro Walter would not conduct that day's concert due to illness—but, he added, everyone present and listening on the radio was going "to witness the debut of a full-fledged conductor who was born, educated, and trained in this country." Incredible, unbelievable. Some people shook their heads and whispered to each other. Some—unfairly, I thought—got up and left the hall. Then Lenny came out of the wings, looking scarily thin and adolescent and as gray as his gray suit, his best and just about only one. He acknowledged the doubtful but polite applause, hopped onto the podium, and proceeded to conduct one hell of a concert—a *succés fou* that nudged some war news off the front pages the next day. As the New York *Daily News* proclaimed, Lenny's last-minute substitution for Bruno Walter was like "a shoestring catch in center field ... make it and you're a hero, muff it and you're a dope. ... He made it." For the Bernstein family—for everybody who heard about it, really—it was just like in the movies.

Lenny was instantly in demand, as a guest conductor, a pianist, a composer, and as a personality. People who knew him (and many who didn't) said they always felt he had it in him to be a brilliant conductor of major orchestras one day. Really? Well, up to that point, conductors of major and minor American orchestras were imported, esteemed Europeans—Toscanini, Koussevitzky, Walter, Ormandy, Mitropoulos, Reiner, Rodzinski—but a born-and-bred American Jewish kid? Out of the question! And yet, amazingly, the subtly predictive suggestion in Bruno Zirato's pre-concert speech on the stage of Carnegie Hall that November Sunday in 1943 came true fifteen years later: Lenny—"a full-fledged conductor who was born, educated, and trained in this country"—was appointed the Music Director of the New York Philharmonic. The precedent was set. An American kid of any background could announce to his parents that he would like to grow up one day to be a famous maestro like Lenny Bernstein and not be put to bed without supper and told to think only about the family business or law school or dentistry. It could be

Two brothers, 1946.

done. It was possible. After all, Lenny Bernstein did it. The successions of Lorin Maazel and, in 2009, Alan Gilbert as Music Directors prove the point.

It is not too great a stretch to compare Lenny's appointment to Jackie Robinson's with the Brooklyn Dodgers eleven years earlier. To my mind, they both represented watershed moments in United States history—singular cultural, sociological events that opened the gates for any talented candidate. Who today flinches or thinks twice about any young person of any stripe making it big in any previously restricted endeavor?

When my brother, inexperienced in dealing with the press, early on described

his father as something of an "ogre" for trying to prevent his son from becoming a musician instead of going into the family beauty-supplies business, Sam, infinitely more inexperienced with the press, came out publicly with his most famous line: "How could I know he would grow up to be a Leonard Bernstein?" It was more than just another funny Samism (for example, he often guarded against the vagaries of fate by advising "Keep your finger crossed"); it was a ringing truth. How *could* he possibly know?

The reason Lenny did grow up to be a Leonard Bernstein was his extraordinary combination of native talent, driven ambition, and good luck. Again, like Jackie Robinson, one needs a great helping of all three to truly succeed. And as it is often said of Jackie Robinson and other stars of all professions, you make your own luck in life.

What this book is about, then, in recognition of the semicentennial anniversary of Lenny's appointment as Music Director of the New York Philharmonic, is what that appointment set in motion—for Lenny himself, for his family, his orchestra, and ultimately millions throughout the civilized world. Those Philharmonic years took in his eleven seasons as the active Music Director, leading the orchestra in New York and on tour over a goodly portion of the planet, and continued during his tenure as Laureate Conductor until his death in 1990. It was an era marked by his being in the forefront of large artistic, social, and political changes, and an era bursting with innovation: experimental music; new approaches in theatre and films; art in and on television; women and minorities appearing on the concert stage; grown-up musical education for children; and more open-minded audiences. New York City was the perfect setting for all this at the perfect time.

As a central figure of the city's frenetic activity, Lenny was the flagrant antithesis of the traditional European-model music director—the hoary master who lived and breathed scores of the classics day and night, usually to the exclusion of all other worldly human functions (a few notable exceptions notwithstanding). Lenny composed Broadway shows, operas, ballet music, film music, serious symphonic works, *lieder*, *divertimenti*, and, as if it were invented just for him, he used live television to bring music of all sorts to places and people never before dreamed possible. He showed the world, whether the world liked it or not, what a talented American could do. He emerged as what I had known him to be since I was a toddler—a great natural teacher, a credit to his scholarly rabbinic ancestors. I received a second-hand Boston Latin School and Harvard education of sorts starting at age three, whenever he was home.

For his nearest and dearest, his growing popularity was nothing short of alarming. We had gotten quite used to Lenny as "the famous musician" but that was mainly in purlieus of more cultural folk. But with his rise to rock-star celebrity on television, we suddenly had to face how celebrated he really was. For instance, Lenny loved movies, movies of all ranks and persuasions. He could get teary at the mere prospect of seeing a Joan Crawford film as much as at, say, *Casablanca* or *Citizen Kane*. He had long ago memorized most of Groucho's deliveries as well as Olivier's declamations in *Henry V*. After dinner with family and friends, he was always ready to head for a likely new film or good rerun, and he would happily stand in line at the Sutton or wherever like everybody else. Once in a while, another queuer would recognize him and, perhaps, ask for his autograph or want to discuss Mahler. But after his regular series of shows on television, everything changed; he was besieged by fans and there was no more just standing in line, and so a special phone call had to be made to a movie-theater manager to sneak Lenny and com-

Mobbed by autograph seekers following a Young People's Concert.

panions in through a side door to roped-off seats—even on Martha's Vineyard. Such was the price of fame, alas.

And, of course, with great fame came great excess: too much publicity, both good and bad (e.g., the Black Panthers episode); unsuccessful innovations (the short-lived Mao jackets for himself and the Philharmonic musicians); overly loquacious lecturing from the podium (even though Lenny cherished the story of the Italian musician who once said to a very long-winded Otto Klemperer at a rehearsal, "Mistera Klemp, you talka too much." Felicia, Lenny's wife, could always make him simmer down when he held forth by reciting that line with the appropriate accent); and his "athletic" conduct as a conductor, which was not put on for effect but came naturally since he never realized he sometimes was practically leaping at the French horns (again, Felicia came to the rescue by convincing him to use a short baton, although at first it would occasionally fly out of his hand towards those victimized horns).

Put it all together, and that was Leonard Bernstein—my brother, Lenny. He was a oner, leading the way, setting the pace and the precedent. I guess they really don't make 'em like that anymore. There has to be a first for everything under the sun, and what follows hereupon spells it out.

Helluva Town: My New York 1943 to 1976

BY ALAN RICH

In lieu of a formal history of the city, Rich was asked to recount his personal version of the New York experience. The music critic's tales of daily life, work, and play mirror the city's moods, from a heady optimism in the post-war boom to the chaos of the 1960s to the dispiriting financial crisis of 1976.

remember it well: arriving at Grand Central Terminal from Boston some time around noon, grabbing a hot dog and an orange drink at Nedick's, making my way uptown on the IRT to Seventy-second Street and Broadway. Nearby, there was a ratty old tenement called The Nevada—it exists no more—and a landlady with a room to rent: no outside window, just an airshaft. Rent was agreed to: twenty dollars a month, if I would walk her seedy, lumbering German shepherd. I unpacked, and strode out to claim my New York.

New York's Upper West Side, the future site of Lincoln Center for the Performing Arts, 1955.

The Nevada, Broadway at 70ᵗʰ Street.

It was early May 1945. Germany had just surrendered; Japan would soon feel the heat of the atom bomb and would follow suit. I had lined up a filing job at CBS (485 Madison Avenue! Magic Address!!), and had a sheaf of my writings (as a stringer music-critic at the *Boston Herald*) that would, I hoped, eventually better my lot, but that could wait. Twenty blocks further uptown, the Thalia on that day was showing a film I had always dreamed of seeing some day: Max Reinhardt's *A Midsummer Night's Dream*. This, after all, was why people came to New York. I had other reasons, as well. One of them was definitely not a useless Harvard pre-med B.A. To my parents' infinite sorrow, I had no intention of following it up; if it hadn't been for a few straight-A music courses I probably wouldn't have graduated at all.

Twice in the previous year my friend Dave Barton and I hitchhiked to New York from Cambridge to see the Metropolitan Opera's *Die Meistersinger* from standing room; before season's end I would see it (always "on foot") four more times, and the next season, six. I had stumbled into the job with the *Boston Herald* on the strength of a bratty letter to the chief critic, Rudolph Elie, picking him apart on a tiny Mozart point. Those were my signature pieces: the Sinfonia Concertante (K. 364) and *Die Meistersinger*. Elie and I got into a Correspondence (capital C) on Mozart, and this led me to a life-changing job. I knew I had to come to New York someday to depose the chief critic of, at very least, the *Herald-Tribune*. Eighteen years later, that would actually take place.

Life on Thirty Bucks a Week

Life on a weekly thirty bucks in wartime New York was not quite as bad as it sounds. On my first day in CBS Network Operations my desk-mate invited me to lunch at the nearby Howard Johnson's and the $1.65 price terrified me; how could people afford such luxury? There were alternatives, however: counter joints (Rudley's, Rikers) with a stuffed-pepper plate for forty cents; or Child's, where you could save on the dinner price by leaving off the veggie; and, of course, the Automats, where the mighty nickel reigned. Once a week I allowed myself a visit to a personal discovery, the darling little English Tea Room on Forty-eighth Street, where a large gray cat lounged across the front table, where Josie knew to save me a tipsy pudding for dessert, and where steak-and-kidney pie seemed as close to heaven as $1.80 could vouchsafe.

Better yet, almost everything in the best of the entertainment world was available to the stable of stance at a proper price. Standing room at the Met went for two dollars, with the outlay of an extra buck to an usher for one of the empty seats, which were numerous, but it meant lining up outside the old building at Broadway

and Thirty-ninth Street, in whatever weather, for as long as six hours on, say, a Lily Pons night. (The current system of pre-sold standing-room tickets is somewhat more merciful.) Most Broadway theaters sold their standing room for $1.20; for that pittance I could pad my memory book, in my first few weeks in New York, with the lively end-of-war musical *Call Me Mister*, the then-baby-faced Marlon Brando in *I Remember Mama*, London's Old Vic, with Olivier's howl of self-recognition in *Oedipus Rex* that I can hear today, and—most memorable of all—the indomitable Laurette Taylor leading the original cast of *The Glass Menagerie*. On the afternoon of Japan's surrender I pushed my way through the jubilation in Times Square and decided on a Leonard Bernstein moment as proper celebration, in the form of a standing-room ticket to a matinee of *On the Town*. I had once walked past Bernstein in the Harvard Yard. I knew him then as the winner of the *Boston Herald*-sponsored

Autographing his new recording of On the Town *for New York's Mayor Fiorello LaGuardia, accompanied by the dancer Sono Osato, who originated the role of Miss Turnstiles in the 1944 production of the Broadway show.*

Musiquiz in 1940, in which I had garnered honorable mention and a record album. Three years later I knew him a lot better and so did everyone else. He and Fiorello LaGuardia were New York's brightest stars in my first New York days.

LaGuardia had been New York's mayor since 1934, and showed no signs of wear and tear. He was an inescapable presence, not as a potentate, more like some slightly belligerent, watchful, apron-clad Mamma. "Did You Make New York Dirty Today?" shrilled a sign on the subway cars, and you could sense that invisible finger waggling behind the sign. "Ah, SHAME on ya, Macy's!!!" I remember him screaming on one of his Sunday broadcasts after Macy's had advertised a line of doggie sweaters when wool was still under ration.

Earthquake on Fifty-fifth Street

Rehearsing the New York City Symphony, 1947.

In 1943, LaGuardia had the city take over the aging Mecca Temple on West Fifty-fifth Street and convert it into the New York City Center of Music and Drama, with tickets priced for the people. The acoustics were terrible; the sightlines were poor; overall shabbiness was a fact of life. "It is not easy," penned the acid-tongued critic George Jean Nathan, "to drink in delicate poetry sitting in a chair whose burst springs assault nether regions already imbedded in souvenirs of chewing gum." But this was LaGuardia's kind of dream: a gathering place for folks to enjoy great art. There was an orchestra, pieced together of freelancers, but given over to the legendary Leopold Stokowski to weld into an ensemble. He did the job for a year but then lost interest; the Hollywood Bowl beckoned. Young Bernstein, fresh from his 1943 come-out-of-nowhere triumph at the New York Philharmonic, but in need of a vehicle to call his own, eagerly grabbed the orphaned New York City Symphony and made it his. Something close to an earthquake hit Fifty-fifth Street on a memorable night in 1947, when Bernstein assembled a cast of actors, singers, choristers, and his orchestra for a performance of the agitprop stage work *The Cradle Will Rock* with all of Mark Blitzstein's score as he had originally dreamed it. I learned that night what it meant to be part of a standing, cheering audience that simply would not go home.

And there was real opera there, too, in that ragtag edifice. On February 21, 1944, the City Center forces—a symphony orchestra, a dance company, theater groups, a burgeoning cul-

tural menu—were joined by a full-fledged opera company, the New York City Opera, which flourishes still. The opera that night was Puccini's *Tosca*, starring the international diva Dusolina Giannini; tickets were priced from seventy-five cents to two dollars.

New York and I began to get along. One of the producers who came past my desk at CBS was a handsome Italian named Dario Soria. His wife, Dorle, was head of publicity at the New York Philharmonic: always good for free tickets. Dario had also begun an import company for a line of Italian opera records, featuring some of the new singers who had emerged since the war and were in demand. I left CBS and went to work for Dario, and Dorle persuaded Irving Kolodin of *The Sun* to take me on as a stringer. New York was mine!

I heard orchestral concerts uptown at Lewisohn Stadium on the City College grounds, where Minnie Guggenheimer, the founder and guiding mama, would call out "Hello, Everybody," and everybody would call back "Hello, Minnie!" Bernstein led many concerts there; Gershwin concerts invariably sold out. An airplane would

(continued on page 21)

West Side Story, *the movie, opened at the* Rivoli *in Times Square in 1961. The first showing was a benefit for the Henry Street Settlement. Tickets to later showings were in such demand that only reserved seats were sold.*

a brother's recollection

On the Town

New York City in the fifties offered unlimited possibilities for young up-and-comers looking for cultural enrichment, with Lenny and the New York Philharmonic leading the parade.

Although I had spent a year in the city as a graduate student at Columbia University, the U.S. Army decided that I should spend two years elsewhere before I was permitted to return to Gotham for a civilian career as a writer. When at last I was settled on the Upper West Side, I learned that *The New Yorker* was in the market for young talent (its older, legendary talent retiring, drying out in various clinics, passing

and—magically it seemed—there I was in an office within shuffling distance of those very idols.

One of my first assignments as a budding "Talk of the Town" reporter, in June of 1958, was covering—by design or chance—a welcome-home outdoor event held at City Hall for the New York Philharmonic on its return from a triumphant seven-week, twenty-one-city tour of Latin America, a tour that neatly countered the treatment suffered by

There were my brother and Mitropoulos, being cheered by throngs, along with municipal dignitaries.

on to greater rewards). And so, as good fortune would have it, I was chosen for a junior editorial position at the one journal I most wanted to write for and with which I had enjoyed a longstanding love affair, thanks in great measure to Lenny's annual birthday present for me of a *New Yorker* subscription that had started in childhood. I dreamed of joining one day the pantheon of brilliant, witty, sophisticated, revered writers I had grown up reading,

poor, abused Vice President Richard Milhous Nixon at a similar geography and time. There were my brother and Dimitri Mitropoulos, being cheered by placard-waving throngs, along with municipal dignitaries and the Department of Sanitation Band. The band's conductor, John Celebre, proffered a white baton to Lenny—who happily and characteristically accepted. All present were thrilled by his spirited reading of "The Stars and Stripes

Conducting the New York City Sanitation Band in "The Stars and Stripes Forever" on the steps of City Hall, 1958.

Dimitri Mitropoulos and Bernstein (front row center) and the Philharmonic being honored by the City of New York for their successful Latin American tour, 1958.

Forever." My "Talk" piece began with an arch reflection on the approaching summer solstice in the city, with all its sweat, fun, and promise, and it ended with the words "in bright sunlight outside City Hall while Leonard Bernstein led the Department of Sanitation Band ... it was summer in New York, no matter what the calendar said!"

For me, that sunny New York City era has evoked several extraordinary memories—with Lenny and his attendant fame as the central source and theme, as he was for his family, friends, fans, and, for that

matter, much of the world. And like all extraordinary memories, especially those of military service, time erases most of the vexations and leaves the laughs. It was truly a great era—notwithstanding the Cold War, Joe McCarthy, the aforementioned Mr. Nixon, and other horrors—full of the call to youth, talent, human improvement, innovation, fame, and fortune.

Everything in New York was opening up for everyone, if you could just hang in there and stick it out through the lean days. Marriage, children, a decent apartment—all

were reasonable quests for me and my coevals. My then-wife, Ellen Siccama, a working actress, and I could even afford a nanny for our kids, thanks to Lenny's wife, Felicia, and her endless supply of eager servants from her native land, Chile. One could get by on less, and one could even afford the luxury of most cultural events.

What with my being Lenny's brother and my accumulating press freebies, I was often in the hot center of things—invited to new film screenings, plays, opening-night parties, and, most memorably, wonderfully late show-biz do's given by the likes of Adolph Green and Betty Comden, Goddard Lieberson, and, once, Tallulah Bankhead. But first and foremost came the regular Thursday night Philharmonic concerts, with reserved family seats in the conductor's box overlooking stage-right whenever Lenny was conducting, which was often enough. Before each concert, little rituals would take place in the Green Room: a tense Lenny would kiss the gold cufflinks that Felicia had given to him early on in their relationship and I would present him with a penny, also for kissing and luck. This latter ritual brought about a limerick of my concoction:

> A nervous conductor
> named Lenny,
> Before concerts he'd soul-kiss
> a penny
> To bring him good luck,
> Playing Schoenberg or Gluck—
> Till Lincoln popped out of
> his fenny.

His good luck held up for just about every concert, although, as we used to say, some were—ahem—better than others. During the ones that were not entirely enthralling, I would amuse myself by scrawling bits of doggerel on Philharmonic programs. For example:

> Miklós Rózsa
>   Is not my favorite composer.
> Brahms charms
>   But Pergolesi drives me crazy.
> I'd rather dine at Taco Bell
>   Than listen to Johann Pachelbel.

(The ones about maestros I'll omit here.)

Amazingly, when I showed the scrawled bits to an exhausted Lenny after the rare not-so-great performance, he'd be cheered a little and then we'd all go out and have drinks at the Plaza Oak Room. There were always the weekend concerts to improve things, he felt, and as for the music critics it was generally agreed that they could rot in whatever circle of hell music critics are consigned to.

It was quite a joyride in Old New York.   —*Burton Bernstein*

New York's Mayor Robert F. Wagner presenting Bernstein with the key to the city, 1959.

come over; Minnie would shake her fists and call upon us to do the same; we were all *mishpocheh*. Damn good concerts they were, too, with the New York Philharmonic under the alias of the Stadium Symphony, for a quarter a seat! Now I could also come in the front door at Carnegie Hall, without, as before, having to bribe the usher. Harold Schonberg was a fellow stringer at *The Sun*; later, at *The New York Times* he would give me my first real job in the city. New York was awash in music critics then: Louis Biancolli and Bob Bagar at the *World-Telegram*, Miles Kastendieck at the *Journal-American*, Harriett Johnson at the *Post*. I don't think anybody took the afternoon papers seriously, of course. We all awaited our morning papers, where we would find the elegant erudition of Virgil Thomson at the *Trib* and the purple thunder of Olin Downes at the *Times*—those tastemakers. A few days later, the delicious, but (alas!) predictable, crankiness of B.H. Haggin, in *The Nation*, a critic of limited tastes explosively expressed, and a famous passion for deriding any and all of his colleagues.

> At Lewisohn Stadium concerts an airplane would come over; **Minnie would shake her fists** and call upon us to do the same. We were all *mishpocheh*.

A Broadening of Horizons

It was a time of discovery in all the arts: Picasso, Klee, and Kandinsky at the Museum of Modern Art upstairs; great, almost-forgotten movie classics downstairs. At the Fifth Avenue Cinema in Greenwich Village there was Cocteau's inscrutable *Blood of a Poet*, which they seemed to run once a month; fine—after a few sittings you could almost figure out what it was about. Down behind Union Square was a hole-in-the-wall movie theater showing Russian films: the great ones from the legendary past: Eisenstein's *Alexander Nevsky*, and other silents by him and Pudovkin.

War's end brought on a broadening of horizons. The city's opera companies began to welcome talent that had somehow been able to survive in wartime Europe and even in Japan. A vast treasury of new recordings on European labels began to trickle into the connoisseur shops. Small groups of us used to hang out at Liberty Music on Madison Avenue, or around the corner at the Gramophone Shop on East Forty-eighth Street as new shipments from England, France, and Germany were uncrated. Names like Aksel Schiøtz, the Danish tenor of melting purity, or Kathleen Ferrier, the British contralto, who could make strong men weak, joined everyone's honor rolls; heartbreakingly, both singers were felled by illness after short

Greeting Louis Armstrong at the rehearsal for the Lewisohn Stadium concert in 1956. Bernstein led the Stadium Symphony, which was actually the Philharmonic, in an arrangement of "St. Louis Blues." The audience included the 80-year-old composer, W.C. Handy.

The New York Herald Tribune *announcement of Bernstein's appointment as the Philharmonic's Music Director, succeeding Dimitri Mitropoulos, November 20, 1957.*

careers, but Ferrier's 1948 American debut, in Mahler's *Das Lied von der Erde*, with Bruno Walter leading the New York Philharmonic at Carnegie Hall, lives on in a CD set of Philharmonic broadcasts.

Record collecting and connoisseurship were greatly encouraged in those postwar years by an almost continual improvement in just the sound of things. FM radio, for example, which had come on in the late 1930s, became the broadcast sound of choice, and the vocabulary sported new come-on terms almost weekly: High Fidelity, Full Frequency Range Recording, 6L6s in Push-Pull. A foolish battle of speeds waged on for a time, with RCA claiming that its little 45-rpm disc, with its goofy little changer, could do the same job as Columbia's continuous 33, but common sense soon prevailed. Much more fun was the battle of the connoisseurs that was waged nightly, and into the wee hours, on FM radio, with the self-styled "musicologists" outdoing one another in dredging up the most arcane repertoire in the name of the newly discovered masterpiece. Most bizarre was a gent who insisted on a single name, DeKoven—his first name was Seymour—who invented a musical style known as "barococo." To fit this ideal, music had to be fast; slow movements were an act of weakness on the part of the composer.

New Food, New Fashions, New Music

That passion for the bygone, however, was joined by wave after wave of newness. Nothing stood still: a "new look" in fashion brought hemlines practically to ground level one autumn, and raised them above the knees the next. One new cuisine after another opened our awareness to the vastness of worldwide flavors and worldwide attitudes about what constituted a proper diet. The great gluttony palaces from a previous era—Mamma Leone's carbohydrate heaven in mid-Manhattan, Luchow's—its carnivore equivalent down in Union Square—were rendered old hat against the exquisite restraints practiced at Henri Soulé's La Côte Basque and Le Pavilion, and a remarkable midtown hole-in-the-wall named (after its martinet of an owner) Pearl's, where everything we thought we knew about Chinese food (i.e., chop suey) was wondrously overturned in a world of new and delicate flavors. And there were the discoveries in the growing ranks of sushi parlors and other Japanese restaurants, which had been virtually nonexistent before the War.

I came to depend pretty much on the Museum of Modern Art as my pipeline to the latest stirrings. One night I watched, bemused, as two grown men on the stage of the small auditorium messed with hand-held phonograph cartridges to produce the kind of staticky sounds that are all that messed-with phonograph cartridges *can* produce. But the noise by *these* guys—their names were John Cage and David Tudor—had a name, Cartridge Music, and that made it legitimate.

"Music," said Cage and his echoing disciples, "is anything we say it is," and that dogma got carried to its extreme fulfillment. Years later—when I had acquired the patience to cope with the motivations that produced white-on-white paintings at the Modern, and musical events in downtown lofts consisting of a burning violin or a single sonority sustained for, perhaps, two weeks (not to mention John Cage's most famous work, his four-minute thirty-three-second piece of silence)—I found myself, more often than not, rushing admiringly to the defense of these very practitioners and taking issue with those who didn't share my enthusiasm. "Mr. Bernstein," I was to write as chief critic in the *Herald Tribune* some years later, on the occasion of an attempt at a festival of contemporary music by the New York Philharmonic, "used everything short of a Flit gun last

Bernstein, along with a group of other admirers, surveying the model of the 1964 World's Fair. The Unisphere, which was the symbol and center of the Fair, is at the far right.

A model for the new Lincoln Center for the Performing Arts on the site prior to construction. From left to right: ballerina Alicia Markova; choreographer Martha Graham; Juilliard President William Schuman and student Dorothy Pixley; soprano Lucine Amara;

Metropolitan Opera Director Rudolf Bing; Lincoln Center Executive Director Reginald Allen; Philharmonic Managing Director George E. Judd, Jr.; Leonard Bernstein; actress Julie Harris; theatrical producer Robert Whitehead.

night to kill off the avant-garde in music."

But I get ahead of myself.

In the late 1950s, I took a couple of years off to finish a graduate degree in musicology and pursue a fellowship in Europe. I returned to New York in time to step up onto the first solid rung on my upward ladder, as one of five members of *The New York Times'* music staff. Harold Schonberg hired me; my colleagues were wise, soft-spoken Ross Parmenter, genial Ray Ericson, Allen Hughes—who would soon move over into dance coverage—and Eric Salzman, a brilliant and fiery supporter of the new. Eric was also a composer, which gave him a solid basis for dealing with the creative groundswells that were making New York exciting and important in the 1960s. Harold, no friend of the avant-garde, thought otherwise, and fired Eric when he declined to abandon his second career. That was Harold. As low man in *The Times* hierarchy I inherited most of the assignments to cover the new and experimental music that got booked into the small Carnegie Recital Hall, or a room at the Donnell Library Center on West Fifty-third Street, at "inconvenient" times like Saturday at five thirty. Names like Yoko Ono, Nam June Paik, and Charlotte Moorman (who played the cello topless) loomed on my horizon as I—a critic who might control their futures—loomed on theirs. I also got to interview the young Pierre Boulez, as he sent his first rumbles across the New York musical scene; the venerable Edgard Varèse; and the new arrivals Yannis Xenakis and Witold Lutosławski, and found it easier to speak their language than I had supposed.

> Names like **Yoko Ono, Nam June Paik**, and **Charlotte Moorman** loomed on my horizon as I—a critic who might control their futures—loomed on theirs.

In 1963, I was offered the top critic's job at the *Herald-Tribune*, the second most important position in New York and, therefore, in the country. Everyone knew that the *Trib* was a doomed paper; still, like a moth in a flame, it had become terminally brilliant, ablaze with great writers (Tom Wolfe, Gloria Steinem), a new design by Milton Glaser, and an over-the-top Sunday supplement called *New York*—started by Clay Felker in 1963—that would outlive the paper. Paul Henry Lang—the distinguished scholar who had replaced Virgil Thomson at the *Trib*, and whom I, in turn, replaced—pleaded with me at our farewell lunch to keep up his good fight against his composer-colleagues at Columbia University on the one hand, and Leonard Bernstein's conducting on the other. I'm afraid I may have let him down.

The good fight: New York's musical establishment and the New York press have always enjoyed a give-and-take relationship. In April 1956, *The Times'* Howard

Upon the Orchestra's return from the 1958 Latin American tour, Bernstein speaks at the welcome-home party given for the Philharmonic on the steps of City Hall.

Taubman unleashed his famous broadside under an eight-column headline "The Philharmonic—What's Wrong With It and Why"; when the dust had settled Leonard Bernstein had been installed to share Dimitri Mitropoulos' podium, and within two years the job would be Bernstein's alone. There were happy headlines and sad: superstar violinist Isaac Stern spearheading a campaign to rescue Carnegie Hall from threatened demolition as Lincoln Center loomed; the Met's Rudolf Bing firing his superstar Maria Callas at the height of her popularity and my writing in 1965, when Callas returned to the Met, that Bing had been wrong to fire her. He attempted to have me fired; my union told him to go climb a tree. I kept a bulletin board (at home) of letters from my spiritual godfather and role model Virgil Thomson, whose desk I had inherited at the *Trib*, telling me that such-and-such a piece was "a honey." I sat at that desk on a November afternoon when the news came down of the Kennedy assassination.

The Birth of the "Arts Supermarket"

The New York Philharmonic's afternoon concert that day was cancelled after the first work; two nights later, Leonard Bernstein went into a television studio and broadcast Mahler's Second Symphony to the nation. By then, the Philharmonic was in its new home at Lincoln Center, which opened its first hall—Philharmonic Hall—in 1962. "Aren't they ashamed?" rumbled Harold Schonberg about the opening week of programming: half a Mahler symphony on Bernstein's inaugural concert with the New York Philharmonic, for example. And then there were those acoustics: "I never saw anything like it," burbled Jacqueline Kennedy on opening night, when asked about the sound at Philharmonic Hall. Samuel Barber's *Antony and Cleopatra* at the new Met wasn't much better, with a gigantic turntable that conked out at a rehearsal for opening night. Only the City Opera's production of Handel's *Giulio Cesare*, which made an overnight star of Beverly Sills despite its violations of the Handelian style, radiated anything close to an unqualified success. Still the crowds welcomed the new spaces; you could have sold out anything in any of the three halls in their first seasons. The fountain on the plaza became one of the city's great hang-out spaces; summer or winter, it was where you found your old friends or acquired new ones.

Nevertheless, the Lincoln Center plan, of bringing a city's major cultural resources together into a centralized "supermarket," whatever the traffic problems it might engender, seemed to make its mark. In 1964, two years after the opening of the first hall at Lincoln Center, Los Angeles opened the three units of its Music Center, joined years later by the sensational Disney Hall; all of them having revitalized not only their cities' awareness of the performing arts, but the whole geography of those cities. London's South Bank, San Francisco, and many other places around the world have also profited from the Lincoln Center example.

With New York City's Mayor John Lindsay.

Meanwhile, I had found a luxurious basement floor-through, plus one upstairs room, on West Eighty-eighth Street for a delightful one hundred sixty dollars (these were the early sixties, remember); it suited me, and my cat Martha, for nearly four years. One November night in 1965, the lights went out: the first of several blackouts to hit the New York area and by far the nicest. It was warm for the season; along Broadway many restaurants served by candlelight, and the lights from New Jersey made a nice backdrop. The transit strike a few months later felt equally civilized. It began during an abnormal warm spell (which, of course, didn't last), but up on the West Side and in several other parts of town (except for Midtown, of course, which was a mess) there were actually folks who took their cars out and drove around offering people rides. I met a couple of these Samaritans, older people; we swapped phone numbers, never got together of course. Later blackouts and strikes were not so pleasant.

The West Eighty-eighth Street idyll ended, in fact, the night I returned home in March 1964, in high exaltation, after

the Met's premiere of *Falstaff*—with debuts by Bernstein and Zeffirelli—to find the place ransacked, records, stereo and clothes gone, Martha in agitation. A friend suggested Rockland County; I wasn't the only one gazing northward and westward as real estate started becoming unreal in New York and the city began to feel less welcoming. I found a three-story, stone house, set into a hillside on the Hudson, tattered but reparable and therefore cheap, in a village called, appropriately, Grand View-on-Hudson, a mere forty minutes from Midtown. With city parking facilitated by press plates, My New York was almost as accessible, and somewhat less scary.

Life in My New York, even from a distance: what a fine mix it had become! Lunch when I was at the *Trib* meant a walk over to Ninth Avenue for Italian sandwiches at great, noisy delis, or a bus ride downtown for dim sum in Chinatown, or just a stroll downstairs to the Artists and Writers Restaurant, which we regulars always called Bleeck's, for the legendary rarebit. Dinner, for the brave at heart,

Rehearsing for his Metropolitan Opera debut in a new production of Falstaff *directed by Franco Zeffirelli, 1964. Front row, left to right, singers Judith Raskin, Mariano Caruso, Rosalind Elias, Andrea Velis, Anselmo Colzani, Norman Scott, Luigi Alva, Regina Resnik, and Gabriella Tucci.*

could be at Sweets, near the Fulton Fish Market, lined up on the staircase for half an hour for a table, then discovering the new shapes and flavors of squid, langoustines, or a fish just in from the sea. New places opening along Columbus Avenue, behind the American Museum of Natural History, were ritualizing the weekend brunch. After Saturday's omelet, there could be a trip down to Fourth Avenue near Astor Place to browse through the second-hand bookstores; new old stuff every week. Then there could be something new to watch, from France or Italy, at the Eighth Street Cinema, with complimentary coffee from Juan Valdez between shows. Isn't memory fun?

A City in Distress

The *Trib* went down, as we knew it would, and merged to become part of a three-headed calf, the *World-Journal-Tribune*. On a May day in 1967, the call came: don't bother to come in. Instead I rushed down to Barclay Street (the *WJT*'s new quarters) and gathered up the scrapbooks my secretary, Rue Canvin, had carefully kept since my first day at the *Trib*. Someday I'll learn how to scan them all into a computer, but at least I was able to rescue my pieces on the premiere of Bernstein's *Kaddish* (my verdict: "might as well be titled 'chutzpah'") and samples of the misguided journalism of B.H. Haggin that eventually turned up in my anthology *So I've Heard*.

At the pinnacle of New York's financial crisis in October, 1975, with the city on the verge of bankruptcy, President Gerald Ford made it clear that he would not initially intervene.

Out of those journalistic ruins emerged *New York* magazine with a gathering of *Trib* writers on the new masthead: Gloria Steinem, Gail Sheehy, Jimmy Breslin; Judith Crist to cover film; myself in my customary aisle seat. In our early days we were swept up in some of New York's most vivid, if frightening days. The day before we held our First Issue party, on April Fools Day 1968, Lyndon Johnson withdrew from the presidential race and Robert Kennedy was due in at Kennedy Airport. A week later Martin Luther King, Jr. was murdered, and Mayor John Lindsay spent day and night in Harlem quieting possible riots, with our Gloria Steinem reporting every moment. Set all this against the background of the Vietnam War at its most explosive, divisive, and frustrating; add a background of the music from Broadway's *Hair*, and another assassination two months later; feed this into a brand-new magazine (with Gloria running out for sandwiches, and isn't that Norman Mailer borrowing a desk to conduct his mayoral campaign, and Tom Wolfe in his all-whites pounding out colorful prose about Lenny's Black Panther partying) and you've got one lively landscape in our fourth-floor walkup over on East Thirty-second Street. Did any journalistic adventure ever endure so adventure-strewn a christening?

As things must, the Bernstein era at the Philharmonic came to its announced end, in May 1969. I think—no, *I know*—that I can still hear, in every bone, that sustained, gorgeously scored D major chord that ends Mahler's Third Symphony. I wish that sublime terminating music had really ended things, instead of obliging me to deal with Bernstein's failed musical for Broadway, *1600 Pennsylvania Avenue*, and, years later, to watch the smoke-wreathed, hunched-over figure at struggling rehearsals in Houston for his opera *A Quiet Place*, in my first week as music critic for *Newsweek*.

> I think—no, *I know*—that I can still hear, in every bone, that sustained, **gorgeously scored D major chord** that ends Mahler's Third Symphony.

Although he would eventually return to the city as a hero, by 1970, both Bernstein and New York City were in some distress: Bernstein's reputation had been well and truly shredded by our own Tom Wolfe and the city had been abandoned by a federal government that was denying its support—a turn of events conveyed most memorably in the iconic *Daily News* headline, "Ford to City: Drop Dead."

A Memorable Bernstein Encounter

In response to President Gerald Ford's statement that Washington would not come to the aid of the city during its financial crisis, New Yorkers threw themselves a Times Square rally celebrating a "United New York." In addition to the politicians' speeches, Bernstein conducted an orchestra of Juilliard students and Robert Merrill sang the "Star-Spangled Banner." At the sight of so many people, Woody Allen quipped, "This is the first time I've been in this neighborhood and not been afraid."

But I would prefer to remember an earlier and happier encounter with Bernstein: It goes back to 1967, I think—something close, anyhow. The wonderful, fearless opera director Sarah Caldwell had brought her Boston Opera down to the Brooklyn Academy of Music for performances of Alban Berg's *Lulu*. I was at the *Trib*; naturally I had to review. My parents, my sister, and my fourteen-year-old niece were visiting from Boston, staying at Grand View. Naturally they had to come along: "My son the critic, etc." Tickets were no problem, nobody even challenged what kind of son takes his mother to see *Lulu*.

Comes intermission, we're all standing there. And who should barge up the aisle but Bernstein. My mother grabs my arm. "Shouldn't you get out of here?" she asks. (She reads my reviews.) No. Bernstein greets me with his trademark hug; in all truth we had met to speak perhaps three times in our lives. I introduce him around. My mother, it happens, plays canasta with several of Bernstein's mother's friends from Brookline, Massachusetts. Bernstein hangs out with us the whole intermission. Hugs and kisses all around—even for me.

That night my father came into my room. "You know," he said somewhat haltingly, "it's not so bad you didn't make it to medical school."

Leonard Bernstein: Humanitarian and Social Activist

BY PAUL BOYER

lame it on Tom Wolfe. For many Americans, Leonard Bernstein's image as a social activist is indelibly associated with a 1970 gathering he and his wife hosted in their elegant Park Avenue apartment that included members of the radical Black Panther party. In a *New York* magazine article and subsequent book, Wolfe skewered the event as "radical chic"—the fatuous pursuit of radical groups by faddish celebrities desperate to keep themselves in the public eye.

Bernstein in Montgomery with singer Harry Belafonte at a rally following the civil-rights march from Selma in March, 1965. At the request of Martin Luther King, Jr., Belafonte had gathered a roster of entertainers to rally the crowd of more than 10,000 on the evening before the marchers converged on the Alabama state capital to press for voting rights.

Bernstein explained that the event had not been an endorsement of the Black Panthers, which espoused armed resistance and socialism, but a fundraiser for their legal defense in the face of FBI harassment. But Wolfe's "radical chic" label stuck. In *The New York Times* obituary for Bernstein, in 1990, a brief paragraph on his social activism mainly rehashed the 1970 brouhaha while largely ignoring a lifetime of engagement with social issues, from racial justice and civil liberties to environmental protection and world peace.

The Making of a Radical

Grandson of a Hasidic rabbi, young Leonard Bernstein absorbed the Jewish concern for ethical principles (along with a love of traditional Jewish music) at Temple Mishkan Tefila in Roxbury, near Boston. At Boston Latin School, founded in 1635, whose sole admissions criterion was academic promise, he observed the principle of egalitarianism in action. With this ethical foundation, he came of age in the turbulent 1930s. Bernstein was fourteen when Franklin D. Roosevelt became president in 1933. His college years at Harvard (1935-39) coincided with one of the most radical and creative eras, politically and culturally, in U.S. history. Indeed, politics and culture often intermingled in the 1930s. New Deal programs supported the arts; government-funded photographers recorded the Depression's human toll. In 1939, the black contralto Marian Anderson gave a government-sponsored recital at the Lincoln Memorial after the Daughters of the American Revolution barred her from Constitution Hall. But many artists and intellectuals of the thirties—including musicians Bernstein admired, such as Marc Blitzstein and Aaron Copland—saw the Soviet Union as leading the way to a socialist utopia. The eruption of fascism in Europe gave rise to the so-called Popular Front movement of the 1930s, when left-leaning writers and artists joined with Communists to battle the fascist threat.

Those were thus heady times for a politically conscious youth like Bernstein. In 1939, his senior year at Harvard, demonstrating the penchant for combining music and politics that would define his career, he organized a campus production of Blitzstein's opera *The Cradle Will Rock*. He loved both Blitzstein's music and the work's radical story, which was set in "Steeltown, USA" and pitted heroic workers against thuggish bosses. In 1937, the New Deal's Federal Theater Project, after funding Blitzstein's work, banned the opera's New York premiere. When Massachusetts authorities followed suit, Bernstein stepped in with his Harvard production. Blitzstein, dogged by his Communist party membership and closeted homosexuality, had a difficult career, but Bernstein remained a lifelong friend and supporter.

Bernstein's senior thesis, "The Absorption of Race Elements into American

At Brandeis University in 1952, Bernstein directed the first Festival for the Creative Arts, which included Marc Blitzstein narrating his English translation of The Three Penny Opera. *Festival programming also included the first performance of Bernstein's* Trouble in Tahiti *directed by Elliot Silverstein, pictured here with Bernstein.*

Music," called for incorporating jazz into the musical mainstream, as George Gershwin had done with *Rhapsody in Blue* and *Porgy and Bess*. Through jazz, Bernstein wrote with youthful exuberance, "Negro music has finally shown itself to be the really universal basis of American composition."

The Apprenticeship Years

Throughout his apprenticeship years—which included his now-famous 1943 New York Philharmonic debut at age twenty-five—Bernstein remained engaged politically. In 1947, concluding a two-year stint as director of the New York City Symphony, he wrote an article for *The New York Times*, "The Negro in Music," in which he attributed the absence of African Americans from the nation's orchestras and opera companies to a lack of early training and encouragement. "This is a social, not a musical problem," he wrote. "Everything we can do to fight discrimination—in any form or field—will ultimately work toward ameliorating the musical situation." Suiting actions to words, he conferred with the New York Urban League on how to bring more blacks into orchestras, and tried to find a position for the young black conductor Dean Dixon. (In 1949 Dixon left America for a career in Europe.)

With Aaron Copland at Philharmonic Hall in 1962. Amid the climate of fear and suspicion that pervaded America in the early Cold War, the lifelong friends and political activists found themselves suspected of being "fellow travelers" with the Communist party.

Bernstein's radical activism, like that of his close friend and mentor Aaron Copland, continued in the early post-war years. In the spirit of the Popular Front, he signed a 1945 *New York Times* ad for the Veterans of the Abraham Lincoln Brigade (a group of American volunteers who had fought in the Spanish Civil War), and judged musical auditions sponsored by the National Negro Congress—both Communist-front groups, according to the United States Attorney General. In 1947, with Albert Einstein, Thomas Mann, Pablo Picasso, and others, he signed a petition supporting the German émigré composer Hanns Eisler, who had been blacklisted after being grilled by the House Un-American Activities Committee (HUAC), then pursuing an anti-Communist witch hunt. That same year, with some fifty Hollywood stars and figures from the New York arts scene, Bernstein signed a manifesto blasting HUAC's Hollywood hearings. In 1948 he backed the third-party presidential candidacy of Henry Wallace, recently

> Suspected of Communist ties, Bernstein had to spend **$3,500 in legal fees** to get his **passport** in 1953. He fumed: "That's what it costs these days to be a free American."

dropped from President Truman's cabinet for criticizing U.S. Cold War policies, and now endorsed by the U.S. Communist party. In 1949, along with Copland, Einstein, Mann, Arthur Miller, Langston Hughes, Charlie Chaplin, and others, Bernstein endorsed a Moscow-sponsored Cultural and Scientific Conference for World Peace, held in New York. *Life* magazine ridiculed the event's U.S. backers as "hard-working fellow-travelers" and "soft-headed do-gooders," but Bernstein was unmoved. Despite the country's increasingly reactionary climate—which led some artists to repudiate their youthful left-wing activities—Bernstein, like Copland, consistently resisted the ideological rigidities of the early Cold War.

His activities caught the attention of the FBI, whose Bernstein file, started in 1943, eventually neared 700 pages. In 1953 (the same year Copland was subpoenaed to testify before Joseph McCarthy's Senate subcommittee), the State Department, citing suspected Communist ties, refused Bernstein's passport application. After paying thirty-five hundred dollars in legal fees to get the ruling reversed, he fumed: "That's what it costs these days to be a free American citizen." When the FBI released his file (or parts of it) in 1994 under the Freedom of Information Act, his daughter Jamie Bernstein commented: "Whenever any liberal cause asked my father [for support] … he said 'Sure,' without doing any investigation into the organization. If it sounded like a nice liberal cause, he would lend his name to it, and the FBI found that alarming."

On the following spread: Pages from Bernstein's FBI file, which was started in 1943 and eventually neared 700 pages. It is noteworthy that at the same time that Bernstein was under surveillance by the FBI for possible Communist associations, he was officially representing the United States in Latin America (1958) and the Soviet Union (1959) on Philharmonic tours.

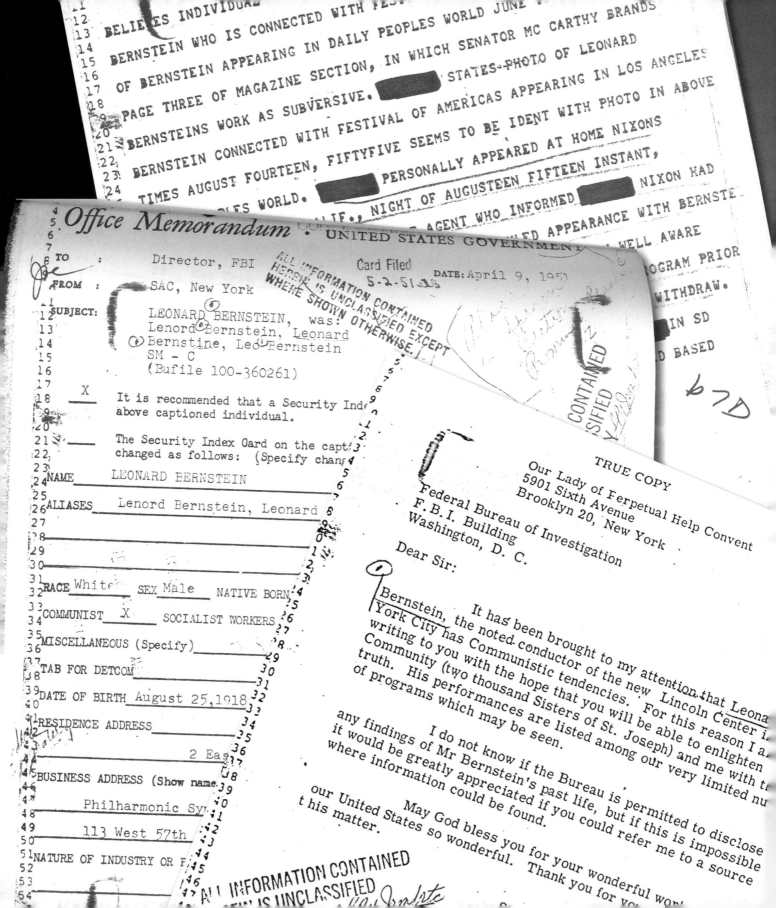

BELIEVES INDIVIDUAL ██████ WITH FES██████
BERNSTEIN WHO IS CONNECTED WITH FES██████
OF BERNSTEIN APPEARING IN DAILY PEOPLES WORLD JUNE ██████
PAGE THREE OF MAGAZINE SECTION, IN WHICH SENATOR MC CARTHY BRANDS
BERNSTEINS WORK AS SUBVERSIVE. ██████ STATES-PHOTO OF LEONARD
BERNSTEIN CONNECTED WITH FESTIVAL OF AMERICAS APPEARING IN LOS ANGELES
TIMES AUGUST FOURTEEN, FIFTYFIVE SEEMS TO BE IDENT WITH PHOTO IN ABOVE
██████LES WORLD. ██████ PERSONALLY APPEARED AT HOME NIXONS
CALIF., NIGHT OF AUGUSTEEN FIFTEEN INSTANT, ██████ NIXON HAD
██████ AGENT WHO INFORMED ██████ WELL AWARE
██████ED APPEARANCE WITH BERNSTE██
██████ PROGRAM PRIOR
██████ WITHDRAW.
IN SD
██████ BASED
b7D

Office Memorandum · UNITED STATES GOVERNMENT

Card Filed
5-2-51

DATE: April 9, 1951

TO : Director, FBI

FROM : SAC, New York

SUBJECT: LEONARD BERNSTEIN, was:
Lenord Bernstein, Leonard
Bernstine, Leo Bernstein
SM - C
(Bufile 100-360261)

ALL INFORMATION CONTAINED
HEREIN IS UNCLASSIFIED EXCEPT
WHERE SHOWN OTHERWISE.

X It is recommended that a Security Ind██
above captioned individual.

____ The Security Index Card on the capt██
changed as follows: (Specify chang██

NAME LEONARD BERNSTEIN

ALIASES Lenord Bernstein, Leonard B██

RACE White SEX Male NATIVE BORN

COMMUNIST X SOCIALIST WORKERS

MISCELLANEOUS (Specify)

TAB FOR DETCOM

DATE OF BIRTH August 25, 1918

RESIDENCE ADDRESS

2 Eas██

BUSINESS ADDRESS (Show name██

Philharmonic Sy██

113 West 57th

NATURE OF INDUSTRY OR F██

ALL INFORMATION CONTAINED
HEREIN IS UNCLASSIFIED

TRUE COPY

Our Lady of Ferpetual Help Convent
5901 Sixth Avenue
Brooklyn 20, New York

Federal Bureau of Investigation
F.B.I. Building
Washington, D. C.

Dear Sir:

It has been brought to my attention that Leona██
Bernstein, the noted conductor of the new Lincoln Center i██
York City has Communistic tendencies. For this reason I a██
writing to you with the hope that you will be able to enlighten
Community (two thousand Sisters of St. Joseph) and me with t██
truth. His performances are listed among our very limited nu██
of programs which may be seen.

I do not know if the Bureau is permitted to disclose
any findings of Mr Bernstein's past life, but if this is impossible
it would be greatly appreciated if you could refer me to a source
where information could be found.

May God bless you for your wonderful wor██
our United States so wonderful. Thank you for yo██
this matter.

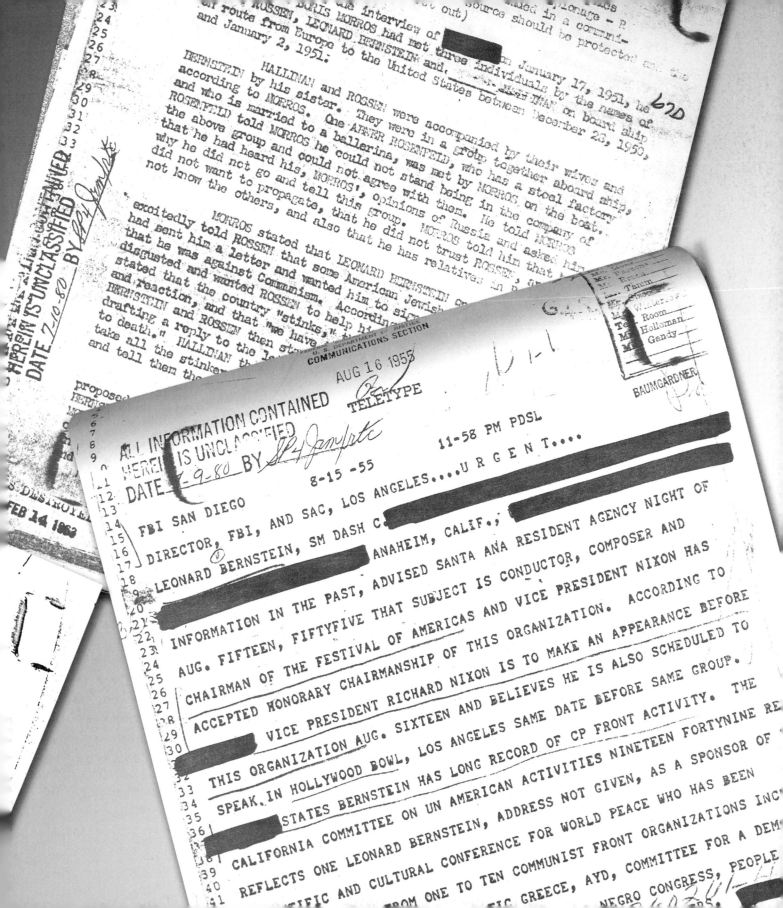

... interview of
BORIS MORROS had met three individuals by the names of
... route from Europe to the United States between December 28, 1950,
and January 2, 1951:

BERNSTEIN, HALLINAN and ROSSEN were accompanied by their wives and
according to his sister. They were in a group together aboard ship
and who is married to a ballerina, was met by MORROS on the boat,
ROSENFELD told MORROS he could not stand being in the company of
the above group and could not agree with them. He told MORROS
that he had heard his, MORROS' opinions of Russia and asked him
why he did not go and tell this group, that he did not trust ROSSEN, and
did not want to propagate, that he has relatives in ...
not know the others, and also that ...

MORROS stated that LEONARD BERNSTEIN ...
excitedly told ROSSEN that some American Jewish ...
had sent him a letter and wanted him to sign ...
that he was against Communism. According ...
disgusted and stated that the country "stinks," ...
and reaction, and that "we have ...
BERNSTEIN and ROSSEN then st ...
drafting a reply to the l ...
to death." HALLINAN th ...
take all the stinker ...
and tell them th ...

proposed ...

U.S. DEPARTMENT OF JUSTICE
COMMUNICATIONS SECTION

8-15 -55   11-58 PM PDSL

BAUMGARDNER

FBI SAN DIEGO

DIRECTOR, FBI, AND SAC, LOS ANGELES....URGENT....

LEONARD BERNSTEIN, SM DASH C.

ANAHEIM, CALIF.;

AUG. FIFTEEN, FIFTYFIVE THAT SUBJECT IS CONDUCTOR, COMPOSER AND
ADVISED SANTA ANA RESIDENT AGENCY NIGHT OF

INFORMATION IN THE PAST,

CHAIRMAN OF THE FESTIVAL OF AMERICAS AND VICE PRESIDENT NIXON HAS

ACCEPTED HONORARY CHAIRMANSHIP OF THIS ORGANIZATION. ACCORDING TO

VICE PRESIDENT RICHARD NIXON IS TO MAKE AN APPEARANCE BEFORE

THIS ORGANIZATION AUG. SIXTEEN AND BELIEVES HE IS ALSO SCHEDULED TO

SPEAK.IN HOLLYWOOD BOWL, LOS ANGELES SAME DATE BEFORE SAME GROUP.

STATES BERNSTEIN HAS LONG RECORD OF CP FRONT ACTIVITY. THE

CALIFORNIA COMMITTEE ON UN AMERICAN ACTIVITIES NINETEEN FORTYNINE RE

REFLECTS ONE LEONARD BERNSTEIN, ADDRESS NOT GIVEN, AS A SPONSOR OF

FIC AND CULTURAL CONFERENCE FOR WORLD PEACE WHO HAS BEEN

FROM ONE TO TEN COMMUNIST FRONT ORGANIZATIONS INC

FIC. GREECE, AYD, COMMITTEE FOR A DEM

NEGRO CONGRESS, PEOPLE

Bernstein himself categorically denied any Communist sympathies. According to his longtime spokesperson Margaret Carson, "His closest political self-definition was that he was a socialist. He said as much. But he never joined the Communist Party." A former State Department cultural-exchange officer observed in a 1994 letter to *The New York Times*: "His habitual comment when international politics entered the conversation was 'Why can't we all live happily together?'" Bernstein himself, looking back, noted: "The 1930s is when I grew up and learned about the world, about music, fascism, anti-fascism. I belonged to more committees, according to *Red Channels* [a right-wing publication listing alleged Communists and "fellow travelers"], than Eleanor Roosevelt. ... The irony is, I've always hated the Communist party!" Said Margaret Carson: "His political involvement was for all humanity. He loved the world and wanted the best for it."

Music and Message

In 1952, during a brief stint as a professor at Brandeis University, Bernstein launched a Festival for the Creative Arts that still continues. The festival program conveys his conception of the relationship of the arts and society in an uncertain post-war world shadowed by nuclear fears:

> This is a moment ... when civilization looks at itself appraisingly, seeking a key to the future. ... The art of an era is a reflection of the society in which it is produced and ... the intellectual and emotional climate of the era. Through [the arts] the patterns of thought and expression which characterize each generation can be analyzed.

This credo—that art reflects social reality, but also influences that reality— places the arts firmly within a larger social/political matrix; it would shape Bernstein's public role and artistic output in the years ahead.

Bernstein's most memorable early melding of his musical genius and his social-activist impulses came in two musicals of the late 1950s: *Candide* and *West Side Story*. *Candide* (1956), a collaboration with Richard Wilbur, John La Touche, and Lillian Hellman, implicitly but unmistakably criticized U.S. politics and mass culture in the Eisenhower era. Like the title character himself, who encounters a brutal and exploitive world blithely ignored by his mentor Dr. Pangloss, Bernstein and his collaborators sought to pierce the surface blandness of the Fifties and awaken America to realities beyond the white suburbs of *Leave It to Beaver* and *Father Knows Best*: racism, poverty, class divisions, Cold War hostilities, radioactive fallout from nuclear tests. Opening in New York soon after Eisenhower's landslide reelec-

Marian Anderson, who first appeared with the Philharmonic at Lewisohn Stadium in 1925, returned there for a concert under Bernstein's direction in 1947. As an African-American, the singer was banned from many venues.

tion victory over Adlai Stevenson, *Candide* got mixed reviews—Walter Kerr in the *Herald Tribune* called it "a really spectacular disaster"—and it soon closed. The year 1956 was not a great one for political satire.

If *Candide* challenged 1950s political culture, *West Side Story* (1957) focused on what Michael Harrington would soon call *The Other America* in his influential 1962 book of that title: the harsh life, ethnic hatreds, and gang violence battering the nation's urban poor. As early as 1949, choreographer Jerome Robbins had proposed to Bernstein an update of *Romeo and Juliet* involving feuding Jews and Catholics in early twentieth-century New York. As librettist, they recruited the blacklisted Arthur Laurents, whose 1945 play (and 1949 film) *Home of the Brave*, exposed American racism. In 1955, the collaborators (plus lyricist Stephen Sondheim) shifted the time to contemporary New York, with its 600,000 Puerto Ricans jammed into Upper West Side barrios, and featured (as Bernstein wrote in his log of the project) "two teen-age gangs as the warring factions, one … newly-arrived Puerto Ricans, the other self-styled 'Americans.' " "Don't be messagy," Bernstein cautioned himself; remember "the fine line between realism and poetry." But the show's message came through. As Bernstein later conceded: "*West Side*

Story is one long protest against racial discrimination. … That is why we wrote it." Reading *Romeo and Juliet* in preparation, Bernstein had scrawled above the prologue: "An out and out plea for racial tolerance."

Brilliantly entertaining, *West Side Story* also addressed the gathering urban crisis. When the show opened, recalled Carol Lawrence, the female lead: "It … touched a nerve in the American public—the headlines were screaming [about gang warfare]." Critic Brooks Atkinson understood: "Instead of glamour, [*West Side Story*] offered the poverty-stricken life of Puerto Rican street gangs, and it did not conclude with … the cliché of living happily ever after. It concluded with the violent death of the chief male character." This dark ending, with Maria mourning Tony after his murder by a rival gang, shocked audiences. (Columbia Records initially refused to issue a record, finding the score too depressing.) Maria's final speech hinted at worse to come: "How many bullets are left?" she lamented. America would soon find out.

"How can it be called a 'musical comedy'?," the journalist Martha Gellhorn wrote her friend Bernstein after seeing *West Side Story*. Without the music and dancing, "people would not be able to bear to look." For Gellhorn, the drugstore scene—in which the Jets' aimless energies explode in the song "Cool"—echoed the era's nuclear fears. "If a man can be nothing, he can pretend to be a hoodlum and feel like a somebody. … It looks to me like doom as much as these repeated H-bomb tests, with the atmosphere … irrevocably poisoned. I think that drug store and the H-bomb tests are of the same family." The U.S. State Department, too, understood *West Side Story*'s ominous social message, and refused to include the show in the U.S.-Soviet cultural exchange program. "The greatest thing we have to sell," Bernstein protested, "is our freedom of expression."

Championing Blacks and Women

The year after *West Side Story*, 1958, when Bernstein became Music Director of the New York Philharmonic, the Orchestra consisted entirely of white males. Indeed, in classical-music venues across America, blacks were almost totally absent. Since the mid-1950s, civil-rights activists had protested such inequities. Sparked by the Supreme Court's 1954 school-integration decision and the 1955 Montgomery bus boycott led by Martin Luther King, Jr., the movement focused initially on the South. But it soon targeted discrimination throughout American society, including the arts. In November 1958, the New York Urban League issued a scathing, statistics-filled report accusing the Philharmonic, other orchestras, the Metropolitan Opera, Broadway producers, and the TV networks of "a pattern of economic discrimination" against black musicians. How would the Philharmonic,

THE NEGRO IN MUSIC

Problems He Has to Face In Getting a Start

By LEONARD BERNSTEIN

THERE'S a concert to be held on the afternoon of Nov. 11, at Town Hall, one that holds special interest for me. The Cultural Division of the National Negro Congress is presenting two unknown Negro artists for the first time, in what they aptly call an "Open Hearing."

I became interested in the problem of the Negro in music some years back, but at no time was it made more graphic for me than when I was auditioning musicians for the New York City Symphony three years ago. I must have heard about 400 musicians, but of this number only three were Negroes. To each of the three I listened eagerly, hoping they would meet the required standards; but in each case they failed. And I don't think it was a lack of talent, but something more serious, a lack of the opportunity for proper training.

In a 1947 New York Times *article, Bernstein attributed the absence of African-American musicians in American orchestras to lack of training and encouragement, and called upon the music world to fight discrimination "in any form or field."*

With Orin O'Brien, the first woman appointed to the Philharmonic.

"the most important institution in our public musical culture" (as *The Nation* called it), respond?

Bernstein—long outspoken on this issue, aware of the Philharmonic's central cultural role, and now spurred by pressure from civil-rights activists—made a point of recruiting black musicians and promoting their careers. In 1958, the New York Urban League informed Joseph De Angelis, the Philharmonic's personnel manager, about a twenty-year-old black violinist from Brooklyn named Sanford Allen. De Angelis recruited Allen for the Philharmonic's 1959 summer series, and in 1961 Bernstein appointed him as the Orchestra's first full-time black member. In May 1962, Bernstein made news again by walking out when a Baltimore restaurant, Miller Brothers, refused to serve Allen. "We made a tremendous protest," Bernstein recalled. Civil-rights demonstrators had been picketing Miller Brothers, and Bernstein's gesture increased the pressure.

In a February 1963 Philharmonic concert, Bernstein replaced the ailing pianist Glenn Gould with sixteen-year-old André Watts, the son of a black GI and his Hungarian wife. (In another breakthrough, *The New York Times* review did not mention Watts' race.) In 1965, Bernstein named the black conductor James DePreist an assistant conductor for the upcoming season. Under Bernstein, the Philharmonic also established a scholarship program for young black musicians.

Bernstein and the Philharmonic were not acting alone, nor were they breaking entirely new ground. As early as 1925, Marian Anderson had appeared with the New York Philharmonic at Lewisohn Stadium, then the Orchestra's summer venue. In June 1947 (two months after Jackie Robinson broke the color barrier in major-league baseball, and eight years before her long-overdue Metropolitan Opera debut) Anderson had again appeared with the Philharmonic at Lewisohn Stadium, this time under Bernstein's baton. In 1957, George Szell had hired black cellist Donald White as a full-time member of the Cleveland Orchestra. Still, Bernstein played a notable role in promoting the cause of black classical musicians.

Meanwhile, the modern women's movement, launched by Betty Friedan's *The Feminine Mystique* (1963), highlighted gender-inequity issues and, again, Bernstein responded. In 1966 he chose Orin O'Brien, a double bassist, as the first woman member (apart from harpists) in the Philharmonic's 128-year history. (The Cleveland Orchestra had women members from its first season in 1918–19, and in 1966 had eleven full-time women members.) In 1967, cellist Evangeline Benedetti joined O'Brien as the second woman member. As early as 1961, Bernstein had invited the famed French music teacher Nadia Boulanger to conduct a full program at the Philharmonic—another first.

A 1966 *Time* magazine article about the "girls" and "lady musicians" invading classical orchestras captures the climate of the times. "Miss O'Brien is as curvy as the double bass she plays," said *Time,* in a piece full of juvenile sexual innuendo. *The New York Times* called O'Brien "as comely a colleen as any orchestra could wish to have."

Bernstein was famously interested in reaching the widest possible audience. His Young People's Concerts, nationally televised from 1958 to 1972, introduced girls and boys of all races and ethnicities to classical music as a source of enjoyment and, for some, a career. Before André Watts' Philharmonic subscription concert debut, Bernstein had showcased him on a Young People's Concert. "I make a special effort to look for black artists [in the Young People's Concerts]," said Bernstein in 1969. "We are dealing with the young, and encouragement is the main thing." Many orchestra members nationwide, including Sanford Allen, would later point to the Young People's Concerts as their introduction to classical music. Indeed, this ranks among Bernstein's major efforts to address racial inequality in classical music, which as early as 1947 he had identified as "a social, not a musical problem."

In 1969, two black musicians, double-bassist J. Arthur Davis and cellist Earl Madison, unsuccessful applicants for Philharmonic chairs, filed discrimination charges with the New York City Commission on Human Rights. In his testimony before the commission, Bernstein, citing his civil-rights record and his efforts to increase black representation in classical music, vigorously denied racial bias at the Philharmonic. The problem, he argued, citing his 1947 *New York Times* article, was a societal one: gifted young black musicians did not receive sufficient early support and mentoring. In its November 1970 report, the commission dismissed the musicians' suit, and found no evidence of discrimination in the Philharmonic's procedure for selecting new members. It did, however, criticize the Orchestra's method of hiring substitutes. Of 277 substitutes hired in the 1960s, the commission found that the sole black, flautist Hubert Lawes, had performed for one week in 1968—when the Philharmonic program included a piece dedicated to the memory of Martin Luther King, Jr. and Senator Robert F. Kennedy. In his testimony, Bernstein had insisted that he had no role in hiring substitutes, while acknowledging his overall responsibility for the process. Had he been aware of the pattern uncovered by the commission, he said, he "would have found it upsetting." (The commissioners didn't explore whether visual observation of the musicians in front of him might have alerted him to the absence of blacks.) Playing as a sub was often a steppingstone to full membership, and the commission suggested changes to give blacks greater opportunity. In response, Philharmonic President Carlos Moseley noted that the Orchestra had already instituted most of the Commission's recommended procedural changes in hiring substitutes.

> In 1969, two black musicians filed **discrimination charges** with the New York City Commission on Human Rights.

Activism Beyond the Podium

Bernstein's civil-rights activism was not limited to the Philharmonic. As the civil-rights and black-liberation movements gained momentum, he was in the thick of it. He served on President Kennedy's National Committee against Discrimination in Housing, and early in 1964 joined Vladimir Horowitz and Erich Leinsdorf in a campaign to urge concert artists to boycott segregated venues. That July, six hundred people attended a jazz concert at his Connecticut summer home to benefit the

NAACP's Legal Defense and Educational Fund. In August he joined Isaac Stern in a benefit concert for the Mississippi voter-registration drive. In September he co-sponsored a benefit for the Congress of Racial Equality. March 1965 found him in Montgomery, Alabama, in solidarity with the Selma-to-Montgomery freedom marchers. "I just wanted to come down to be with you," he told the ten thousand marchers. (In a 1968 report to President Johnson, the ever-vigilant FBI noted: "Information has been developed that Mr. Bernstein has been active in the Civil Rights movement.")

Bernstein's Philharmonic position and his growing fame boosted any cause he espoused, and they were many—the National Committee for a Sane Nuclear Policy (a test-ban organization); the International Rescue Committee; the American Civil Liberties Union; the National Conference of Christians and Jews; the United Nations Children's Emergency Fund—the list goes on. Sometimes "Mrs. Leonard Bernstein" (Felicia Montealegre) appeared as sponsor of an event, but Bernstein always gladly lent his name, and often helped in more palpable ways, both on and off the podium.

Bernstein waits to testify with Philharmonic Managing Director Carlos Moseley at the New York City Commission on Human Rights in September 1969, as complainants Earl Madison and J. Arthur Davis enter.

Anti-Vietnam War protests in the later 1960s won Bernstein's fervent support. On October 13, 1966, he focused an entire Philharmonic concert on the horrors of war, and included *The Airborne Symphony* by his controversial friend Marc Blitzstein on the program. "The effect on the audience was profound," noted *The New York Times*. A 1967 visitor to his home noticed on the reading table the anti-war *Nation* magazine and *Viet-Nam Witness* (1966) by Bernard B. Fall, a scholar and journalist killed in Vietnam that year. In January 1968, he collaborated with lyricists Betty Comden and Adolph Green on a song entitled "So Pretty," for an anti-war fundraiser, Broadway for Peace, held at Philharmonic Hall; the song was performed by Barbra Streisand, with Bernstein himself at the piano. As 1968 unfolded, he supported the anti-war candidacy of Senator Eugene McCarthy; then of Robert Kennedy; and, after Kennedy's assassination, McCarthy again. At a Madison Square Garden rally before the Democratic convention, Bernstein told the audience that the nomination of Vice President Hubert Humphrey, who was closely identified with the war, would "almost surely [lead to] civil bloodshed."

At an October 1969 event sponsored by Brandeis University, Bernstein attacked

A founding member of Another Mother for Peace, Felicia Bernstein hosted the press announcement for the new anti-Vietnam War group at the Bernstein's Park Avenue apartment, 1967. The group, which became well-recognized through its sunflower logo, asked mothers across the country to mail Christmas cards to the President and members of Congress urging "an end to the killing."

the "MIC," the "military-industrial complex," criticized by President Eisenhower in his 1961 farewell address. In tones evocative of Allen Ginsberg's 1955 poem "Howl," he declared: "MIC is a monster that is eating up America alive.... This monster feeds on selfishness; it is nourished by greed; and it operates mostly in secrecy. Now and then we catch a glimpse of it, bellowing fire, smoke, pollution and corruption into our lives." In a hectic few days in November 1969, Bernstein attended a Times Square anti-war rally; joined three hundred thousand protesters in Washington; and, back in New York, participated in a reading at Riverside Church of the names of GIs killed in Vietnam.

Still Hoping for Utopia

Retiring from the Philharmonic in May 1969 as Music Director, Bernstein undertook a demanding schedule of composing, guest appearances, and recording dates. Through it all, his social activism continued unabated. As new issues arose, he responded. In 1970, he was enlisted as a supporter of Earth Day, promoting environmental awareness—the same year as his infamous brush with the Black Panthers. In a June 1980 commencement address at Johns Hopkins University, Bernstein sketched a vision of unilateral U.S. disarmament that recalled the idealism of the now-distant 1949 World Peace Conference and John Lennon's 1971 antiwar ballad "Imagine." Envision an America no longer armed to the teeth, Bernstein exhorted the graduates. What an example to the world! Perhaps the Soviet Union would follow suit and become a democracy! "Think of the relief at no longer having to bluster and sabre-rattle...; think of the vast new wealth, now available to make life rich, beautiful, clean, sexy, thoughtful, inventive, healthful, fun!" What did the Hopkins students and their families, on the cusp of the Reagan era, make of all this? Bernstein's utopian vision seemed from another age, if not another planet, but he was being true to himself.

Bernstein backed the nuclear weapons freeze campaign of the early 1980s, a grassroots movement that attracted millions. As his sixty-fifth birthday approached in August 1983, he urged friends who wished to honor him to wear blue armbands supporting the freeze. He endorsed a new organization, Musicians against Nuclear Arms, and its October 1983 Lincoln Center benefit concert for Physicians for Social Responsibility, a leader in the freeze campaign. On August 6, 1985, the fortieth anniversary of the atomic bombing of Hiroshima, he conducted a memorial concert in that city as part of a Journey for Peace world tour with the young Japanese violinist Midori. In 1987, honoring his late wife, he established the Felicia Montealegre Fund to support Amnesty International, an organization devoted to the cause of political prisoners.

A final flowering of Bernstein's unique genius for blending art and politics came in December 1989, after the fall of the Berlin Wall, when he conducted Beethoven's Ninth Symphony in concerts in both East and West Berlin with an international orchestra that included musicians from the New York Philharmonic. In a classic Bernsteinian gesture, he substituted the word *Freiheit!* (freedom!) for Beethoven's *Freude!* (joy!) in the final chorus. Recalled one orchestra member of that moment: "I shall always remember how his face lit up."

At an October 1990 Carnegie Hall AIDS benefit concert, James Levine eulogized Bernstein, the scheduled co-conductor, who had died two weeks earlier of lung cancer. What more appropriate coda to a lifetime spent at the vital center where music, politics, and social commitment converge?

A Life of "Action and Passion"

Tom Wolfe was not alone in ridiculing Leonard Bernstein's social activism. In 1967, as Bernstein's anti-Vietnam War activities intensified, *New York Times* music critic Harold C. Schonberg, adopting the persona of his comic alter ego, "Dr. Flabbergast," described a world ruled by musicians. Imagining a U.S. administration headed by President Isaac Stern, with Bernstein as Secretary of the Interior and other musical notables in various cabinet posts, Flabbergast exults in his fractured English: "There will be great changes in America. Fresh winds over the wasteland of American politics will blow."

The conservative guru William F. Buckley dismissed Bernstein as a "useful idiot"—Lenin's phrase for naïve liberals who embrace causes they don't understand. The critic Hilton Kramer lumped him with Norman Mailer, Allen Ginsberg, and others as examples of artists and writers who believed that "to be an American intellectual was to be anti-American." A more generous *New Republic* obituary observed: "Romantics have always shuttled between the sublime and the ridiculous, between spirituality and celebrity, between seriousness and delight; and Bernstein was perhaps the last American Romantic."

Whatever the critical carping, the public took Bernstein to its heart, not only for his musical genius and his delight in spreading his love of classical music as widely as possible, but also for his unapologetic concern for the poor, the oppressed, the exploited, and the victims of war and totalitarian regimes. Of the musical giants of his generation, none so fully addressed the public issues of the day. Even the most dedicated artist, Bernstein believed, was also a citizen, implicated in the well-being of the larger society. His epitaph might well have been Oliver Wendell Holmes' observation: "As life is action and passion, it is required of a man that he should share the passion and action of his time, at peril of being judged not to have lived."

a brother's recollection

Paying the Price

Lenny's activist stances placed him squarely in a harsh media spotlight during turbulent times, but he never backed away from the principles in which he wholeheartedly believed.

In all the fifty-eight years that Lenny was my living, breathing brother, the notorious Black Panther event and its aftermath marked the only time Lenny and I had a serious feud—serious enough so that we didn't speak or meet face to face for at least two months. While all of us Bernsteins reveled in family spats galore—about matters ranging from anagram-game eruptions to tennis line-call debates—they could be quickly healed with a hoary private joke or a surprise dunking in a

The New York Times and Tom Wolfe of *New York* magazine. As a writer-journalist of some experience, I simply couldn't believe it. Lenny was still naïve about the press, even after decades of harsh lessons. But this was throwing a fat kudu to a pride of lions, a Brazilian tot to the piranhas. How could the sponsors of the event be so monumentally dumb?

My then-wife, Ellen, and I were both invited to the affair, but I intuitively declined with a weak excuse, sensing that I wouldn't be happy

He never understood why what he saw as clear common sense and human decency was not accepted by everybody else.

lake or pool. Not so with that Black Panther party in 1970 at Lenny's Park Avenue penthouse.

It wasn't that I disagreed with the political motives behind the event; like Lenny and Felicia I heartily believed (and still do) in equal justice under the law for one and all. What infuriated me beyond brotherly loyalty was the sheer stupidity of their inviting the press—especially acerbic, quidnunc Charlotte Curtis of

there. Ellen, however, attended and later reported back to me, mentioning that some press people were there by invitation. My shock turned to fury the next day when I read Charlotte Curtis' piece in *The Times*. The result was my two-month break with Lenny and Felicia: no communication, no meals together, no concert-going, no anagram marathons, no private family jokes, no nothing. It was a miserable time for everyone

SPECIAL ISSUE
Tom Wolfe on Radical Chic

JUNE 8, 1970

New York

Free Leonard Bernstein!

Letters to the Editor of The Times

Panthers' Legal Aid

To the Editor:

As a civil libertarian, I asked a number of people to my house on Jan. 14 in order to hear the lawyer and others involved with the Panthers 21 discuss the problem of civil liberties as applicable to the men now awaiting trial, and to help raise funds for their legal expenses.

Those attending included responsible members of the black leadership as well as distinguished citizens from a variety of walks of life, all of whom share common concern on the subject of civil liberties and equal justice under our laws.

The outcome of the Panther 21 trial will be determined by the judge and jury. That was not our concern. But the ability of the defendants to prepare a proper defense will depend on the help given prior to the trial, and this help must not be denied because of lack of funds.

It was for this deeply serious purpose that our meeting was called. The frivolous way in which it was reported as a "fashionable" event is unworthy of The Times, and offensive to all people who are committed to humanitarian principles of justice. FELICIA M. BERNSTEIN

New York, Jan. 16, 1970

New York's reaction to the Bernsteins' hosting of a fundraiser for the Black Panthers was immediate and brutal. Picket lines manned by the right-wing Jewish Defense League were set up in front of Bernstein's apartment building, Lenny was booed by Philharmonic subscribers and universally vilified in the press; even J. Edgar Hoover instructed the FBI to send anonymous letters to everyone who attended the event highlighting the "Panthers' anti-Semitic policy." A hostile editorial appeared in The New York Times referring to the "so-called party" as "elegant slumming," claiming that it "mocked the memory of Martin Luther King, Jr." Felicia Bernstein strongly defended the event with a letter to the editor. Amyas Ames, Chairman of the Philharmonic's Board, released a statement of support for the Orchestra's Laureate Conductor, but it was not enough to stem the unbridled fear and vitriol that the Bernsteins' actions unleashed. By June, only a year after Bernstein was lionized by both the audience and critics at his grand Philharmonic Farewell, New York magazine dedicated nearly an entire issue to Tom Wolfe's scathing account of the event, topping it off with a mocking cover image entitled "Free Leonard Bernstein!"

concerned, but we had all dug into our set positions. Finally, after a lot of negotiations among family and friends, a truce was arranged, and Lenny and I made up with many *abrazos* in the Philharmonic Hall Green Room as the last of the post-

Lenny paid a price for his open-mouthed activism, but that never deterred him from being a warrior for what he felt was right.

concert fans departed. To everybody's relief, all was forgiven—if not quite forgotten thanks to Wolfe's coinage of the term "radical chic," which has become an enduring part of the American vernacular. Lenny, on occasion, could be an easy mark for ridicule, but certainly by more adept wits than *The Times'* music critic Harold C. Schonberg or culture maven Tom Wolfe.

Lenny paid a price, all right, for his open-mouthed activism—above and beyond Tom Wolfe and the Black Panther incident—but that never deterred him from being a fervent warrior for what he felt was right. He was ready to combat Nazis, bigots, whatever, if need be. He never

understood why what he saw as clear common sense and human decency wasn't accepted by everybody else. In one unforgettable incident, he came face to face with a colleague, Herbert von Karajan, who had made a choice he found unfathomable. This is how Lenny told me the story of the strange encounter at La Scala in Milan, more or less in these words:

I figured, what the hell! As much as I disliked the bastard, he was the distinguished Dirigent*, after all. I was very nervous about the whole thing, so I thought it should be private, just the two of us in my hotel room. I found out he liked Scotch, so I managed to get hold of a bottle of Ballantine's, my favorite and perhaps his. He entered the room and we shook hands, greeting each other in a polyglot mix. I couldn't bring myself to call him Herb—the name of our family dentist in New York—so I avoided calling him any proper name*

at all. When we stood across from one another, I was happy to note that he was a bit shorter than I am, which evoked a shared observation about how audiences always think a conductor is taller than he really is, because of the podium. Ha ha. Big joke. As the Ballantine's diminished, our chitchat became less stilted with some gossip about opera singers and conductors and orchestras, but we both studiously avoided the one subject I was most interested in and he was least interested in—to wit, Austrian Herbert von Karajan joining the Nazi party before the 1938 Anschluss. That, to Austrians, was the mark of the real Nazi. Every time I looked at him I saw in my mind's eye that famous concert at the Paris Opéra during the German occupation, with von Karajan on stage, facing an audience filled with Nazis. After about an hour or so, the Scotch almost drained dry, the verboten subject somehow—I'm not sure how—came up. He sighed and said that back then he was so ambitious he would have joined anything to succeed. I couldn't bring myself to mutter another word of substance,

While on tour with the Philharmonic in 1959, Bernstein is joined in Salzburg by Herbert von Karajan (left) and his wife and Dimitri Mitropoulos. Karajan had conducted the Philharmonic in Beethoven's Ninth Symphony the previous November in New York.

and neither did he. We were both exhausted and fairly drunk, and so we parted ways never to speak of the subject again.

Lenny, the man of principle, was also "a fierce patriot," as he once described himself. He worshipped the United States of America in the truest, most honest way. One of the bitterest disappointments of his life came at the outset of World War II, when he was classified 4-F—not acceptable for military service—because of asthma. He firmly and intellectually believed in the Constitution and American justice, as his musical *1600 Pennsylvania Avenue* (a sincere attempt, but hopeless flop) proved.

A favorite story of his took place in the summer of 1941 during his threadbare days trying to make a living in New York City. He was nursing a drink in a Greenwich Village bar with his close friend Adolph Green and a few others, one of whom was a certified American Communist Party member. Lenny and the Communist were arguing heatedly about the Molotov-Ribbentrop nonaggression pact, which paved the way for the German invasion of Poland and the start of hostilities; Lenny was for all-out war against the Nazis, the Stalinist was for peace with them, as dictated by the party line. As the argument grew smokier and more alcoholic, a newsboy suddenly appeared in the bar, hawking a tabloid with the screaming headline that the Nazis had just invaded the Soviet Union. The dedicated Communist grabbed a copy of the paper and shouted for all to hear, "We'll kill the bastards!"

—*Burton Bernstein*

Bernstein's Musicals: Reflections of Their Time

BY CAROL J. OJA

Just as the American musical was reaching one of its peaks of productivity and popularity in the 1940s, an extravagantly gifted young composer appeared on the scene. He was handsome and charismatic, and the camera loved him. This was of course Leonard Bernstein, whose talent in composition was equaled by his ability as a conductor, teacher, and television personality. The 1940s and 1950s turned out to be a Bernstein moment: an era of seemingly endless American aspirations, when the classical and popular worlds had close enough ties that a musician with the urge to migrate between the two could do so in high style.

Exuberantly exiting the National Theater in Washington, D.C. during out-of-town tryouts for West Side Story, *1957.*

"A group of youngsters" cooking up a show: Bernstein, Adolph Green, Betty Comden, and Jerome Robbins put their heads together for On the Town, *which had its premiere in 1944.*

As one reporter put it during the summer of 1957, not long before the premiere of *West Side Story*, Leonard Bernstein was "the coolest cat in long-hair circles."

Bernstein's work for the theater eventually spread over three decades, divided into two not-so-equal parts. The first period extends from *On the Town* (1944) to *West Side Story* (1957), and includes five shows that brim with exuberant energy, intellectual curiosity, political conviction, and artistic innovation. Most of them were set in urban America, with its struggles and opportunities, and they focused on youth. They ended up contributing some of the legendary soundtracks of American culture. The second wave began in the 1970s, after Bernstein had taken a long break from composing for the commercial stage. On the whole, these later works received less acclaim. They included *Mass* (1971) and *1600 Pennsylvania Avenue* (1976), as well as the opera *A Quiet Place* (1983), which falls outside the scope of this essay. By the 1970s, Bernstein was middle-aged. His drive for social relevance remained intact, as did his urge to fuse diverse musical styles, yet this time around he struggled to find a voice at a time of extraordinary social and political volatility. Consistently throughout his life—and particularly in his works for musical theater—Bernstein embraced the goal of being relevant to the person on the street, and he searched for a language through which the popular and classical worlds could fuse compatibly.

Enough time has passed so that Bernstein's contribution to the stage stands ready—more than ready—to be studied as a whole. What binds the Bernstein shows? What are the flashes of personality that make them stand apart from their contemporaries? What do they tell us about key moments in American culture, from World War II through the Bicentennial? Following is a bird's-eye view of Bernstein's works for the commercial stage and the themes that animate them, including their celebration of youth, their commitment to cultural fluidity, their focus on urban life, and their persistent attention to political issues of the moment.

Setting the Standard

Youthful high spirits and timeliness certainly characterized *On the Town* of late 1944. The show represented Bernstein's first collaboration with Betty Comden, Adolph Green, who wrote the book and lyrics, and the choreographer Jerome Robbins. Oliver Smith, a rising stage designer, was also part of the team. "A group of youngsters" was cooking up a new work, as *Variety* put it in 1944; they were led by George Abbott, a veteran Broadway director and the "adult" in the group. When *On the Town* had its debut, the tide of World War II was turning in favor of the Allies, yet victory was by no means assured. Capturing a sense of suspension— of being perched on the brink—the show puts the war front and center. It depicts a trio of sailors named Chip, Ozzie, and Gabey who set off on a one-day leave in New York City, bent on finding women. A palpable sense of bittersweet evanescence hovers over their zany amorous pursuits. Time passes, so does youth. Comedy distracts. But danger lurks—even death—once the battle resumes.

With *On the Town* Bernstein set a standard that his most successful shows would draw on: Find the best possible creative team (preferably young), and develop a working process that is deeply collaborative. Straddle the cultural divide, even trounce it, incorporating stylistic norms from the concert world, opera, pop songs, and commercial theater. Include as much dance as possible—in fact, make it central to telling the story. Engage with the contemporary world and its politics, but don't offer up simplistic solutions. In short: be provocative, be relevant, and have a whale of a good time in the process.

The collaborators as performers: Betty Comden and Adolph Green do their own particular interpretation of "Carried Away," from On the Town, *on the 1959 national television program "The Humors of Music," with Bernstein at the piano.*

In rehearsal for the premiere of Trouble in Tahiti *at Brandeis University, 1952. The feminist storyline, set in suburbia, dealt with social constrictions of the day.*

When Bernstein began his theatrical career during the 1940s, many average Americans still experienced classical music as part of their daily lives, while Broadway's shows and tunes provided the hits of the day. Crossing over was commonplace, with musical genres of all kinds turning up alongside one another on radio bands and in record bins. Leopold Stokowski conducted a string of classical favorites for *Fantasia*, the now-classic Disney animation of 1940. The violin virtuoso Jascha Heifetz made a recording with Bing Crosby, and became well known for his arrangements of popular tunes by composers such as Stephen Foster and George Gershwin. Meanwhile, the choreographer Agnes De Mille, who began her career with the American Ballet Theatre, moved back and forth from modern ballet to Broadway. She choreographed *Oklahoma!* (1943), which gained instant fame as a landmark in integrating text, music, and dance, and went on to shape the dance for a string of major shows, including *Carousel* (1945), *Brigadoon* (1947), and *Gentlemen Prefer Blondes* (1949).

Fusing the High and Low

In the same year as *Oklahoma!* Bernstein made his now-famous debut with the New York Philharmonic—an event captured on the radio—and it brought him overnight acclaim as a star conductor. Meanwhile, he, Robbins, Comden, and Green were seeking a new generation's version of crossing over and integrating dance. They certainly looked to *Oklahoma!* as a model, but they pushed its "integrations" even further, although with far less credit in the history books. They tied together all the various components of their show—dance, book, lyrics, music—shaping a brazen fusion of high and low with numbers like "Carnegie Hall Pavane" and "I Get Carried Away," and a hilarious buffo ensemble featuring Judge Pitkin W. Bridgework, a comic cuckold. Their female characters were smart, independent, and sexually aggressive—"Rosie the

> "When I'm with composers, I say I'm a **conductor**. When I'm with conductors, I say I'm a **composer**."

Riveters" with hyped-up hormones—and they too signaled a high-low mix. Hildy drives a taxi cab. Ivy is a rising singer who studies at a studio in Carnegie Hall. Claire has a career as an anthropologist. "Bernstein bridges the gap between the Tin Pan Alley idiom and Copland-Stravinsky so successfully," wrote the critic Henry Simon in the short-lived New York newspaper *PM* soon after the premiere. "The highly expert ballet music and the smart Broadway songs seem to be all of a piece. The lyrics belong to the tunes, the tunes to the orchestration, the dancing to both, and all of them to the high-spirited, youthful vitality of a swift-moving show."

On the Town signaled another theme in Bernstein's relationship to Broadway—that is, a cluster of interlocking tensions that would continually pull him from the podium to the pen, and from writing for the commercial stage to doing so for the concert hall. It represented a real-life quandary that came to be part of the spin surrounding this brilliant young star. His dilemma—managing his time and coping with an abundant and multi-faceted talent—came to embody the kind of mega-achievement that Americans valued during the post-war years. Already, with this first show, Bernstein was telling reporters that it might be his last. "*On the Town* represents a six-month period out of my life," he said in an interview from 1944 in *PM*. "I'm primarily a conductor. It's not easy to grow as a conductor when you're diverting your energies in so many other directions." Podium or creative solitude? The urge could strike from either direction. "When I am with composers,"

On the Town's *cast included African-Americans, integrated into an ensemble that represented people of various races living harmoniously side-by-side in the bustling city. Among the chorus members is Lenny's and Burton's sister, Shirley, (ninth from left) who went by the stage name Shirley Anne Burton.*

Bernstein stated in *Vogue* in 1956, "I say I am a conductor. When I am with conductors, I say I am a composer." The reporter quipped: "When anyone asks his secretary, she says, 'He is busy.' " In following the trail of Bernstein's life and work, one finds recurrent statements of this sort. "In an age of specialization," *Time* magazine declared in a cover story in 1957, Bernstein "refuses to stay put in any cultural pigeonhole."

Politics Set to Music

Two of the preceding quotations about *On the Town* come from *PM*, a daily newspaper whose left-wing stance brings us to a central topic in the Bernstein saga: that is, the degree to which progressive politics inflected his work for the stage. *PM*, published between 1940 and 1948, clearly recognized Bernstein as someone whose music had the kind of political orientation that was worth following. But the political messages in Bernstein's shows were rarely confrontational or didactic. There is little of the overt agitprop practiced by his mentor Marc Blitzstein, whose *The Cradle Will Rock* of 1937 took aim at big business and the patronage of high art. Bernstein knew that show well and performed the music repeatedly over the years, but with his own *On the Town*, he avoided direct political statements. Rather, the politics emerged through the overall ethos of the show, with its competent women and oblique references to Roosevelt-era populism (such as the politicized phrase "the people" in "New York, New York," the show's famous signature song). Perhaps its signal achievement in the sociopolitical realm involved assembling a cast that included six African Americans, yielding the "first time" that "a mixed cast" had been "completely integrated" on Broadway, as the *People's Voice*, another progressive paper, reported in February 1945. The show demonstrated, the article continued, "a thoroughly normal presentation of people [of mixed races] living their lives—and having loads of fun doing it. … It's the biggest, most important thing that has ever happened to Negroes in the American theatre."

Trouble in Tahiti, Bernstein's next major work for the theater, put social commentary at the fore. Its premiere took place at Brandeis University in June of 1952—eight years after *On the Town*—and the work was billed as a "one-act opera." Yet it, too, confounded standard categorizations, with a production on Broadway in 1955 as part of a triple bill entitled *All in One*. (Also included were Tennessee Williams' one-act play *27 Wagons Full of Cotton*, starring the young Maureen Stapleton, and a performance by the tap dancer Paul Draper.) *Trouble in Tahiti* captures one day in the life of a suburban couple whose marriage is careening out of control. It is a feminist drama which sympathetically portrays the social constrictions endured by the wife (Dinah), and critiques the culture of consumerism and conformity so emblematic of affluent Americans in the 1950s. The Broadway production of *Trouble in Tahiti* featured Alice Ghostley as Dinah, and the fact that she was hired to star in an "opera" on Broadway exemplified the high-low suppleness of the era. Ghostley's background lay thoroughly in the commercial world. She made her Broadway debut in *New Faces of 1952*, and she later became familiar in households across the U.S. as Esmeralda in the sitcom *Bewitched*. With *Trouble in Tahiti*, she apparently "stop[ped] the show," as Bernstein's long-time secretary Helen Coates reported in a letter to Bernstein, who was conducting in Italy at the time.

> It is hard to overstate the degree to which the **concert and popular** worlds had respect for one another during the **mid-twentieth century.**

It is hard to overstate the degree to which the concert and popular worlds had respect for one another during the mid-twentieth century. *Trouble in Tahiti* was not the first so-called opera to appear on Broadway. Gian Carlo Menotti's *The Consul* premiered at the Ethel Barrymore Theatre in the spring of 1950 and enjoyed a solid run before moving to La Scala. Others followed, including a revival of *Four Saints in Three Acts*, a modernist opera by Virgil Thomson and Gertrude Stein, which opened at the Broadway Theater in April of 1952. A highly publicized revival of Gershwin's *Porgy and Bess*, starring Leontyne Price, William Warfield, and Cab Calloway opened in the spring of 1953 and probably became the most famous of them all.

This hybrid genre of "Broadway opera," as the composer Ned Rorem once dubbed it, provides a meaningful context for understanding Bernstein's remaining shows from the 1950s, starting with *Wonderful Town*, which premiered in late February of 1953 at the Winter Garden Theater. It reunited the creative team of *On the Town*, with Betty Comden and Adolph Green as authors of the lyrics and George Abbott as director. This time, Donald Saddler—making his Broadway debut—was the choreographer, with Jerome Robbins assisting "in an advisory capacity." Even though *Wonderful Town* has subsequently been somewhat eclipsed by its more famous Bernstein successors, it was a major hit at the time, beaming as one of the brightest lights in a theater season that had otherwise been "not particularly auspicious," according to *The New York Times*.

Wonderful Town exhibited crossover with the same subtlety and hilarity as *On the Town*; like *Trouble in Tahiti*, it brought together performers from the worlds of popular entertainment and opera. Rosalind Russell, who starred as Ruth, was one of the great Hollywood comediennes of the day. Edith (Edie) Adams, who played

Eileen, was making her "legitimate theater debut," as the *New Haven Register* put it, having gained popularity on the television show *Kovacs Unlimited*. George Gaynes (as Bob Baker) had appeared in *The Consul*, and Warren Galjour (The Guide) had been involved with the NBC Opera Theater. The score, too, was all about synthesis, with a dynamic synergy of diverse styles animating just about every page. At first glance, *Wonderful Town* appears as musical comedy in the classic sense. But viewed up close, it becomes apparent that the show also drew upon opera and operetta, as in the delicious bravura of the song "What a Waste" or the brilliant ensemble writing of "Conversation Piece."

Wonderful Town's *cast and creators. From top left, Adolph Green, Bernstein, producer Robert Fryer, John Bruno, Rosalind Russell, Betty Comden, and Edie Adams.*

At War With the Cold War

Wonderful Town, like other Bernstein shows, featured a feisty woman—the character Ruth—who is smart and proud of it. In the show, Ruth, a writer, and her sister Eileen, an actress, move to New York from Ohio, intent on establishing themselves professionally. They quickly discover that the city can be indifferent to young talent. The show originated with *My Sister Eileen*, a collection of stories from the late 1930s by Ruth McKenney, who was almost as well known for agitprop texts as for screwball comedy. The journalist Heywood Broun once dubbed her the "Red Gracie Allen," and she and her husband Bruce Minton were among the many American intellectuals and creative artists who were forced into exile because of

A souvenir program for Candide, *which subtly mocked the era's anti-Communist witch hunts while affirming the importance of human relationships.*

Cold War purges (they lived in the United Kingdom).

Wonderful Town, too, had a political agenda, albeit one that was deeply encoded. Early 1953, after all, represented an especially intense period in the hearings of the House Un-American Activities Committee and the Senate Permanent Subcommittee on Investigations (the latter chaired by Senator Joseph McCarthy), and any display of left-wing sympathies could carry extreme consequences. Evidence suggests that the creators of the show tested ways to speak out. Sketches for an early version of the lyrics for "What a Waste," for example, include a draft verse that profiled a figure named "Eric the Red" (these manuscripts are housed in the Bernstein Collection at the Library of Congress). With deceptive zaniness, the verse confected a story about an exiled Viking from the tenth century who could not get past Saint Peter because "He's a red, he's a red, there's no room in heaven for him." And the show's opening number, originally entitled "Self-Expression," was changed during tryouts to "Christopher Street." Yet the concept of "expressing oneself," which certainly was a hot-button topic in McCarthy's America, still turned up in the lyrics—a rousing, albeit wacky, send-up of Greenwich Village as a site of creative and personal freedom.

> Bernstein saved his strongest **anti-McCarthy** statement for his next show, *Candide,* a re-imagining of Voltaire's **classic satire.**

In retrospect, however, it appears that Bernstein saved his strongest anti-McCarthy statement for his next show, *Candide*. It premiered at the Martin Beck Theatre in December of 1956 and presented a re-imagining of Voltaire's classic satire from the eighteenth century. True to form, its creative team drew on the best in the business—Lillian Hellman (book); Richard Wilbur, John La Touche, Dorothy Parker, and others (lyrics); Irene Sharaff (costumes); Tyrone Guthrie (director); Lehman Engel (music director); Barbara Cook and Robert Rounseville (stars). Here, again, protest was embedded in a swirl of camp and fanciful historical metaphor. At the opening, Dr. Pangloss teaches Candide and Cunégonde that, as the song title suggests, they are living in "The Best of All Possible Worlds." The two young people then set off around the globe, confronting repeated traumas, including rape and physical abuse. In Lisbon, they are subjected to an Inquisition, providing a thinly veiled commentary on the Congressional anti-Communist hearings in the lyric, "What a day, what a day, for an auto-da-fé." By the end, Candide and Cunégonde resolve to face their fate and forge ahead. The work ends with "Make Our Garden Grow," a hymn-like affirmation of the importance of human relationships.

Perhaps the most telling contemporaneous context for *Candide* came with Alan Jay Lerner's *My Fair Lady*, which was also based on a classic text, George Bernard Shaw's *Pygmalion*. But what a difference in tone! Whereas *My Fair Lady* transported the audience to another time and place, spinning a tapestry of beautiful tunes ("I Could Have Danced All Night," "I've Grown Accustomed to Her Face"), *Candide* offered up rowdy (even raunchy) cynicism, constantly challenging both the mind and ear. It's not surprising then that *Candide* had a rough critical ride and has continued to struggle over the years, going through multiple versions. This was an opera for the commercial stage, a Broadway score filled with complex vocal ensembles and demanding virtuosity. Or as *Variety* put it in 1956: "a classic story, beautiful score, virtuoso staging, brilliant performance, exquisite production—and remote box office potential."

Reinventing Candide

In many ways, *Candide* remains enigmatic, which is central to its identity. It retains a reputation as a somewhat troubled show, at the same time as its cultural traction has been substantial and it continues to be a pliable vehicle for ever-new conceptions. In 2004, the New York Philharmonic mounted a successful semi-staged version of the show, conducted by Marin Alsop and starring Kristin Chenoweth. Directed by Lonny Price, it updated the story by inserting contemporary signifiers, such as portraying the judge at Candide's Inquisition as Donald Trump. A production in 2006–07 by Robert Carsen—mounted both at the Théâtre du Châtelet in Paris and at La Scala in Milan—took the updating of *Candide* even further by construing the show as a parable of American moral deterioration in the late twentieth century. Carsen's vision lampooned imperialism, consumerism, mass-market entertainment, and the Bush administration. His conclusion—true to Bernstein's inspirational intent—turned "Make Your Garden Grow" into a plea for responsible stewardship of the environment.

Candide, then, can be viewed from multiple perspectives. It's an allegory of the wandering Jew; Candide and Cunégonde, after all, are diasporic figures, sent off to roam the globe, and at times the score references minor melodies that evoke the *shtetl*. It's also a celebration of the pleasures of the body. Cunégonde's sexuality is omnivorous, which was striking for a female character within the context of the restrictive social mores of the 1950s. And it contains some of Bernstein's most rapturous music, from numbers such as "Glitter and Be Gay," with its razzle-dazzle fusion of coloratura and camp, to "It Must Be So," with a text that expresses resignation with a whisper of hope. Its overture, which has become a staple of orchestras around the world, is often performed by the New York Philharmonic without a

In process: The production team observes a West Side Story *rehearsal, 1957. From left, producers Robert E. Griffith and Harold Prince, choreographer-director Jerome Robbins, lyricist Stephen Sondheim, composer Leonard Bernstein, playwright Arthur Laurents, assistant director Gerald Freedman, associate producer Sylvia Doulie, and an unidentified member of the group.*

conductor as a tribute to Bernstein. All this circles back to the word "enigma." *Candide* probes and ponders. It guffaws. But it avoids tidy solutions.

The next Bernstein show was the most famous of all: *West Side Story*, which opened in September of 1957. Its mammoth achievement, both artistically and commercially, overshadows all other Bernstein works for the stage. Just as *Candide* retold Voltaire's novella, *West Side Story* recast Shakespeare's *Romeo and Juliet* as a tale of urban violence and immigrant ethnic strife. Youth once again stood in the spotlight. This time the focus was on teen gangs, with an edge of brutality and verisimilitude. The creators intentionally eschewed established stars, casting young, unknown actors, including Larry Kert, Carol Lawrence, and Chita Rivera. The show's lyricist was also young and unknown—a twenty-seven-year-old named Stephen Sondheim. With the remainder of the creative team, familiar figures returned: Jerome Robbins as director and choreographer, Oliver Smith as scene designer, Irene Sharaff as costume designer. The book was by playwright Arthur Laurents, and the producers were Harold Prince and Robert E. Griffith.

Taking on the Concrete Jungle

Critics grasped the innovations of *West Side Story* with exceptional acuity. This was no sleeper waiting to be understood by future generations, but an instant cultural icon. Brooks Atkinson of *The New York Times* called it "profoundly moving," adding that it was "as ugly as the city jungles and also pathetic, tender, and forgiving." He recognized the centrality of Robbins' choreography, noting that "the ballets convey the things that Mr. Laurents is inhibited from saying because the characters

600 ROOKIE POLICE TO PATROL IN WAR ON YOUTH GANGS

Assigned to Night Beats in City Tinder Areas—Club Workers to Be Shifted

YOUTH SHOT DEAD IN EAST HARLEM

Two Others Are Wounded— Police Investigate Link to Three Teen-Age Gangs

An apparent outbreak of gang warfare in East Harlem last night brought death to one teen-ager and wounds to two others. The police were investigating the possibility that three rapid fire shootings

are so inarticulate." And Walter Kerr of the *Herald-Tribune* commented on how the music, from start to finish, conveyed the "sorry and meaningless frenzy" of these teens' lives.

Yet again, Bernstein was involved with a show that confronted political conundrums. Who should take responsibility for the fate of these desperate urban kids? Why do humans resort to bloodshed, which consistently hurts more than helps? How do immigrants fit into a new home when ethnic difference starkly sets them apart? At the time of *West Side Story*, these questions carried urgency. The West Side of Manhattan—particularly the neighborhoods from Hell's Kitchen to Washington Heights—was in the midst of a disturbing wave of youth crime. "Five youths displaying their prowess before a gang of fifteen girls critically wounded a boy on the West Side last night," read the opening of a *New York Times* story in March of 1956. "Four youths were arrested last night in

Headlines about gang violence lent currency to West Side Story'*s story line, with tenement fire escapes serving for the balcony scene of an urban* Romeo and Juliet. *Opposite page: original cast members rehearse "The Rumble" scene.*

the aftermath of a teenage gang fight in Washington Heights in which one young-ster was fatally stabbed," read another article in August of 1957. Many such stories were appearing. Bernstein, Robbins, and Laurents had been at work on their show for some time before this violence erupted. Their original title had been *East Side Story*, and the show had been set on the Lower East Side, with a focus on tensions between Catholics and Jews. Along the way, they shifted the emphasis to a current crisis and moved the action across town. Whatever the locale, "an out and out plea for racial tolerance" remained central, as Bernstein jotted down on his personal copy of *Romeo and Juliet*, now housed at the Library of Congress.

Of all the Bernstein shows, this one achieved the most deeply integrated fusion of otherwise disparate musical worlds. "Dance at the Gym" spins through popular Latin genres and gestures. "Cool" conjures up the post-bop world of jazz pianists Lennie Tristano or Dave Brubeck. "One Hand, One Heart" uncannily unites a hymn with a pop song, set to the meter of a waltz. "Gee, Officer Krupke" draws on the comedic agitprop of Marc Blitzstein. And with the "Tonight" quintet, Bernstein once again created a masterpiece of ensemble, one that rivals the best of such moments in European opera.

If the historical corollary to *Candide* was *My Fair Lady*, that for *West Side Story* was Meredith Willson's *The Music Man*, which opened three months after the Bernstein show. The contrasts are similar: melodious nostalgia vs. hard-edged real-ism, a purebred musical lineage vs. deeply rooted miscegenation, Eisenhower's America vs. Kennedy's (which, of course, was still on the horizon). Willson romanti-cized the American heartland, while Bernstein confronted its urban jungle.

(continued on page 80)

a brother's recollection

Easy Laughter of a Grand Wit

Being part of the Bernstein family meant sharing in Lenny's raucous love of joke-telling, and also being privy, at times, to the very moments that sparked his inspiration as a composer.

My first real exposure to Lenny's connection to Broadway began about the same time as his, not long after my first real exposure to the concert world, which was not all that long after his, also. In late 1944, when I was twelve, *On the Town* arrived in Boston for some strengthening tryouts under the veteran hand of the show's director, George Abbott. My sister, Shirley, fresh out of Mount Holyoke, got a

of out-of-town trials and errors. My parents had only a dim idea of what Lenny and Shirley were doing, and they were never really sure where I was. No matter that my grades and extracurricular activities waned, it was worth it; I was a front-row witness to the birth of one of the more remarkable, fresh Broadway musicals of all time—and the start of several brilliant careers.

What impressed me most about the show was the wit and humor that

Humor burst from every scene, even the ones with a touch of wartime gravity.

job singing in the chorus thanks to our Lenny, who had gotten his job writing the musical with friends Adolph Green, Betty Comden, and Jerry Robbins thanks to his sudden fame as a conductor and composer. I played a lot of hooky from my nearby school, watching those fascinating show-biz folk rehearse at the Colonial Theatre and in various hotel rooms, as they threw out numbers that weren't quite working, put in new numbers, stayed up all night, and withstood the notorious agony

burst from every scene, even the ones with a touch of wartime gravity. This was true of just about all of Lenny's compositions: for instance, his dour first symphony, *Jeremiah*, had a whimsical reference to a liturgical theme that brings a smile to every kid who has gone through a bar mitzvah; his *Mass* had shockingly light moments; and, of course, there were the downright hilarious shticks in *Wonderful Town*, *Candide*, *West Side Story*, and other opuses.

Humor was part and parcel of

Lenny with Army Band members at El Morro Castle in Puerto Rico. Burton's commanding officer insisted on this visit and photo.

the man. Music essentially meant joy for Lenny; indeed, it was the title of his book *The Joy of Music*. He cherished all kinds of humor—good, bad, clean, dirty, witty, broad, ethnic, politically correct, ridiculing, loving. As a lad, he co-invented a private funny language called Rybernian, which still evokes laughs among the privileged few who can understand it. Telling a joke—the longer and more ethnic the better— always turned into a major performance. Lenny insisted on rapt attention during his recitation, going so far as to once shout at some dinner guests who were whispering while he was mid-joke, "Everyone shut up but me!" It was a line we threw back at him many times thereafter and it never failed to make him laugh; he was generally good at laughing at himself as well as at others. The others he laughed at and

Original West Side Story *cast members rehearse the "Mambo."*

with were his nearest and dearest: Adolph and Betty, Mike Nichols, Mike Mindlin, Goddard Lieberson, Martha Gelhorn, and his immediate family.

When it came to judging what would make a successful Broadway show, Lenny wasn't always on target. He didn't like to be reminded of his pronouncement that Alan Jay Lerner and Frederick Loewe were making a big mistake by turning Shaw's *Pygmalion* into a musical called *My Fair Lady*. I also must admit to a bit of misjudging when Lenny was working on what would become *1600 Pennsylvania Avenue* and he shared the plot and some tunes with me: I proclaimed it a brilliant concept. As we all know now, that show was one of his few disasters. That wasn't so funny for anyone. Nor was the tension in the room when he played for the family his somewhat less disastrous quasi-opera *A Quiet Place*.

As brilliant as Lenny was, he searched at times for inspiration. When he was having particular difficulty with lyrics for his *Mass*, Shirley came to the rescue. She had long since given up her unpromising musical-comedy career and had entered the producing and agenting part of show business. Tipped off about a talented student named

Stephen Schwartz at Carnegie Mellon University, she traveled to Pittsburgh to check him out. Check him out she did; she signed him up as a client and recommended him to Lenny. Schwartz helped save the day.

I, too, made a very small contribution to Lenny's Broadway *oeuvre*. For my sins I, as a lowly grunt, was sent by the U.S. Army to an infantry regiment in Puerto Rico—an assignment surprisingly less agreeable than duty in Korea, where I was supposed to go in the first place. In 1955, when I was transferred to a cushier posting in San Juan, Lenny

feuding teenage gangs, not unlike those in *Romeo and Juliet*. It was originally supposed to be about Catholics and Jews on the Lower East Side of Manhattan, but they decided to update it by moving the setting to the Upper West Side, which was then experiencing Anglo-Puerto Rican friction. He admitted he had an ulterior motive for his visit to San Juan: Could I take him to some of the cruddy *boîtes* I had boasted of frequently in my letters so that he could hear some authentic native music? So off we went to the cruddiest *boîte* I knew. It

The brother-writer as an infantryman in Puerto Rico.

As the "Mambo" number began I heard the distinctive signature riff of that San Juan quintet.

wrote to congratulate me on my good fortune and said that he'd like to come down for a visit. I wangled leave time, booked him into the Condado Beach Hotel, and proceeded to show him the sights, as best I knew them. He casually mentioned that he had been meeting with Arthur Laurents and Jerry Robbins about a show involving

featured a quintet of house musicians who played interesting mambos and such, and every number had a little signature riff by way of introduction. After a while, I noticed that Lenny had jotted down some notes on a napkin.

Two years later, I attended a run-through of *West Side Story*. Sure enough, as the "Mambo" num-

ber began I heard the distinctive signature riff of that San Juan quintet, fewer than ten notes that have since become part of Broadway lore. After the exciting run-through, I charged Lenny with the crime of rank plagiary. He confessed his guilt but he said that he had no idea how to make amends to the unsung quintet, nor did I. He cited similar misdemeanors by Haydn, Mozart, Brahms, and, more recently, Copland. I also pointed out that the song "Somewhere" was oddly reminiscent of the *Adagio* movement of Beethoven's Fifth Piano Concerto. "Alas," he sighed. So goes art, which is *longa*.

—*Burton Bernstein*

This time there was no problem about box-office potential as there had been with some earlier Bernstein shows. *West Side Story* sold tickets galore, and over time, it has become one of those rare artistic creations that captures a core sense of national identity—a bit like Beethoven's Ninth for the Germans. It not only gave voice to the anxieties of a particular historical moment, it also delivered central themes about life in the United States: ongoing struggles with urban violence, deeply rooted racism, fear of the newest immigrants. *West Side Story*'s reach got a huge boost from the 1961 film, starring Natalie Wood and Rita Moreno, which itself has become a classic. Meanwhile, *West Side Story* also entered American culture as a mainstay of the repertory for high schools and regional theaters. Its angular rhythms—especially its finger snaps and the distinctive musical shriek heard during the rumble as Bernardo stabs Riff—have become cultural signifiers, as instantly familiar as the opening of George Gershwin's *Rhapsody in Blue* or the tag of Bob Dylan's "Blowin' in the Wind." And how many Americans have said their vows to "One Hand, One Heart"? Not long before the premiere of *West Side Story*, Bernstein told a reporter for the *Daily Worker* that it was "the hardest thing I've ever done," and it turned out to be a challenging act to follow, especially once Bernstein began as Music Director of the New York Philharmonic in 1958. Over the next decade-plus, various ideas emerged for new shows, but none took off.

A Plea for Peace

Bernstein returned to the stage in 1971 with *Mass*, which was subtitled *A Theatre Piece for Singers, Players and Dancers* and was commissioned for the opening of the Kennedy Center in Washington, D.C. It combined the Latin text from the Roman liturgy with lyrics by Bernstein and Stephen Schwartz. While setting a Catholic ritual might seem an odd choice for a composer of Jewish heritage, Bernstein made a habit of taking on unexpected challenges. In this case, the commission was initiated by Jacqueline Kennedy Onassis in honor of her late husband John F. Kennedy, who were both devoted Catholics. Bernstein's admiration for the youth and idealism of J.F.K. had been enormous.

Although *Mass* was not a Broadway effort, its dramatic conception represented a fundamental extension of Bernstein's work for the commercial stage. *Mass* epitomized the notion of a hybrid, infusing age-old tradition with up-to-the-minute cultural gestures: church choirs rubbed elbows with rock, Catholicism met elements of Jewish tradition, deep-seated beliefs confronted skepticism. It captured the crisis of faith of the 1960s and 1970s. Scored for a Celebrant (i.e., a priest), mixed choir and children's choir, Street Singers, and Altar Servers, the work begins with a united affirmation of belief in God. But that solidarity fractures, reaching a climax at the

moment of Communion, when the Celebrant becomes overwhelmed by doubt. At one of the holiest points in Catholic ritual, he hurls the chalice-like objects with which he has been invested to the ground. His faith is gradually restored, and *Mass* ends with the traditional benediction "Go in peace." In 1971, at the height of the Vietnam War protests, those words resonated mightily.

Mass has had extensive exposure over the years, including a PBS broadcast in 1974 and numerous stagings at colleges and universities, where it has become a staple of the repertory. But its initial reception was rocky, and it remains controversial. Catholics and other devout Christians, writing in publications such as *Sacred Music* and *The Catholic Standard*, called it a "perversion of the liturgical act," a "sacrilege." Others loved its probing skepticism. "There were those, especially among the youthful members of the audiences," conceded Harold Schonberg, Bernstein's longtime nemesis at *The New York Times*, "who screamed and applauded and cheered and cried and said it was the most beautiful thing that they had ever heard."

Alvin Ailey choreographed the premiere production, and his dance company performed, yielding an integrated cast. Once again, youth provided the fuel.

Bernstein at the premiere of Mass *at the Kennedy Center, 1971. The work's youthful cast and probing skepticism proved popular with young audiences.*

The original cast of 1600 *Pennsylvania Avenue, a show that explored the history of the White House through stories of its occupants, whether presidents or servants.*

Stephen Schwartz, who collaborated with Bernstein on the lyrics, was then twenty-three, and Bernstein promoted him as "a genius." Bernstein scored the work for a boys' choir and a rock band, in the manner of *Godspell* or *Jesus Christ Superstar*, both of which appeared on Broadway around the same time. *Mass* was aimed at teens, and it emerged just as rock and folk started to gain currency in houses of worship. Yet its composer, even in this most irreverent work, remained tied to Western concert traditions. "If the text of *Mass* is potentially offensive," the critic David Schiff has observed, "the music reveals the composer to be in full command of his musical and theatrical powers, moving between styles and moods effortlessly and to great effect."

Bernstein's final attempt at a Broadway show came with *1600 Pennsylvania Avenue*. For the first time in a Bernstein theater work, youth was not center stage. The musical was a collaboration between two Broadway eminences in their late fifties; both born in 1918, both Harvard graduates. Bernstein conceived *1600 Pennsylvania Avenue* together with Alan Jay Lerner for the United States Bicentennial in 1976. But rather than marking the nation's birthday with a celebration of the red, white, and blue, Bernstein and Lerner launched a critique. The show explored the history of the White House through the stories of its occupants, and it placed a focus on race relations, with servants getting as much stage time as presidents. "The subject is not the presidency but the house," Bernstein stated firmly in an interview in the *Philadelphia Inquirer*. "Both the house and play become metaphors for the country." The work premiered not long after the Watergate scandal and responded to the death of John F. Kennedy, as well as Martin Luther King, Jr.

Unfortunately, both the message and the medium of *1600 Pennsylvania Avenue* failed to capture public support. It appeared in a Broadway season that was far from fallow, and that included premieres of *Chicago* (John Kander and Fred Ebb), *A Chorus Line* (Marvin Hamlisch), and *Pacific Overtures* (Stephen Sondheim). In many ways, these shows were the descendants of *West Side Story*, while *1600 Pennsylvania Avenue* struck out on its own, not exactly plugging into Broadway conventions but not successfully challenging them either. Despite some glorious music—including "Take Care of This House" and "Duet for One"—and extensive advance promotion, the show essentially died on arrival, lasting for only seven performances. With it, Bernstein's production for Broadway came to an end.

Bernstein's Vision

Looking back on Bernstein's singular achievement in the theater, his strength can appear to hold the seeds of his weakness. His open-mindedness and stylistic nimbleness generated a provocative combustion of opera, operetta, and musical theater that delighted audiences and critics, but left him struggling to define himself and his art. In the concert world, the "higher" the art, the more prestige it garnered. Yet Bernstein was constantly drawn back into the less-prestigious popular realm, and to his belief that the two worlds could successfully be merged. Every new work for the stage reactivated the struggle, and his vision of a brand-new, yet-to-be-labeled hybrid. "The form will be of wider range by far than musical comedy," he told an Albany reporter in 1953, "yet not in the traditional opera form, nor again in the form of Menotti whose *Amahl and the Night Visitors* was so widely seen on television." To realize this vision, he consistently leapt onto a high wire, turning perilous pirouettes as he balanced an array of styles and genres. When all is said and done, that sense of danger might be what most animates the Bernstein shows. Each tackles new problems. Each shoots the moon. And, as time passes, that perception of living on the edge continues to engage and challenge audiences the world over.

Bernstein's last musical, 1600 Pennsylvania Avenue, debuted in the wake of the Watergate scandal, which had brought down the presidency of the most recent White House occupant.

Leonard Bernstein and Television: Envisioning a Higher Purpose

BY TIM PAGE

"Ever since I can remember I have talked about music, with friends, colleagues, teachers, students and just plain, simple citizens…"

—*Leonard Bernstein, 1959*

n addition to his distinctions as composer, pianist, and conductor, Leonard Bernstein was also the most influential music teacher in history. A big claim, of course, but it stands up to analysis. I met the man only four or five times (and then briefly), but thanks to his many appearances on television I can say that I studied with Leonard Bernstein, and so did most of my contemporaries.

At a rehearsal for a CBS Omnibus *program, c. 1960.*

Indeed, if you grew up in the United States between 1955 and 1970, and you care enough about music to be reading this book, you are almost certainly one of Bernstein's students, too. And, fortunately, the programs are still extant, permitting the man Virgil Thomson called "the ideal explainer of music, both past and present" to extend his reach far beyond the grave.

Bernstein made his first television appearance in 1954. To put matters into context, remember that five years earlier only one in ten Americans had even *seen* a television. When Arturo Toscanini began his historic telecasts with the NBC Symphony Orchestra in 1948, there were no more than 350,000 sets in the entire country, and more than half of those were in the New York area. Toscanini was already in his eighties when the series began, but he appeared on ten programs, most of them about an hour long, between 1948 and 1954, after which he retired and the ensemble was summarily disbanded. By then there were more than 20 million television sets in the United States and an estimated 44 percent of the population was tuned in.

The new medium's power and influence continued to grow: in 1960, almost

90 percent of Americans would own a television. By 1981, when the Metropolitan Opera telecast Richard Strauss' *Elektra*, it was estimated that more people saw and heard the work on that single night than the sum total of every man, woman, and (God forbid!) child who had held a ticket to a live performance since the world premiere in 1909. One night! And then consider the number of television appearances Bernstein made in his prime—the early appearances on *Omnibus* and the long years with the Young People's Concerts—and you come up with a staggering total of potential "students."

For those of us who were raised in rural surroundings, far from concert halls and subscription series, watching and listening to Bernstein take us through music four times a year, whether Beethoven, Strauss, Gershwin—and even, on several occasions, the Beatles—was like a passport into another world. Bernstein took naturally to the television medium, and with his concise, cogent explanations, his balletic movements, his poetic face—suffering and ecstatic—he seemed the very personification of the art of music.

Rehearsals for live television programs. Opposite page: the lights required for early broadcasts were so bright that many Orchestra musicians donned sunglasses to protect their eyes during a 1958 Young People's Concert rehearsal.

Dionysus Meets Chaplin

What contrasts he presented! His leadership was simultaneously Dionysian and impeccably controlled, fiercely impulsive yet carefully thought through. Bernstein was Chaplinesque in his pantomime, capable of conveying the essence of a particular measure with such acuity and grace that watching him was like reading a map of the score. Much of the time, he wiggled and danced like an orgiastic surfer, carried aloft on waves of sound. But, when he wanted to, Bernstein could also be a tremendously economical conductor, with a tight little beat that was scarcely visible yet produced the intended results.

And he understood television from the start. Here is the beginning of Bernstein's first show, a program on Beethoven's Fifth Symphony presented on CBS's *Omnibus* on November 14, 1954:

> We are going to try to perform for you today a curious and rather difficult experiment. We're going to take the first movement of Beethoven's Fifth Symphony and rewrite it. Now don't get scared; we're going to use only notes that Beethoven himself wrote. We're going to take certain discarded sketches, intending to use them in this symphony, and find out why he rejected them, by putting them back into the symphony and seeing how the symphony would have sounded with them. Then we can guess at the reason for rejecting these sketches, and, what is more important, perhaps we can get a glimpse into the composer's mind as it moves through this mysterious creative process we call composing.

It was perfect, it was poetry, it was a grand game, it was an excavation, we were invited to play composer—indeed, for a moment, to be *Beethoven!* What sentient being, adult or child, could resist following Bernstein wherever he might have taken us from there? Half an hour later, having explored this most familiar music and made it sound brand new, the young conductor wrapped up his argument, in words so eloquent that they should be posted on the bulletin board of every conservatory or music school:

And so Beethoven came to the end of his symphonic journey, for one movement, that is. Imagine a whole lifetime of this struggle, movement after movement, symphony after symphony, sonata after quartet after concerto. Always probing and rejecting in his dedication to perfection, to the principle of *inevitability*. This somehow is the key to the mystery of a great artist; that for reasons unknown to him or to anyone else, he will give away his energies and his life just to make sure that one note follows another *inevitably*. It seems rather an odd way to spend one's life, but it isn't so odd when we think that the composer, by doing this, leaves us at the finish with the feeling that something is right in the world, something that checks throughout, something that follows its own laws consistently, something we can trust, that will never let us down.

Always the teacher. Opposite page: in rehearsal for a Philharmonic Young People's Concert at Philharmonic Hall with his daughter Jamie in a preferred seat, 1962.

Civilizing the "Vast Wasteland"

The title *Omnibus* was taken from the Latin ("for all; for everyone"). The hour-long program ran on Sundays from 1952 to 1961, initially on CBS, later on ABC and finally on NBC—surely the only program to have run on all three of the major networks. But that was hardly its only distinction. Sponsored by the Ford Foundation and hosted by Alistair Cooke, *Omnibus* offered diverse and intelligent programs about the sciences, the arts, and the humanities and remains a high point in the history of commercial television. After the quiz-show scandals broke in the late 1950s, *Omnibus* was regularly cited as exemplifying television's higher aspirations amidst what FCC chairman Newton N. Minow would later famously describe as a "vast wasteland."

Those "higher aspirations" were very much in the air in those early days of television, as the new medium's potential was being debated and explored. The celebrated newscaster Edward R. Murrow articulated the hopes of some, on October 15, 1958, when he spoke in Chicago at the annual convention of the Radio and Television News Directors Association. Criticizing the networks for programming "decadence, escapism and insulation from the realities of the world," he envisioned

a higher purpose for television: "This instrument," Murrow said, "can teach, it can illuminate. … Yes, and it can even inspire." Bernstein's programs on *Omnibus* put those aspirations into practice.

You can find all seven of Bernstein's *Omnibus* scripts in his first book, *The Joy of Music*, which was originally published in 1959, and was most recently reissued by Amadeus Press (2004). From the beginning, where television was concerned, Bernstein operated in the general vicinity of what might now be described as multiculturalism, with a taste that was wide-ranging and bracingly catholic. With equal clarity, he explored the conventions of the American musical theater, the syntactic structures of jazz, and the radical innovations of Stravinsky. And in an era when most conductors treated their art as a mysterious metaphysical shamanism that defied rational analysis, Bernstein actually took the time to explain just what he was doing up there on the podium.

> The great newsman **Edward R. Murrow** envisoned a higher purpose for television: "This instrument can teach, it can illuminate . . . it can even inspire."

His program on Bach was unusually personal. Bernstein admitted straight away that the composer's music had meant very little to him until he reached the age of seventeen. "Before that Bach had meant only some pretty monotonous stuff I sometimes heard at concerts and on the radio, plus some piano pieces I was given to practice." Still, by the end of the program, after comparing Bach to Beethoven, Rachmaninoff, César Franck, Tchaikovsky, "oriental folk music," jazz, "Frère Jacques," "Three Blind Mice," and more, while returning again and again to the *St. Matthew Passion*, Bernstein had made a brilliant popular (indeed, populist) argument for Bach, a composer who was then probably more revered than loved. At a moment in time when crossover was still in its infancy, this man and this medium—two powerful popularizers—joined forces to bring classical music to a vast new audience in a new way.

The Bach program, his penultimate creation for *Omnibus*, was telecast in 1957, which turned into Bernstein's *annus mirabilis*. This was the year that his masterpiece *West Side Story* came to Broadway, establishing a new musical style that captured urban tensions and rhythms; meanwhile, only a few blocks north of Manhattan's theater district, Bernstein was appointed Music Director of the New York Philharmonic, the oldest orchestra in the United States, then in residency at Carnegie Hall. It really was the best of both worlds, and only Bernstein could negotiate them both so effortlessly.

Being interviewed for a telecast from the American Pavilion in Moscow, during the Philharmonic's groundbreaking tour to the Soviet Union in 1959.

During his tenure with the Philharmonic, he altered the standard repertoire (I wonder whether Mahler's symphonies would have attained their current popularity without Bernstein's inspired and evangelical advocacy). He helped win a new, academic respectability for jazz and rock. Most important, perhaps, he proved that an American conductor, educated in this country, need no longer look to Europe for certification—a declaration of independence that had roughly the same effect on our homegrown musicians that Ralph Waldo Emerson's *The American Scholar* had on nineteenth-century poets, essayists, and philosophers.

Music Education for the Masses

It was as the New York Philharmonic's Music Director-Designate, on January 18, 1958, that Bernstein would lead the first of the fifty-three televised Young People's Concerts, which would prove one of his proudest legacies. He did not invent mass music education for young people. The peripatetic Theodore Thomas—who led the New York Philharmonic from 1877 to 1891—also had a profound effect on the dissemination of concert music in America, through a series of youth programs in Chicago in the late 1800s. And in 1924, a full three decades before Bernstein's first *Omnibus* program, Ernest Schelling—who was, like Bernstein, a pianist, conductor, and composer—started the long-running New York Philharmonic Young People's Concerts at Aeolian Hall on West Forty-second Street. The series proved so

(continued on page 97)

a brother's recollection

The Maestro's New Medium

Initially seeing little place for himself in television, Lenny, the born teacher and natural performer, soon embraced its potential for entertainment and edification.

The funny thing about Lenny and television is that when he first saw the new contraption he was not very impressed, and even after several encounters with the medium he displayed no particular affection for it. For one thing, he was never much good at handling mechanical devices, with the notable exception of the piano; to him, television was just another tech-

business. Sam, feeling his oats in the late 1930s, had developed a line of original beauty products under the rubric Avol Laboratories, and he was talked into promoting the abortive venture by mounting a fifteen-minute radio program called *Avol Presents* on a local Boston station. The artist that Avol invariably presented was none other than a young Leonard Bernstein at the pianoforte, ripping

He was never much good at handling mechanical devices, with the notable exception of the piano.

nological novelty of the postwar age. He seemed to like some newscasts, documentaries, late-night movies, and anything involving Sid Caesar and Imogene Coca. But I believe he saw very little potential for himself in the medium.

Lenny had some considerable experience with radio, however. His premiere as a performer while still a teenager was sponsored by our father, Samuel J. Bernstein, owner and president of the Samuel J. Bernstein Beauty Supplies Company, who had presumed that his older son would one day take over the family

through such light favorites as *Malagueña* and *Hora Staccato*.

Years later, as an established, celebrated musician, and no longer Sam's successor in the beauty-supplies game, Lenny was an occasional guest on Clifton Fadiman's witty, cerebral radio quiz program, *Information Please*. Adolph Green (an autodidact, if there ever was one) enjoyed accompanying Lenny to the studio on those occasions, and his presence in the audience evoked one of the myriad Adolph-and-Lenny stories, told well and often at parties. Although Lenny was a big T.S. Eliot

Television cameras offer an aerial view of the conductor's movements.

fan, he drew a total blank when Fadiman asked him a question about a famous Eliot poem. Adolph, seeing Lenny pale with the inexplicable lapse, suddenly raised a leg high enough for Lenny to notice and started madly adjusting his trouser cuff. Lenny, barely able to control his laughter, shouted out, "The Love Song of J. Alfred Prufrock." quickly adding a line from the poem, "I grow old, I grow old, I shall wear the bottoms of my trousers rolled." Fadiman and the audience were awed.

As Lenny and Felicia became an item, culminating in their 1951 marriage, television took on a whole new meaning for him due to her emergence as one of the great leading ladies of early television drama. Her acclaimed appearances—in vehicles such as in Henry James' *The Wings of the Dove*, on those live, primitive, yet polished series like *The Kraft Television Theater* and *Studio One*—convinced her husband that television had real potential for art, education, and perhaps even for Leonard Bernstein. Lenny was a born teacher, a habitual pedagogue who relished instructing one and all, young and old, with a maxi-

Soprano Veronica Tyler was a featured performer on the 1964 national telecast "What is Sonata Form?"

mum of joy and a minimum of pain. I have attested to this fact herein and elsewhere many times, as have Lenny's children, Jamie, Alexander, and Nina; my children, Karen and Michael; and God only knows how many thousands or perhaps millions of others. His inclination to teach was probably rooted in his rabbinic heritage, most cogently passed

and right up to the last minute before air time, various Bernstein offices, abodes, and dressing rooms were filled with smoke, half-consumed sandwiches and drinks, and scattered piles of messy paper. Robert Saudek, the major force behind *Omnibus*, and his staff worked every bit as hard as the star to wring out a script acceptable to Lenny, the tech-

His inclination to teach was probably rooted in his rabbinic heritage.

down by our father, Sam, who though a businessman by trade, never passed up an opportunity to edify others—alas in his favorite subject, Judaism. Few of Lenny's viewers were aware of how much dogged work went into the dozens of television shows that he made over the years. He was so adept at displaying an easy, casual manner that his performances evinced what the Italians call *sprezzatura*, something that appears to be born whole, effortlessly and spontaneously. The truth, of course, was that I rarely saw Lenny work harder on any projects than on those TV scripts. Weeks before any given telecast

nicians, the budget, the musicians, logic, knowledge, and art.

Lenny was truly a dedicated worker who loved working with others—a natural collaborator tossing out ideas from his notes on yellow legal pads to his equally dedicated co-workers until a graceful, accessible product mysteriously came to be. He believed deeply in teaching the world what he knew and felt, and hoped that maybe in the process he was making the planet a little smarter and more agreeable. The best way to do this, ironically, turned out to be television. For him and for so many others it was, indeed, the happy medium.
—*Burton Bernstein*

```
                                    22

              BERNSTEIN (CONT'D)
   In music composers can make these
   surprises in lots of different ways - by
   making the music loud when you expect it
   to be soft, or the other way around; or
   by suddenly stopping in the middle of a
   phrase; or by writing a wrong note on
   purpose, a note you don't expect, that
   doesn't belong to the music.  Let's try
   one, just for fun.  You all know those
   silly notes that go -
   SING:  SHAVE AND A HAIRCUT - 2 BITS


   O.K. Now you sing "Shave and a Haircut",
   and the orchestra will answer you with
   "2 bits" and see what happens.
   ORCH:     ILLUSTRATE


   (IF NO LAUGH)
   Now, you see, you didn't laugh out loud.
   (IF LAUGH)
   Now most people don't laugh out loud about
   musical jokes.  That's one of the things
   about musical humor: you laugh inside.
   Otherwise you could never listen to a
   Haydn symphony: the laughter would drown
   out the music.  But that doesn't mean a
   Haydn symphony isn't funny.

   ag               (MORE)
```

Always prepared. This excerpt from the script for "Humor in Music" shows how carefully Bernstein and his team planned.

popular that it grew to ten programs per year before the decade was out; starting in 1930, CBS presented about five Young People's Concerts on the radio each year. After Schelling's death in 1939, the concerts were supervised by Rudolph Ganz, Wilfred Pelletier, and Igor Buketoff. Upon rare occasions, a Philharmonic Music Director—notably John Barbirolli—would step in to lead a program or two. But Bernstein took the programs more seriously than any of his predecessors, viewing them as one of his most sacred and important duties.

As fate would have it, a new medium, which could reach a much wider audience than had been previously possible, had emerged to further the mission of this telegenic young maestro, with his passion for education. From the beginning, the *New York Philharmonic Young People's Concerts with Leonard Bernstein*, as the show was officially titled, was a tremendous critical and popular success. "Mr. Bernstein threw his young audience an awful lot of ideas, and he hurled them pretty fast," *The New York Times* critic Harold C. Schonberg observed the day after the first program. "He conducted excerpts by Beethoven, Mussorgsky, Tchaikovsky and, of all composers, Anton von Webern. The children listened to the wispy ultra-modernist with much more complacence than do their parents. As a matter of fact, they liked it." Schonberg continued: "How much of this the children absorbed remains to be seen, but it cannot be denied that Mr. Bernstein held their attention. No paper airplanes flew, nor was there a mass exodus to the watering points of Carnegie Hall."

> **"Mr. Bernstein** threw his young audience an awful lot of ideas, and he hurled them pretty fast."
>
> —Harold C. Schonberg, *The New York Times*

The titles of Bernstein's programs are indicative of his wide-ranging interests: "What is a Concerto?"; "Jazz in the Concert Hall"; "The Sound of an Orchestra"; "What Does Orchestration Mean?"; "Humor in Music"; "Unusual Instruments"; "The Latin American Spirit." As early as 1967, years before Ives-mania hit the United States, he assembled a program entitled "Charles Ives: American Pioneer." He did not ignore contemporary music: there were tributes to Hindemith, Sibelius, Shostakovich, and Stravinsky (the last two composers were then still living and Hindemith had only recently died). Aaron Copland's charming children's opera, *The Second Hurricane,* was presented in its entirety. Meanwhile, Bernstein illustrated sonata form by singing the Lennon-McCartney hit "And I Love Her," much to the delight of his audience.

Every year after 1960, Bernstein gave a forum to developing instrumentalists

On the set of "The Drama of Carmen," 1962, with tenor William Olvis and mezzo-soprano Jane Rhodes, Bernstein contrasts Bizet's original opéra-comique version, which included spoken dialogue, with the later grand-opera form.

and conductors on an episode called "Young Performers." The roster of Bernstein's discoveries is impressive: pianists André Watts and Horacio Gutiérrez; violinists Sergiu Luca, Elmar Oliveira, and Young Uck Kim; cellists Stephen Kates and Lynn Harrell; bassist Gary Karr; harpist Heidi Lehwalder; conductors James DePreist and Edo de Waart. On the December 23, 1963 broadcast, Bernstein presented a sixteen-year-old composer named Shulamit Ran who played the world premiere of her Capriccio for Piano and Orchestra. In 1991, she would win the Pulitzer Prize for composition, only the second woman to be so honored.

> "The Philharmonic's conductor has the **knack of a teacher** and the **feel of a poet.**"
>
> —*Variety*

Variety summed up Bernstein's appeal succinctly: "The Philharmonic's conductor has the knack of a teacher and the feel of a poet," it said. "The marvel of Bernstein is that, like the writer of television melodrama, he knows how to grab attention and how to carry it along, measuring just the right amount of new information to precede every climax."

Panoramas and Close-Ups

Meanwhile, Roger Englander, Bernstein's producer and director, was equally innovative in his approach to the show's visual presentation. There were panoramic long shots and tight close-ups of soloists, which helped bring a verisimilitude to the occasion. One of Englander's favorite effects was to let the camera pan across the faces of audience members as they listened raptly to Bernstein. I can remember the envy I felt for those lucky children—far away in glamorous New York, listening to Leonard Bernstein tell them about music. "What goes into the televising of a Young People's Concert?" Englander asked, rhetorically, in an essay that accompanied the series' tenth-anniversary season. "The basic formula is a relatively simple one. First assemble more than a million dollars' worth of mobile color television equipment. [remember, these were 1960s dollars!] Combine with 75 highly trained programming and engineering specialists and place everything and everyone in and around Philharmonic Hall. Add a famous conductor narrator in the person of Leonard Bernstein, 106 excellent symphony musicians and shoot for one hour. ..."

At the peak of its popularity, during the years when CBS presented four Young People's Concerts a season, the series was also carried in nine European countries—Italy, Germany, Belgium, Austria, Norway, Denmark, Finland, the

Netherlands and Portugal—as well as in Argentina, Japan, the Philippines, Australia, and New Zealand. During Bernstein's first ten years, the show won nine Emmy Awards, three awards from Sigma Alpha Iota (a national fraternity for professional musicians, teachers, and students of music), and three Thomas Alva Edison awards as the Best Children's Television Program of the Year. Initially, the telecasts emanated from Carnegie Hall, but they moved (with the Philharmonic) to Lincoln Center in 1962. After 1966, all concerts were telecast in color; those who know the Philharmonic's home, Avery Fisher Hall, only since its renovation in 1976, will be startled by the plush, purplish color of the original house.

When Bernstein left the Orchestra in 1969, he still returned to conduct several of the following season's Young People's Concerts. In the 1970–71 season, he presented "A Copland Celebration" and a virtuoso exploration of *Also Sprach Zarathustra*, entitled "Thus Spake Richard Strauss." The last two programs were devoted to "Liszt and the Devil" (Bernstein was a passionate advocate for Liszt's *Faust* Symphony) and, finally, *The Planets*, a presentation of Gustav Holst's beloved suite, complete with Bernstein's own improvisation of a theme for Pluto, which won and later lost its status as a planet after Holst had finished his work.

In 1972, it was announced that Michael Tilson Thomas, a Bernstein protégé who was then the music director of the Buffalo Philharmonic and the principal guest conductor of the Boston Symphony Orchestra, would lead the next two seasons. Tilson Thomas was a creative host—one memorable episode traced the distinc-

Backstage monitors capture every move during the Moscow broadcast, 1959.

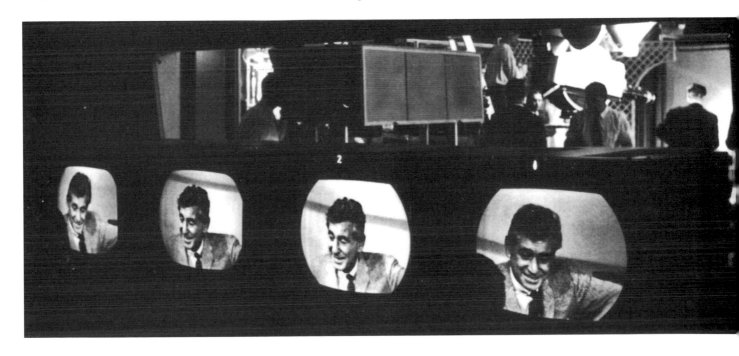

Young People's Concert,
Carnegie Hall, 1960.
Sometimes the audience
at home had a better view
of the action than those
sitting in the hall.

tions between music and noise—but television was changing and there were fewer
viewers. For one thing, by the early 1970s, young viewers and their parents had
many more choices. In addition, the major networks were no longer so concerned
about their public duty, and music education in this country was becoming something of a scandal. Watching the old YPC programs, it is startling to realize that
Bernstein presumes a greater musical knowledge on the part of his children than
most critics would presume from their grown readers in the twenty-first century.

Bernstein's television career did not end with those final YPCs; it stretched on
until the last year of his life. In 1973, he delivered the Charles Eliot Norton
Lectures at Harvard University. Entitled "The Unanswered Question" (the title was
borrowed from Charles Ives) and inspired by the linguistic theories of Noam
Chomsky, the series was videotaped and presented in its fifteen-hour entirety on
WGBH and WNET, in 1976, and was also published in book form. In addition,
there would be telecasts from Tanglewood, from London's Royal Albert Hall, and
from the Frederick R. Mann Auditorium in Tel Aviv. And between 1972 and 1983,
Bernstein collaborated with the Vienna Philharmonic on two monumental televised
series: one of the complete Brahms orchestral works, the other, *Bernstein/Beethoven,*

a survey of that composer's nine symphonies. Finally, few of us who were alive in that amazing autumn of 1989, when anything and everything seemed possible, will forget the supercharged rendition of Beethoven's Symphony No. 9 that Bernstein led in the beautiful rubble of what until weeks before had been the Berlin Wall. He called on the chorus to substitute the word *Freiheit!* (freedom!) for Beethoven's *Freude!* (joy!). If it sounds a little corny now, it didn't back then, in the days before the concept of "freedom" had been officially and routinely debased. Rarely had Beethoven's celebration of universal brotherhood, both tub-thumping and celestial, rung out with such resonance, as boundaries dissolved, soldiers went home, Europe was remade, and we dared to hope that a better world might be on the way. And all of it brought to viewers around the world via television, the medium that Bernstein had embraced so enthusiastically early in his career and had made his own.

Using an old Victrola to illustrate his point on a Philharmonic Young People's Concert. 1960.

It is hard to believe that Bernstein has been gone the better part of two decades, and that he never knew the Internet or DVDs or even YouTube, where one can find so many of his lectures and performances immortalized. Yet we may be grateful that he understood television so well and used it so wisely. For this reason, among many others, Bernstein—like his friend Glenn Gould, who came to eschew live performance in favor of performing only on recordings—is one of a handful of performing artists from the past who remain a permanent part of our present.

Forever Young

Some words Bernstein wrote about the Young People's Concerts in 1968 can stand as his credo. "These concerts are not just concerts— not even in terms of the millions who view them at home," he wrote.

> "They are, in some way, the quintessence of all I try to do as a conductor, as a performing musician. There is a lurking didactic streak in me that turns every program I make into a discourse, whether I utter a word or not; my performing impulse has always been to share my feelings, or knowledge, or speculations about music—to provoke thought, suggest historical perspective, encourage the intersection of musical lines. And from this point of view, the Young People's Concerts are a dream come true, especially since the sharing is done with young people—that is, people who are eager, unprejudiced, curious, open and enthusiastic. What more could an old incorrigible pedagogue ask for? I hope I shall never have to give these concerts up; they keep me young."

Through these remarkable telecasts, Bernstein is *forever* young—and so is the art of music.

a brother's recollection

Leonard Bernstein's Separate Peace with Berlin

What follows is a very personal account of one of the more famous Philharmonic tours abroad. It was a piece I wrote for Esquire magazine in 1961, where it appeared in a somewhat different and lengthier form. Then, as now, it was a labor of great fun and devotion.

Since it first went into the tour business with an expedition through darkest New England in 1910, the New York Philharmonic has performed on four continents, in thirty-five foreign countries, forty-three of the United States, and two hundred seventy-eight cities. And although he has only been the Orchestra's Music Director and Conductor since 1958, Leonard Bernstein has led the

Lenny's way across the Atlantic. A seven-week trek through the continental United States, Canada, and Hawaii had taken Lenny to one-night stands at such cities as Las Vegas, Memphis, Chattanooga, Birmingham, San Diego, and Charlotte. Suddenly, there was to be one other little stop before the tour was completed—West Berlin.

The Berlin junket—the purpose of which was to perform two con-

As a demonstration of faith in the troubled city, a Ford Motor Company Vice President suggested a visit by the Philharmonic

Philharmonic through at least half of the above statistic. Now this information might not unduly alarm the average music lover, but it unquestionably has added more than a few gray hairs to the heads of Leonard Bernstein and his immediate family. I know because I've actively been the conductor's brother for twenty-nine years. In my particular case, the anxiety was accompanied by verdant envy at not being along. That is, until last year, when an extra plane seat became suddenly available on

certs at the annual West Berlin Music, Drama, and Arts Festival and to tape a Leonard Bernstein and the New York Philharmonic television show for American viewing—came about because of a precedent-setting subsidy from the Ford Motor Company, the Philharmonic's television sponsor. Early in 1960, Charles Moore, a Ford vice-president, visited Berlin and found that the United States would be inadequately represented at the forthcoming festival. As a demonstration of faith in the

The conductor and the writer on board their flight to Germany.

troubled city, he suggested a visit by the Philharmonic. Thus, for the first time in history, an American corporation, dedicated to making a profit, happily put up $150,000 for an orchestra's tour.

Lenny arrived back in New York on September 18 for a day's rest before the hop to Berlin. He had his customary post-tour look of Marley's Ghost and had the voice, or lack of same, to match. Once en route to Idlewild, I was informed that Robert Saudek and his associates, who

were producing the television show to be taped in Berlin, were also coming along. Like most tired people, Lenny was cranky. "All day long I've been longing for something," he said hoarsely, "and now I know what it is. What I'd really like is a bowl of crisp corn flakes and milk. God, what I'd give for that!"

A touring orchestra has much of the quality of a busload of high-school seniors visiting Washington, D.C., during spring vacation. First of all, there is the inevitable class

cutup—in the Philharmonic's case, Jack Fishberg, a cheery, owlish first violinist. It was hot in the jet before it took off, and Fishberg lost no time in removing his shirt and parading around telling jokes in his T-shirt, pants, and workingman's suspenders. Somehow, he succeeded in gaining access to the stewardess' microphone, and before anything could be done to stop him, he announced to the passengers in a fake Russian accent: "Hallo, this is your keptan. Plizz tek your sits, or I

"A touring orchestra has much of the quality of a busload of high-school seniors."

refuse to tek off." George E. Judd, Jr., a Bostonian, and the Orchestra's infinitely patient and wise Manager, subdued the violinist before any more advisements could be made. When the real captain made an announcement in a thick Dutch accent, nobody paid any attention to it.

As in any group of high-school seniors worth their salt, there are the class lovers—those insatiable fellows to whom every girl is an automatic challenge. The Philharmonic has two admirable speci-mens—both violinists and both darkly handsome—Alfred Breuning and Robert de Pasquale. They had already cornered the harassed stewardess in the galley and were wangling appointments with her for later in the flight. "Really, I have loads of work to do now," she was saying to them sweetly, as I passed through on the way to my seat.

I strapped myself in next to Lenny, and by 7:30 we were airborne. Once we had leveled off, various members of the Orchestra filed up to their leader to pay their respects, a solid-ified tour tradition by this time. Most had little speeches prepared on what an "artistic success" the summer tour had been; how happy, though tired, they were; and how they were looking forward to the coming season. One of them, Richard Nass, the English hornist, preferred to talk about Berlin. "All I want to do," he said, waving his ready-mixed Martini, "is to go back to the house in Berlin where I was born and throw stones at it or something." Lenny listened to each musician with a curious blend of weariness and humility. He thanked them all and was careful to point out how much they as individuals helped to make the tour a success. When the last musician had wandered back to his seat, Lenny said to me, "I know, from other Philharmonic flights that there won't be a minute's sleep tonight. You wait and see."

The serving of dinner (*salade aux fruits de mer, filet mignon grille maître d'hôtel, petits pois au beurre, pommes rissolées,* etc.) kept the passengers, for the most part, in their assigned seats and also gave me my first chance to speak to Lenny about the trip and the television show. He seemed most concerned with the Ford subsidy and what it could mean to American art. "I still think government support of art is on the way," he said, "and I'm all for it. Meanwhile, it is the responsibility of the wealthy corporations to support our artistic institutions privately—that is, until generous government support, with a minimum of strings attached, is forthcoming. Someone has to do the

"What I'd really like is a bowl of crisp corn flakes and milk. God, what I'd give for that!"

work the government should do, otherwise we'll be in an artistic vacuum. And everybody stands to gain from this kind of support—the nation, the artists, the audiences, the company that finances the artists—everybody. That's why this Ford Berlin tour is important; because it will show the potential of subsidizing art."

I asked him how the television script was coming. He said he was worried, for one thing, by whether the audience of German students would understand his thesis that Beethoven's music comes closest to universal greatness because of the German genius for development— the intricate broadening of a simple idea into a universal comment. "I'm

not so bothered really about talking Beethoven to Germans in English as I am about whether they'll get my allusions," Lenny said, lighting a cigarette. "For instance, the way it stands now, I'm going to show how development works by pointing out that from a seemingly insignificant local truth—namely, that Seventh Avenue is a one-way street—literally dozens of grander truths of universal interest can be developed and drawn. Seventh Avenue is one way because of the New York traffic problem. The New York traffic problem is bad because a lot of Americans can afford cars. A lot of Americans can afford cars because our economy and standard of living are high, which brings us to capitalism—you see, we're already on a subject that involves all mankind—and then on to world economic, social, and political affairs. The problem is, will the Germans relate to the Seventh Avenue reference, or should I make it into more of a local Berlin thing? We've even had research done on whether there are one-way streets in Berlin. It turns out there aren't any. I don't know, it's something the Saudek people and I will have to figure out once we get there. It'll mean a hell of a lot of rewriting, and there's so little time, what with the concerts."

Lenny was also uneasy about the end of his script, where he dedicated the performance of the Beethoven First Piano Concerto in C major to the most immediate universal goal of world peace. Since the program was to be taped on the second day of Rosh Hashana, the Jewish New Year, Lenny planned to recite, in Hebrew and in English, the benediction: May the Lord lift up His face to you and give you peace.

"The benediction fits perfectly into the spirit of the dedication," Lenny said, a trifle defensively, "and

it does have the ring of universality about it. And, anyway, I feel so damn guilty about being in Berlin, of all places, over Rosh Hashana. Besides, I honestly don't think it will do the Berliners any harm to hear a little Hebrew once in a while." He stretched back in his seat, looking like a man who had fully made up his mind. One of the associate producers on the Saudek staff sat down in

"I feel so damn guilty about being in Berlin over Rosh Hashana. Besides, I don't think it will do the Berliners any harm to hear a little Hebrew."

the third seat and broke his short spell of contentment. "Lenny," she said, "can I talk with you a minute, or are you going to sleep?"

"There'll be no sleep tonight," Lenny announced tragically, bringing his seat into an upright position. "What is it?"

"Well," she went on, "I've been having some second thoughts about the Rosh Hashana bit at the end of the script. I tried it out on a few of my friends—who are by no means stiff-

necked—and some of them seem to think that since the TV show will be shown around Thanksgiving, the Jewish benediction will be a little out-of-place, if you know what I mean."

"I don't," Lenny said sourly.

"Well," she explained, "they think Thanksgiving is basically a Protestant holiday, and some people might be—well, not offended, but think it's bad timing. Personally, I think it's fine, but I can understand the argument for the other point of view."

"Ridiculous!" Lenny said, loosening his tie. "First of all, we'll have the announcer or somebody explain that the program was taped during Rosh Hashana, and, secondly, what could be more appropriate than this ancient benediction at Thanksgiving, which is, even more appropriately, a universal holiday, when you get right down to it. And anyway, it's that Hebrew in Berlin on Rosh Hashana that will really make this show for me."

"I guess you're right," she said.

"Don't worry," Lenny said in a tone that was meant to be comforting.

"Have you thought any more about the Berlin local example?" she asked.

Lenny thought for a moment. "Maybe we can do something with Tempelhof Airport. I don't know, I'm too tired now. Let's think about it once we get there. We'll have a meeting tomorrow afternoon, at the Hilton."

It has become a tradition with the Philharmonic to feel toward the pilots of their planes as an appreciative Carnegie Hall audience feels towards the Orchestra after a good concert. Whenever one of their planes makes a safe, smooth landing, the entire group bursts into hearty applause and cheering, usually led by Jack Fishberg. "That sound of tires touching down on a runway and applause means tour-time to me," Lenny said, as we land-

Receiving a warm welcome at Tempelhof Airport in West Berlin.

ed perfectly at the Frankfurt Airport, seven hours after we left Idlewild. "I hear that sound in my dreams, and so does the Orchestra. They've spent half their lives in planes over the past three summers. They feel every landing like a Beethoven symphony."

In Frankfurt, we were transferred to two smaller DC-6 planes—the largest Berlin's Tempelhof Airport could accommodate. The pilot of Plane A felt obliged to couch his in-flight remarks in musical terms. "We'll be heading *molto allegro* to Berlin," he announced, "over a few measures of East Germany. ... Down there on the right is Eisenach, where

the composer J. S. Bach was born. ... And up ahead on the left is a Russian military airfield. There's a MIG taking off now."

"They wouldn't dare shoot us down. We're artists!" joked one of the musicians.

When the DC-6 landed at Tempelhof—always a thrill as the wings almost brush the adjacent buildings—the musical pilot got the loudest ovation, it was reported, of any Philharmonic flier to date.

At the Berlin Hilton—a building indistinguishable from any other Hilton—the Philharmonic men who had arrived before us by bus were

Bernstein at the piano, playing and conducting Beethoven's First Piano Concerto during the televised concert from Berlin.

milling about the lobby. While most of them said they were going to spend the free day sleeping, a few hardies were already grimly setting out for some sightseeing. Lenny, after arranging with Robert Saudek for a script meeting in his suite at 3:30, went to sleep. "I think I'm getting bronchitis," he said. "That's all I need."

I was feeling a little wheezy myself, so I went to sleep, too, in the suite I was sharing with Lenny. I was awakened around four o'clock by Lenny's voice coming from the other room.

"Personally," he was saying, "I don't see why they can't imagine what Seventh Avenue traffic is like, even if they never saw it." There was a round of detailed discussion on that point and I dozed off again. I reawakened a few minutes later to hear Lenny say, "All right, all right, then it's Tempelhof. Let's make it something like this: It's noisy in Berlin. Why? Because planes land all the time at Tempelhof Airport, and Tempelhof is right smack in the middle of the city. Why can't a more distant airport be used? Because Berlin is a political island, that's why … and so on to

world conflict and power politics. How does that sound?" They agreed it sounded pretty good. "I still like Seventh Avenue better," Lenny said. I showered, shaved, dressed, and went out into the cold drizzle of Berlin to have a look around.

Miles of prosperity line the Kurfürstendamm and its adjacent streets, and when I had my afternoon's fill of it, I headed back to the Hilton. The script meeting was breaking up as I entered the room. "Then it's all agreed," Lenny was saying to Saudek. "Tempelhof and the Hebrew, right?" Saudek nodded his head. He looked like a man who would have agreed to a show on Buxtehude's mother-in-law at that point.

"I'll take care of the revised stuff, Lenny," said one of the Saudek associates, as she led the way out. "You get some sleep."

Lenny fell into the largest of our room's many bright-purple chairs and allowed a cigarette to droop rakishly from his lower lip. "Actually, I should go right to sleep," he said to me. "I'm *collapso profundo*, but do you know what tonight is?" I nodded because I knew what he meant; it was the first night of Rosh Hashana. We examined a copy of *Berlin Programm*, looking under "Jüdische Gottesdienste" for a nearby synagogue. We were amazed to find five choices, the nearest being at 13 Joachimstaler Strasse. "I can't believe there are enough Jews to fill five synagogues in this city!" Lenny exclaimed. "What are they all doing here?" I answered that we'd find out if we hurried. We rounded up some likely companions and off we went by Mercedes-Benz taxi.

There are no Hitlers, Goerings, Himmlers, or Goebbels in the Berlin telephone directory, but there are thirty-five Cohns and twenty Bernsteins. What this proves, I'm not exactly sure, but the Orthodox synagogue on Joachimstaler Strasse was filled to capacity when we arrived. We were wordlessly offered skullcaps and prayer books and ushered to the only empty space left on the floor. Several people stared at us for a few seconds and then turned nervously back to their praying. Lenny cocked his ear at the singing and whispered to me, "These people aren't Germans. I can tell by their accents. They're Poles. What do you make of that?" Lenny seemed strangely depressed by his discovery.

The service ended and worshipers began filing toward the door. Lenny struck up a conversation in pidgin English with a ruddy-faced fellow. Lenny asked him where all the German Jews were; the man replied that as far as he knew they attended a reformed synagogue across town. There were just two thousand Jews left in West Berlin, he said, and three thousand in the East; he never went to any other synagogue but this one, so he didn't know much about them. We asked him if he wanted to stay in Germany, and he answered with a shrug.

Lenny was up early the next morning, Thursday, for a full day of on-camera rehearsing with the

The producer looked like a man who would have agreed to a show on Buxtehude's mother-in-law at that point.

Orchestra at the Grosser Sendesaal des Senders Freies Berlin, a large radio studio where both the concerts and telecast were to take place. He arrived back in the hotel room late. He had just been told that that night's concert was to begin at 7:50, which was any minute now, because of a radio broadcast. "And this on top of the day to end all days," he moaned. "At the rehearsal we had American producers,

English technicians, and German television cameramen. As if the language barrier weren't bad enough, they've got to adjust the cameras one way for the Eurovision telecasts and another way for our taping. And the hall we play in has the acoustics of ninety hi-fi sets at full blast. It's impossible to get balances right. I'm so tired I can hardly see any more. I really think this has been the worst day of my life. The only thing that saved it was that the Orchestra was moved by my script. When that happens, I must say it almost seems worth it all." We wolfed a quick dinner in the room, and then we dashed off to the concert hall.

The Grosser Sendesaal of the SFB seats only eleven hundred persons, but it looks larger because of its light-wood paneling. Music played there has the crisp, brittle sound of electronic music, and the brass and winds being on tall risers doesn't soften the blow any. Yet, there was an infectious, intimate feeling in that stark hall, and the audience had little of that "O.K., show me" look that so many audiences do.

I have heard enough of Lenny's concerts to know when one is destined to be a triumph. From the *Candide* Overture on, I knew this was going to be one of them. Lenny and the Orchestra seemed to sense it, too; they played the remainder of the program—Roy Harris's Third Symphony, Copland's *El Salón México*, and Tchaikovsky's Fifth—like overcharged batteries. The audience wouldn't leave the hall. They stamped their feet, yelled "Bravo," and insisted on bringing the conductor back for nine curtain calls. After his ninth bow, Lenny tried his German again and explained haltingly that the Orchestra had a lot of work ahead, but they would play the "Infernal Dance" from Stravinsky's *Firebird* as an encore. This was worth three more bows and would have gotten more, but Lenny held up his hands in a desperation gesture and the musicians dashed off stage, as if obeying a secret cue.

It will never cease to amaze me what a genuine ovation will do for Lenny. He can be gray-green and sunken-eyed with fatigue, but with a round of sincere applause he can bounce right back with the resiliency of Herb Elliott on the last lap of a mile race. Backstage, Lenny looked suddenly healthy, energetic, and vital and he was in rare form at a

Lenny can be gray-green and sunken-eyed with fatigue, but with a round of sincere applause he can bounce right back.

reception given by the SFB and Berlin Festival managements. He signed dozens of autographs (occasionally playing the *enfant terrible* by drawing goatees and mustaches on his program picture first); charmed countless *Frauen* and *Fräuleins* into fits of giggling; interviewed a young Japanese conductor who wanted to come to New York (and who turned out to be Seiji Ozawa); posed with several government officials; and had a talk with Sydney Gruson, *The New York Times'* Germany correspondent,

In his dressing room following a concert, with Philharmonic President David Keiser.

about the television script.

Ready to leave, Lenny had invited several shocked Berliners to come along to the Rififi, a low-down night club of some fame. Three did accept—two lovely girl students and a stringy, sensitive young man who was interested in music. The handsome Philharmonic violinist Al Breuning was disconsolate at having been stood up by a Pan American stewardess he had invited to the concert, so he came along, too. There were sporadic entrances of half the Philharmonic. The regulars at the Rififi never knew what hit them; they simply stared at us all unbelievingly.

We ordered drinks and settled back to view the famous Berlin nocturnal scene, which was getting more American by the minute. The three German youths whom Lenny had invited along—Barbara, Jutta, and Michael—appeared increasingly ill-at-ease. Lenny began to speak to them and they relaxed somewhat, in a kind of worshipful way.

"Do you like rock-'n'-roll, Barbara?" Lenny asked the blonder of the two girls.

No matter how exhausted, Bernstein seemed always to have energy for the local nightlife wherever he toured.

"Yes, sometimes," she answered, "but not like in this place. I just heard it for the first time two years ago when I came to West Berlin from East."

"Have you always lived in Berlin?" Lenny asked.

"Yes," she said.

"How old are you?"

"I'm twenty-one years," she answered.

Lenny looked into his drink for a moment. "Isn't it amazing?" he said. "You were born when I was finishing college and the war was just breaking out here. All I could think of that year was how much I hated Germans."

"We cannot blame you," Michael said.

"The world stinks," someone who was on his second drink mumbled.

"Oh, it's not so bad," Lenny said. "Here it is 1960 and here we are, sitting together in Berlin listening to ghastly American popular music. Where else could this happen but in the world? I hope you kids are coming to the taping tomorrow, because that's what it's all about."

It was a late but pleasant evening at the Rififi.

The next day, Friday, Lenny became the first musician known to recorded history to play and conduct Beethoven's First Piano Concerto three times for three different audiences within a twelve-hour period. He was at the SFB hall at nine o'clock in the morning, an hour before the Orchestra, for make-up and a final script conference. Then, at ten o'clock, there was a dress-rehearsal taping of the television show before an exuberant audience of Berlin students.

"It went like a dream," Lenny told me during the break between the morning and afternoon tapings. "They seemed to understand the point of the script and they liked everything. You know the part where I play a little of the Beethoven as a German, a Frenchman, a Russian, and an American might play it. Well,

they laughed. Really, I never expected the script to work so well, and then they actually burst into applause at the Hebrew prayer. It was a joy to behold; I felt like crying. I almost fainted three times from tiredness, but it was worth it. Now, let's hope the afternoon session goes as well."

The afternoon taping didn't go as well. A completely new audience of students, just as exuberant as the

"They actually burst into applause at the Hebrew prayer. It was a joy to behold; I felt like crying."

first, was present, but a series of mechanical difficulties with the teleprompter broke up the continuity of the script and made Lenny's line of thought harder to follow. The delays, while the teleprompter was fixed, drained a lot of the vitality from both Lenny and his audience. By the time he arrived at the Hebrew benediction, the students had pretty much forgotten the point he was trying to make by it. They were slightly stunned at hearing the Hebrew, but finally burst into strong applause.

Backstage, Lenny had slipped into a dark, limp depression again. "It was lousy," he was saying to a consoling group around him. Shirtless and gray-green in color, he stretched out on a couch. "It just didn't work like it did this morning. This morning, the kids were hepper to English and caught all the subtleties and the Beethoven sang and everything worked. This was a debacle. And the Rosh Hashana thing

didn't work, either. Dammit!"

William Graham, the director of the show, entered the dressing room and said, "Sorry about the teleprompter, Lenny, but a beautiful job on your part. It looked great on the monitors."

"Yeah, grand," Lenny grunted. "Well, maybe we can use some of the dress-rehearsal tape."

An aide popped in and said there were a lot of kids outside who wanted autographs. "Tell them I'm too tired to sign anything," Lenny said.

"But tell them nicely."

The aide left and came right back in again. "One of them says he was with you and your friends last night in some bar. His name is Michael something."

Lenny got up from the couch. "All right," he said, "tell him to come in, if he wants to."

"I'm sorry to bother you, Mr. Bernstein," Michael said, poking his head through the doorway. "I enjoyed the program very much and I want to thank you for making it for us here. Barbara and Jutta want to thank you, too. Would you sign something for us, please." He proffered his program. "I would especially like it if you would write the Hebrew prayer you spoke today."

Lenny smiled and painstakingly wrote out the Hebrew letters of the benediction and signed his name. He handed the program back to Michael and shook his hand warmly. "I'm glad you enjoyed it," he said. "Thank you."

The boy left and Lenny slowly got into street clothes. He suddenly looked as if he could rally enough spirit to perform the second concert and have another go at the Beethoven Concerto that night. "Maybe it wasn't so bad after all," he said, then sighed.

I saw the Thanksgiving telecast of the Berlin concert in the presence of its star and the rest of the Bernstein family. I don't particularly relish watching Lenny watching Lenny on television; he fidgets constantly, criticizes every camera shot, screams at wrong notes and late entrances, and generally can't stand the sight of himself ("My God, do I really look like *that*?"). Needless to say at this point, the Berlin show was especially nervewracking for him and the rest of us. Yet, Lenny was uncharacteristically silent throughout. He winced sharply at some piano clinkers and unconsciously cleared his throat when he sounded hoarse on the screen. But as soon as the final Ford commercial shocked us out of Berlin, Lenny stood up and raised his arms exultantly. "How about that?" he shouted. "It wasn't bad at all. I would've liked another crack at the Beethoven, though."

—*Burton Bernstein*

An Idealist Abroad

BY JONATHAN ROSENBERG

*W*hat a thrilling world this could be, *if only we knew we would never again have to indulge the brutal sin of war-making. … Instead of wasting our energies in hostility and our wealth on weaponry, we could send art to the moon, exalt our Pasternaks instead of isolating them. We could feed and house and clothe everyone forever; lick cancer in a week; harness the sun's energy; learn a few languages; talk, travel, grow, and love. If our musical mission has made any slight contribution to that eventual state of affairs, we are humbly grateful, and we are particularly grateful to President Eisenhower for making our mission possible.*

—*Bernstein's closing remarks following his 1959 Moscow concert program telecast nationwide in the United States.*

Author Boris Pasternak attended the concert at the invitation of Bernstein and his wife, Felicia. It was Pasternak's first public appearance after being named persona non grata *by the Soviet authorities for his willingness to accept the Nobel Prize in Literature for* Dr. Zhivago.

To the list of Leonard Bernstein's many roles—conductor, composer, pianist, and educator—we must add one more: idealist. Believing deeply that art and politics were interconnected, Bernstein was certain that music could help bring peoples together by inspiring them to transcend the political forces that pushed them apart. But Bernstein was also an iconoclast. One of the most outspoken classical musicians of the post-war period, he was not afraid to express sentiments that lay outside the political mainstream. No symphony conductor before or since was as rhetorically daring as Bernstein, who articulated views that challenged the reigning conventions of Cold War America. In an era when the national security state was expanding dramatically, Bernstein advocated peace while others prepared for war. He argued that it was essential to provide funds for basic human needs, while others said it was necessary to produce more missiles. And he extolled the virtues of international cooperation while others warned that it would be folly for the United States to let down its guard against an aggressive enemy.

Fighting a War with Violins and Trumpets

If Bernstein was willing to give voice to such unconventional sentiments, the U.S. government conceived a quite different role for classical musicians, seeing them as allies in the East-West struggle. Government officials embraced the notion that the splendor of a symphony orchestra could fortify America's relations with its friends and provide sonic ammunition that could be targeted at its foes. The U.S. government thus sent orchestras overseas in an effort to display the fruits of liberal democracy to allies and adversaries, believing that violins and trumpets could help win the Cold War.

During the 1950s, the New York Philharmonic under Leonard Bernstein was one of several ensembles that participated enthusiastically in this cultural offensive, crossing the oceans under the sponsorship of the President's Special International Program for Cultural Presentations, which was administered by ANTA, the American National Theater and Academy. On such journeys, Bernstein conducted everything from Beethoven to Barber for music lovers the world over—whether in Rio, Buenos Aires, Budapest, Warsaw, or, most memorably, in the Soviet Union in 1959, when he led the Orchestra in some of the most compelling performances in its history. Including the government-sponsored tours of the late 1950s, Bernstein conducted the Orchestra on a total of ten overseas trips between 1958 and 1976, playing some two hundred fifty concerts outside the United States and Canada. This essay will consider three of those tours—the extraordinary journeys to Latin America, the Soviet Union, and Berlin—when music and politics were intertwined.

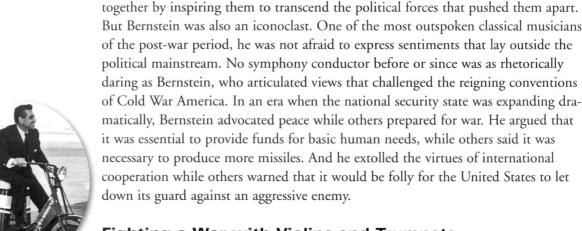

Thrilling the welcoming crowds, Bernstein takes a spin on a motor scooter upon his arrival at the airport in Lima, Peru, 1958.

The Orchestra in Latin America

Bernstein's first foreign tour with the Philharmonic came in 1958, when the Orchestra visited Latin America from April to June, performing in twelve countries and twenty-one cities over a seven-week period. (Three years earlier, before Bernstein's tenure began, the Philharmonic had undertaken its first tour under ANTA sponsorship, playing a month of concerts in Europe.) Bernstein conducted the majority of the concerts on the 1958 tour, sharing podium duties with Dimitri Mitropoulos, the Orchestra's other Principal Conductor. (Bernstein became the Orchestra's sole Music Director the following season.) By every measure, the trip was an enormous success, although even in the late fifties many Latin Americans harbored considerable animosity toward the United States. But the hostility that was aimed at the political leadership of the United States contrasted sharply with the enthusiasm and affection the

Relishing the unscripted moments to make friends, Bernstein stops for a shoeshine and photo with street kids in Lima.

Philharmonic encountered in the concert halls and stadiums of Latin America, where the public reaction to the tour was uniformly enthusiastic, even euphoric. The continent had never before witnessed orchestral performances of this caliber, and in city after city the ovations were described as "delirious," "frenetic," and unlike any that had ever been seen.

In the first program, played in Panama City, Bernstein demonstrated his formidable skills on the podium and at the piano. Leading the Orchestra in works of Mendelssohn and Copland, the young maestro also played Ravel's Piano Concerto in G, a work he performed several times on the tour, winning tumultuous applause on each occasion. According to one Chilean paper, Bernstein knew how to "give to each of the interpretations an exceptional sparkle," while another spoke of the "rare and precious present" the U.S. State Department had bestowed on the country. It could be summed up, the critic reported, "in one word: sound," the quality of which was a "sensual delight without comparison." A Peruvian critic noted that the tour "affords us the opportunity of witnessing the heights of perfection which may be reached as a result of constant effort and practice."

Along with the national anthems of the United States and the host country, the U.S. government required the Orchestra to play at least one piece by an American composer at every concert. In fact, the American compositions that Bernstein and Mitropoulos selected—music by Barber, Copland, Gershwin, Roy Harris, or William Schuman—were vetted by a U.S. government-appointed committee, the Music Advisory Panel, which was charged with evaluating the suitability of the music to be played. While the panel also hoped that the Orchestra would perform music by Latin American composers, it was not as insistent on that point, and a government official assured a Philharmonic administrator that playing such music "is only a suggestion, not a requirement." As it happened, the Orchestra complied with this request up to a point, performing works by either the Brazilian composer Carmago Guarnieri or Mexico's Carlos Chávez on one-third of the tour's thirty-nine concerts.

Bernstein's talents as a cultural ambassador were hardly confined to the podium and while overseas, he represented the United States with devotion and vigor. Throughout the 1958 tour, the exploits of this handsome, charismatic, young American were avidly followed by the public and the press. In the words of one

> In city after city the **ovations** were described as "delirious," "frenetic," **unlike any** that had been **seen before.**

Rarely turning down an invitation to participate, Bernstein joins in with a traditional dance group during the Philharmonic's Latin American tour, 1958.

Orchestra official, he "attended press conferences without number, luncheons, dinners, celebrations of local playing and dancing, good, bad, and indifferent," and "charmed the old and fascinated the young." Moreover, Bernstein could communicate in English and Spanish, an invaluable asset, given the Orchestra's goals in Latin America. Those who watched him were amazed by his vitality. The Philharmonic's Board President, David Keiser, worried that Bernstein might not be getting enough rest, writing that "he certainly does burn the candle at both ends." But Keiser noted that Bernstein had not missed a single concert or a rehearsal, and had given his best at every performance, despite "poor halls, inadequate dressing facilities," and "second class, poorly tuned" pianos. Merely keeping up with it all, without having to conduct, Keiser observed, was "a full-time occupation."

No matter how exhausting the schedule—and these trips were draining for the conductor and his players—Bernstein relished the opportunity to present his

With a band of Peruvian musicians during the 1958 South American tour. As always, Bernstein was tireless in his efforts to sample and celebrate local culture.

Orchestra to peoples outside the United States. More than that, he loved seeing the world and seized every opportunity as completely as he could. In Lima, Bernstein entertained onlookers by charging about an airfield on a motor scooter, an escapade captured in the local press. On a flight over the Andes, he headed to the cockpit to co-pilot the Orchestra's plane as it made its way to still another destination. According to one account, five minutes later the plane dropped dramatically, causing several musicians to become sick. Many were convinced the maestro had been at the controls. From the Hotel del Lago in Maracaibo, Venezuela, Bernstein wrote exuberantly to the Philharmonic's offices in New York of his exploits: "Today has been a joyful one of waterskiing and sun in this glorious place." He also wrote of his admiration for the Orchestra: "So far the trip is wonderful; success, fun, no major illness, everyone loves us, everyone in the Orchestra loves everybody else; they play like angels." And then he looked toward his future with the Philharmonic. "I am tired but very happy; and with every concert I feel the Orchestra is more and more my Orchestra."

Crossing paths with then-Vice President Richard Nixon, who was also on a goodwill tour of South America on behalf of the United States.

Although the Bernstein-led export of U.S. culture was working brilliantly, U.S.-Latin American political relations remained tense. While the Orchestra was touring, in April 1958, Vice President Richard Nixon also visited the continent in an attempt to shore up relations with U.S. allies to the south. He attended the inauguration of the Argentine president, and stopped in Uruguay, Peru, and Venezuela, among other places. He met with an angry reception in several cities, and in Caracas, Nixon and his wife Pat were spat on. Worse still, his limousine was stoned by enraged citizens, who were no doubt upset that the United States had once supported the dictator Marcos Pérez Jiménez, whom the Venezuelans had overthrown a few months before. Before Nixon's driver managed to escape the melee, a Secret Service agent had drawn his gun, saying, "Let's get some of these sons-of-bitches." The car finally sped away, but its occupants had feared for their lives.

A Meeting with Nixon

Soon after, when Nixon reached Quito, Ecuador, the conductor and the future president had a chance to exchange thoughts on politics and music. While Nixon was holding a press conference at the U.S. Embassy, Bernstein made his way over. Upon learning that the conductor was there, the Vice President offered praise for the musician, spoke fondly about his collection of Bernstein recordings, and invited him to say a few words. Never reluctant to engage a crowd, Bernstein noted that the two men were on similar missions in Latin America, though he acknowledged Nixon's job was tougher since the Philharmonic was sharing music, while Nixon was discussing tariffs and other less exalted matters. Bernstein praised Nixon for the good job he was doing, and that was that, or so it seemed.

That evening, the two wound up next to one another at a diplomatic dinner and got to talking about their respective challenges, a conversation Bernstein recalled with characteristic idealism: "I reported to the Vice President tumultuous receptions; record crowds; cheering, stamping audiences; kisses; roses; embraces; while he reported to me the unpleasant, distasteful incidents" he had endured. Bernstein speculated as to why they had had such different experiences. After all, both were on goodwill missions. And both were "vulnerable to the same demonstrations of anti-Yankee feelings." But the musicians had "music on [their] side," and "if we are really serious about communicating with one another," he said, then "we can never overestimate the good that comes from artistic communication." For Bernstein, the significance of the Philharmonic's global mission was undeniable. "When we touch one another through music," he observed, "we are touching the heart, the mind, and the spirit all at once."

The essence of that mission—and its significance for the U.S. government at the height of the Cold War—was made clear to the Orchestra upon its return by President Eisenhower and Vice President Nixon. In a letter sent to the Philharmonic, Eisenhower praised the members of the Orchestra for their "excellent accomplishment" overseas. By sharing their skills with the United States' neighbors to the south, he wrote, the country had "drawn closer to the ideal of mutual understanding and friendship which is our goal." For his part, the vice president expressed "delight at the success" of the Latin American tour and hoped such programs would continue in the years to come. Future concerts would make it possible, he wrote, "to reach even deeper into the hearts and minds of our friends around the world."

Penetrating the Iron Curtain

The following year's tour was even more politically charged, as Bernstein and his Orchestra played not just for America's allies, but in countries whose regimes were less congenial to the United States. The ten-week trip to Europe in 1959, including performances in Eastern Europe and the Soviet Union, was arduous: fifty concerts, twenty-nine cities, seventeen countries. To this day, it remains one of the most dramatic in the Philharmonic's history. As before, the journey was funded by ANTA, and the foreign policy aims were explicit. The American government hoped that wherever the Orchestra performed—whether in London, Paris, Warsaw, or

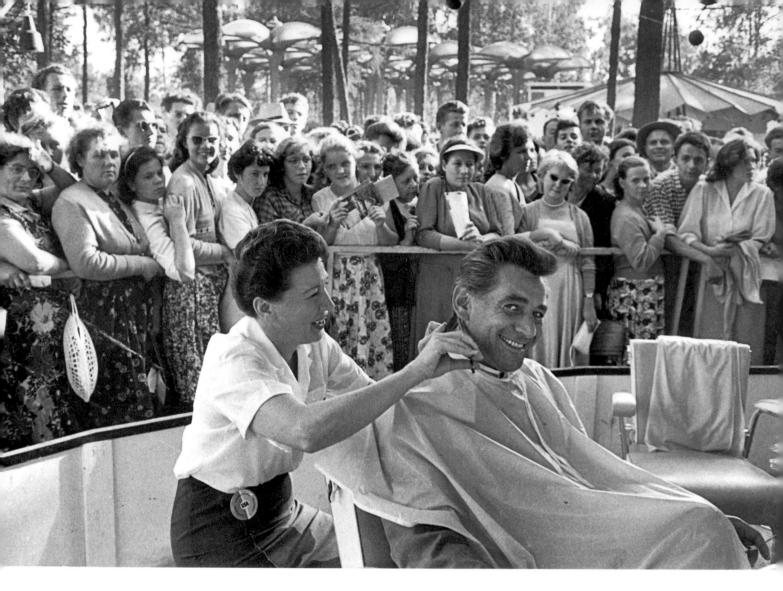

At the American pavilion of an international trade fair in Moscow, where demonstrations extolled the benefits of everyday life in the U.S., Bernstein showed the Soviet crowds how Americans get a haircut.

Moscow—the artistry of Leonard Bernstein and the Philharmonic would elevate the standing of the United States in the eyes of the world. Over many weeks, Bernstein would display his extraordinary talents as a conductor, educator, and cultural ambassador. Equally clear would be his signature idealism.

The high point of the trip, which took the Orchestra to many of Europe's great cities, was the concerts behind the Iron Curtain, which marked the first time the Philharmonic had played in countries under communist rule. While the Orchestra garnered marvelous reviews in Greece, Turkey, and Lebanon, the concerts in the Soviet Union, culminating in a glittering September 11 farewell program in Moscow, were as dramatic and passionately received as any the Philharmonic had ever experienced. The columnist Art Buchwald memorably summed up the response of the Soviet people, writing that it was "one of the greatest receptions any body of musicians has had in Russia since Rasputin was a pup."

The first set of concerts in Moscow in late August (the Orchestra would return there two weeks later after playing in Leningrad and Kiev) was not without controversy as Bernstein got into a scuffle in the press with a Soviet critic. In a wide-ranging piece, the reviewer Alexsandr Medvedev described Bernstein as "immodest" and "conceited" because he had turned to the audience to explain the modern idiom in Charles Ives' *The Unanswered Question*, which the Orchestra was poised to play. Worse still, Medvedev asserted, Bernstein had played the piece a second time, even though the audience had been unmoved by the American work. How dare Bernstein lecture on music to a Soviet audience? And what possessed him to force his listeners to endure for a second time something they had clearly disliked? "Some kind of show is being played under the title 'Bernstein Raises the Iron Curtain in Music,'" Medvedev observed.

> How dare Bernstein lecture on music to a **Soviet audience?** What possessed him to force listeners to endure for a second time something they **clearly disliked?**

Bernstein fumed. Firing back, he called the review "an unforgivable lie and in the worst possible taste." The audience had demanded an encore of the Ives with their rhythmic clapping, he declared. He had merely obliged. And he would continue to speak to Russian audiences when he thought an explanation was necessary. Sounding like a Cold Warrior, he said he was miffed because critics in the United States expressed their own opinions, whereas in Russia, "every word printed is official one way or another." The tempest soon faded, the reviews (even the Soviet ones) were superb, and the Orchestra continued its travels around the Soviet Union, returning to Moscow a few weeks later for its final performances in the capital.

A Message From Moscow

On the night of September 11, at the Great Hall of the Tchaikovsky Conservatory, Bernstein would conduct the Orchestra's farewell concert in Russia. But earlier that day—a day filled with music—Bernstein led a program that was recorded for American television. Before an audience of Muscovites, including the composer Dmitri Shostakovich, the Philharmonic played the first movement of his Seventh Symphony, a riveting performance preceded by a thirty-minute lecture in which Bernstein brilliantly explored what he saw as the similarities between American and

Russian music. Illustrating his comments with excerpts from the music of Copland and Shostakovich played by the Philharmonic, Bernstein used the podium as a bully pulpit to assert that Russians and Americans, though fearful of one another, were really quite similar. And he was not just making that rather stunning assertion to the Russians, for the program would shortly be aired on U.S. television. What would both peoples make of Bernstein's claim that Russian and American music reflected a similar attitude toward the wide open spaces of the Siberian frontier and the American West; that both cultures were "gigantic melting pots" able to absorb all kinds of cultural influences; that both peoples laughed at the same jokes; that they were, in fact, "natural friends"? Brimming with irrepressible optimism, an idealistic Bernstein stated that the United States and Russia had "come a long way toward being close together," and argued that they must continue to strengthen their relationship, not just because "we two giant nations cannot afford to be unfriendly, but also because it is so natural a thing for us to be close to each other." In watching the program today, one is struck by the hopefulness etched on the Russian faces in the audience. Countless men and women appeared genuinely moved by the conductor's message.

An Invitation to Pasternak

The evening concert was an even more remarkable event, as the Orchestra played the Beethoven Seventh and Shostakovich Fifth Symphonies with blazing intensity. Making the night especially memorable was the presence of two giants of Soviet culture, Shostakovich and the famed writer Boris Pasternak, whom the Soviet government had recently reviled for his work, and who had been living in forced seclusion. The preceding year, Pasternak had been awarded the Nobel Prize in Literature for his novel *Dr. Zhivago*. After accepting the prize, he was excoriated in the Soviet press and expelled from the Soviet Writers' Union, which compared him to a "pig, who dirties the place where he sleeps and eats." Forced to reject the prize by Soviet authorities, who objected to the book's anti-Communist character, Pasternak announced that he had made a mistake and would not accept the award. Publicly disgraced, he was now living an isolated existence outside Moscow.

Pasternak's presence at the Philharmonic's final Moscow concert—his first public appearance in almost a year—was the result of the intervention of Bernstein and his wife, who had injected themselves into the middle of a political controversy. Hoping to meet the author during the tour, Bernstein had invited Pasternak to the concert. In response, the novelist had written to Bernstein, accepting his invitation and offering one of his own. Would the Bernsteins come for a meal at his dacha? The exchange of messages proved difficult, but Mrs. Bernstein would not give up.

On a spur-of-the moment visit to the author's home, she managed to track him down as he walked near his rural retreat and the meeting was arranged. For the Bernsteins, the visit to Pasternak's home was unforgettable. "We hit it off, straight away," Bernstein recalled. "We talked for hours about art and the artist's view of history." Especially impressive was the Russian's knowledge of music and its centrality in his life. "Very often, authors talk rot about music," Bernstein said, "but Pasternak talks with a musician and has something to say." Bernstein even played bits from *West Side Story* for the author. Most of all, the American cherished hearing Pasternak expound upon "aesthetic matters."

In a sense, the Philharmonic's final concert in Moscow allowed Bernstein to share his own aesthetic sensibility with the distinguished Russian. During the intermission that night, Pasternak made his way to Bernstein's dressing room. The sixty-nine year-old author, struggling under the weight of an oppressive regime, called the slow movement of Beethoven's Seventh, "a tragic expression of the tragedy of existence." "I have never felt so close to the aesthetic truth," he said. "When I hear you, I know why you were born." Bernstein was overcome, and with his wife at his side, he remained silent. "I only want to listen, not speak." Later that evening, at the triumphant conclusion of the Shostakovich Fifth, as the crowd stood and roared, Shostakovich, who years earlier had also been persecuted by the Soviet regime, rushed to the stage to embrace Bernstein. The two men bowed repeatedly, as a dozen girls handed flowers to the performers. In Bernstein's dressing room, Pasternak once again conveyed his appreciation. "Thank you. You have taken us up to heaven," he said, as the two embraced. "Now we must return to earth."

Following the Philharmonic's performance of his Symphony No. 5, Shostakovich climbed onto the stage to embrace Bernstein and to recognize the musicians, a moment viewed by millions who watched the concert telecast back in the U.S.

Beethoven and Politics in Berlin

The next year, the Philharmonic again traveled overseas, as Bernstein led the Orchestra on a brief visit to play two concerts at the West Berlin Music, Drama, and Arts Festival, where it would also tape a program to be aired in the United States. (For an evocative personal account of the journey, see Burton Bernstein's essay, "Leonard Bernstein's Separate Peace with Berlin.") While the 1960 trip was sponsored not by the government, but by the Ford Motor Company, its political significance was clear. Berlin was one of the most contested places on earth, and it had been a focal point of Cold War tensions since the late 1940s. If U.S.–Soviet tensions ever exploded into all-out war, many believed Berlin would be the flashpoint. Shortly before the visit, a Ford executive wrote to the Philharmonic's Manager George Judd about the upcoming performances. "All of the people in Washington … are really excited about the idea because of what Mr. Bernstein and the Philharmonic will be able to do for this country" by playing a part "in strengthening and warming German-American relations."

The day after the first Berlin concert, before an audience of German students, the Orchestra taped Beethoven's First Piano Concerto with Bernstein as conductor and soloist, a performance that was broadcast a few weeks later on U.S. television. A brilliant showcase for Bernstein's gifts, the event allowed him to play, conduct, and teach. He would even speak about politics and God. Bernstein began by repudiating the notion that certain musicians were uniquely suited to play particular pieces. One did not have to be Russian to play Russian music. Today, he said, musicians everywhere grow up hearing all kinds of music and are "stylistically sophisticated." Delivering a message that undermined the idea of innate national and ethnic differences to an audience of young Germans was a bold gesture, but Bernstein was far from finished.

In an intriguing juxtaposition, he explored what he called the universal character of German music. It could not be quarantined, Bernstein said, for German music transcended ethnic and national categories. Nevertheless, it possessed one distinctive attribute, a quality that made it unique: the idea of musical development. Development, Bernstein claimed, is "the fountainhead of everything we call symphonic," the key to the whole German symphonic idea. He demonstrated this at the piano by playing excerpts from the Beethoven concerto he was about to perform. After brilliantly illustrating the centrality of development in German music, which he related to the analytical nature of the German mind, Bernstein suggested that when linked to creative energy, development gave German music its universal character.

His musicological lesson completed, Bernstein the educator became Bernstein

One of the stops on the 1959 tour was Istanbul, Turkey. Bernstein and his wife, Felicia, explored the city's streets and culture. Philharmonic Manager George Judd, Jr. is pictured at far left.

the political idealist and spiritual guide. Explaining why his band of New Yorkers had crossed the ocean to perform the music of Beethoven before a German audience in Berlin, he said, "We have come to take one more step through this kind of cultural exchange along the paths of international understanding that lead to peace." The "heyday of narrow nationalism is, or should be, over." It was necessary to cultivate the "understanding that exists on a level as deep as musical communication, a direct, heart to heart, mind to mind contact." With words that surely resonated in a vulnerable city, he asserted that only this "kind of rapport can bring us peace, which is the immediate and necessary goal of this modern world." The Philharmonic dedicated its performance of the Beethoven to peace, he said, with "special reverence on this sacred day of Rosh Hashana." Bernstein intoned a Hebrew prayer, which he then translated into English. "May the Lord lift up his face to you and give you peace." With that, he sat down to play the Beethoven.

> "Cultural **exchange** . . . international **understanding** . . . lead to **peace**. The heyday of narrow nationalism is, or should be, over."

The German critics wrote rapturously about the Philharmonic's concerts in Berlin, highlighting the group's "incomparable virtuosity" and "technical perfection." The Orchestra made "every musical heart beat faster," and its conductor was described as a "magician," who captivated audiences with his every movement. "Youthful and slender," he was an "electrifying" presence on the podium, "a *Wunderkind*," who was "greeted with shouts of joy." But beyond the countless glowing reviews, the Orchestra's trip to Berlin pointed to something far more lasting, to an idea Leonard Bernstein embraced wherever he performed. In a troubled world, the Philharmonic's conductor believed that music possessed a distinctive power that could advance the cause of international cooperation and human understanding.

Postscript: Berlin 1989—The Idealist Returns

Although Bernstein's subsequent foreign tours would draw large, enthusiastic crowds and achieve critical success, they were not as overtly political as were the earlier trips. One exception came in late 1989, less than a year before Bernstein died. In December, the seventy-one year-old maestro took eight players from the New York Philharmonic to join an international ensemble in Berlin for concerts on both sides of the crumbling Berlin Wall. It was an historic moment of the twentieth century, for the division of Europe, which had lasted some forty years, had come to an end. And in Berlin itself, which had been a divided city for twenty-eight years, the era of forced separation and political oppression was no more. It was a joyous time, and Bernstein had been asked to help mark the rebirth of freedom with performances of Beethoven's choral masterpiece, the Ninth Symphony. He called the city's unification "the most exciting thing that has happened in my lifetime, historically."

Bernstein conducted an orchestra comprising musicians from East and West Germany, and from the four victorious allies in World War II: the United States, Britain, France, and the Soviet Union. In memorable performances of the Beethoven, Bernstein placed his distinctive mark on the symphony's final movement by altering the text in the "Ode to Joy," which was based on Friedrich Schiller's eighteenth-century poem. The original word *Freude!* (joy!) would be replaced by *Freiheit!* (freedom!), which, given the occasion, seemed entirely appropriate. While Bernstein's tinkering with the original displeased some, he claimed this was "a heaven-sent moment to sing the word '*Freiheit!*'" "If not now, when?" he asked, noting that he had "always heard [freedom] as the subtext of the symphony. So why not make it the text?" Beethoven would "give us his blessing," Bernstein observed. On Christmas Day, millions watched the historic concert from Berlin, which allowed the aging conductor a final glorious moment on the world stage. Yet again, America's idealist on the podium had used music to inspire people to transcend the political forces that had kept them apart.

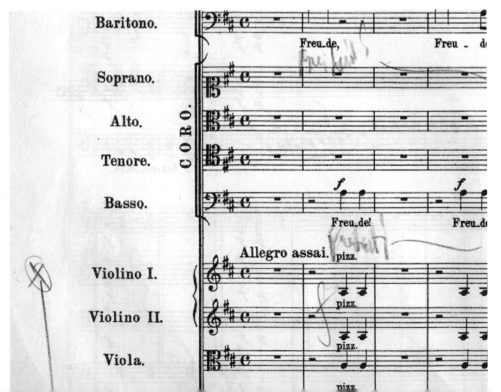

The score Bernstein used for his 1989 performances of Beethoven's Ninth Symphony marking the fall of the Berlin Wall shows his decision to replace the word Freude! *(joy!) in the choral parts with an emphatic* Freiheit! *(freedom!) to emphasize the spirit of the occasion.*

The Philharmon[...] 57th S[...]
113 West 57th S[...]
Telephone: COlum[...]

Date.......February 4th 1958

[Ler]nard Bernstein

[P]rograms - General Plan
[S]eason 1958-1959

The season is divided into seven periods of four weeks each, except for the final period, which is six weeks. I will conduct periods 1,3,5, and 7.

The over all point of my eighteen weeks is a general survey of American Music from the earliest generation of American composers to the present. This does not mean that any one program will be made up entirely of American music, but rather that this music is featured or emphasized as the consistent factor running through my programs. The programs of the guest conductors are being so planned as to comple- ment mine by placing emphasis on music of other nationalities.

My first period of four weeks will feature music by the earliest generation of American Composers; approximately one significant work a week by such composers as Ives, MacDowell etc. These works, or "point pieces" would be surrounded by pieces of more standard, classic nature, Baroque or Romantic. For example, it might be possible to open each of these concerts with a Concerto of Vivaldi, thus running a parallel line of consistency against the line of the American music. It might then be possible to follow each of the American works with a "schlagger," Brahms, Tschaikowsky or Beethoven.

The second period will be shared by Schippers and von Karajan, and it is my hope that Schippers will, in his two weeks, emphasize some aspect of contemporary music of Italy or Scandinavia, and that von Karajan, in his two weeks will feature some- thing new in German music along with his Beethoven. I then return for four weeks with programs featuring American music of the 20's, exemplifying the "Jazz-Boot- leg" spirit, similarly framed by more standard pieces.

Barbirolli then appears with four weeks featuring British music.

I then return with four weeks featuring American music in the 30's, with emphasis on its~seriousness, simplicity and proletarianization.
         ∟new

Then comes Mitropoulos with four weeks featuring French music. In fact it is Mitropoulos' wish to turn his four weeks into a "Salute to France," which I heartily endorse.

I then return for the final period of six weeks, which will have a double point: the 200th anniversary of Händel's death, and naturally the latest generation of American composers, who have grown up since the war.

At the end of this season, I feel that the public will have a sense of accomplis[...] and of an intelligent survey of a great variety of music so that they can feel the season as an entity. In making these programs it is my hope that variety not be sacrificed for unity, but that an effective balance of the two can be The only problem in my mind at this moment is the satisfactory integration o[...] into the over-all plan, but I feel sure that this can be done.

Columbia Records is very much interested in the idea and they will coopera[...] maximum in integrating their recording plans to conform with our plans.

As Music Director:
A Quest for Meaning and Identity

BY JOSEPH HOROWITZ

The over all point of my eighteen weeks is a general survey of American Music from the earliest generation of American composers to the present. ... The programs of the guest conductors are being so planned as to complement mine by placing emphasis on music of other nationalities. ...

At the end of this season, I feel that the public will have a sense of accomplishment and of an intelligent survey of a great variety of music so that they feel the season as an entity. In making these programs it is my hope that variety will not be sacrificed for unity, but that an effective balance of the two can be maintained. ...

—From a memo entitled "Programs: General Plan/Season 1958-1959," dated February 4, 1958, a few months after being named Music Director of the New York Philharmonic.

Principal Conductors of the New York Philharmonic, from top: Anton Seidl, Gustav Mahler, and Arturo Toscanini. Opposite page: After they shared the conducting position for the 1957–58 season, Bernstein succeeded Dimitri Mitropoulos as Music Director in the fall of 1958.

The resulting 1958–59 programs were received "with enthusiasm" by the New York Philharmonic Music Policy Committee (about which more in a moment). David Keiser, the President of the Board and a committee member, remarked that the Philharmonic had for some time wanted a "master or global" repertoire plan. Why Bernstein felt a need to organize his first season so systematically, why he felt impelled to emphasize American works, and why Keiser was so grateful and supportive may only be fully apprehended once the Orchestra's long history—including decades of artistic drift and a 1956 call for vigorous housecleaning in *The New York Times*—is taken into account. In this context, the Bernstein agenda was a necessary corrective. And his means for pursuing it—his singular powers of advocacy—were redoubled by powers of inquiry: by a need to know that was equally singular.

What Came Before

For the early conductors of the Philharmonic, choice of repertoire was a paramount function. New York audiences were still acquiring a knowledge of the symphonic canon, and little-heard music by the likes of Beethoven, Weber, Mendelssohn, and Spohr was centrally significant. Later, when Wagnerism galvanized American classical music, Theodore Thomas included forty-seven Wagner compositions on the seventy-eight subscription programs he led between 1877 and 1891. Of Anton Seidl's eighty-one subscription performances between 1891 and 1898, thirty-nine featured at least one Wagner work. Thomas and Seidl were missionaries for the new or otherwise unfamiliar. That was their job.

Nine years after Seidl's early death in 1898, Gustav Mahler took over. Mahler declared his intention to "educate the public." He organized "historical" surveys beginning with Bach. He offered lots of Wagner, including six all-Wagner programs. In the final months of his abbreviated regime lasting fewer than two seasons (too ill to conduct by late February 1911, Mahler returned to Vienna to die), he registered a fascinating predilection for thematic organization. And Mahler was not shy about presenting his own symphonies and songs. But Mahler's unexciting successor, Josef Stransky, was not a missionary program-builder. Stransky was eased out in 1923 by a new and dynamic Philharmonic Board Chairman, Clarence Mackay. It was Mackay's opinion that, with its long season, the Philharmonic would benefit from some variety on the podium. He engineered the appointment of Willem Mengelberg beginning in 1922. Beginning in 1925, Wilhelm Furtwängler—another great European name—was a frequent Philharmonic conductor. But Mackay's chief goal was to lure Arturo Toscanini from Italy—and he did, beginning in 1926.

Mengelberg, during his nine New York years, remained conductor of Amsterdam's Concertgebouw Orchestra. Furtwängler, a Philharmonic conductor

for three seasons, remained conductor of the Berlin Philharmonic. Toscanini severed his ties to La Scala, but considered himself too old to undertake even half a Philharmonic season. One result was that the Philharmonic became dependent upon the "guest conductor." Another was that the Orchestra failed to consolidate a bold repertoire profile comparable to what Thomas, Seidl, and Mahler had initiated. Toscanini, who dominated the Philharmonic's identity through 1936, was a notoriously conservative programmer: 40 percent of his Philharmonic repertoire comprised music by Beethoven, Brahms, and Wagner. In fact, the main source of artistic continuity during the post-Stransky era was another Mackay appointee: Arthur Judson, who became the Philharmonic's Manager in 1922 and who would retain that post for thirty-four years.

With Toscanini's resignation, the need for a single dominant New York Philharmonic leader to undertake nearly the entire season was self-evident. The chosen leader was the thirty-six-year-old John Barbirolli—an infamous wrong turn. Judson eventually felt impelled to write to his factotum, Bruno Zirato: "Why is it that every important novelty given in N.Y. is done by Boston, Philadelphia or some other visiting orchestra? I have the feeling, we are asleep: we'd better get up on our toes, musically. … Other conductors find new works and new ideas. That's B's job: why doesn't he do it?" Zirato replied, "We have been telling him that it is up to him to make interesting programs and he has failed us. There is nothing that we can do any more, I am afraid."

Barbirolli was let go in 1941. Two years later, Artur Rodzinski was named "Musical Director"—the first Philharmonic conductor so titled. Rodzinski elevated the playing level, but a rancorous relationship with Judson cut short his New York career in 1946. The 1950 appointment of Dimitri Mitropoulos brought to the Philharmonic an important conductor of important twentieth-century music—and important performances of Mahler, Schoenberg, Webern, and Berg ensued. But Mitropoulos' programs seemed to many erratic, even unfathomable. On April 29, 1956, *The New York Times* published a full-page analysis, "The Philharmonic—What's Wrong With It and Why," by Howard Taubman. Taubman was dire: "During the 1955–56 season the New York Philharmonic-Symphony rarely sounded like an orchestra of the first order. Its programs lacked an over-all design and were often badly balanced, being either top-heavy or flimsy." Taubman fingered Mitropoulos for bearing "the heaviest responsibility" and called for his replacement. Of the Orchestra's programs, he further wrote that their arrangement "appears to be haphazard, depending on the conductors and soloists who happen to be engaged for the sea-

A marked page from Bernstein's score of Charles Ives' Second Symphony, used at the 1951 world premiere. Written in is, "And crown thy good with brotherhood."

son. Convenience often takes precedence over design, and the whims of individuals receive too much leeway." Of the Philharmonic's new Board President, Taubman wrote: "David M. Keiser ... told this observer that a music committee of the board had been named during the past season and that it would keep a close watch on programs. This is a good move and may lead to improvements."

The Music Policy Committee Taubman mentioned had been formed in 1955. A meeting on April 23, 1957, registered the committee's predilections. Unlike certain disgruntled members of Stokowski's Philadelphia board, unlike Judson and Zirato in their dealings with Mitropoulos, it would not bristle at new works. It evidently agreed with Taubman. In spring 1957, Bernstein was named co-conductor with Mitropoulos for 1957–58. In fall 1958, he was named sole Music Director as of 1958–59.

Bernstein had conducted fifty-one New York Philharmonic subscription concerts in the seasons that preceded his co-conductorship. In terms of repertoire, the most momentous occurred on February 22 and 23, 1951: the premiere perform-

Members of Bernstein's "Older Generation" of American composers: John Becker, Carl Ruggles, and Wallingford Riegger.

ances and broadcast of an unknown American masterpiece half a century old: Charles Ives' Symphony No. 2. Barbirolli's entire tenure had not produced so important a musical event. Bernstein would repeat Ives' Second in 1958, 1961, and 1967. He also recorded it with the Philharmonic in 1958 and 1987. In fact, Bernstein began his first season as Music Director with William Schuman's *American Festival Overture*, the Ives' Second, and Beethoven's Seventh. The die was cast.

A New Age

The Schuman and Ives works began Bernstein's promised "general survey of American Music from the earliest generation of American composers to the present." Interspersed with European works during Bernstein's eighteen weeks, the survey was necessarily far from comprehensive. By the 1950s, three decades of modernist revisionism had erased memories of American music before World War I. Bernstein paid no attention to America's four most important mid-nineteenth century composers: Louis Moreau Gottschalk, William Henry Fry, George Bristow, and Anthony Philip Heinrich. But he was intrepid in revisiting such turn-of-the-century figures as George Chadwick, Arthur Foote, Henry Gilbert, and Edward MacDowell. These—plus Ives, John Becker, Carl Ruggles, and Wallingford Riegger, all of more recent vintage—comprised his "Older Generation."

The second installment of Bernstein's American survey, "The Twenties," featured works by Aaron Copland, Edgard Varèse, and George Gershwin. Segment three, "From the Crash through the Second World War," offered music by Samuel Barber, Randall Thompson, Roy Harris, Walter Piston, Roger Sessions, and Virgil Thomson. "The Young Generation," finally, included Grant Beglarian, Kenneth Gaburo, Irving Fine, Lukas Foss, Ned Rorem, and William Russo.

Toscanini had reserved the right to concentrate on music he loved. Bernstein's survey reflected his enthusiasm for America and a sanguine approach to its classical-music growth. He had in mind an evolutionary ladder. In fact, his knowledge and affection for such composers as Chadwick, MacDowell, and Foote was no greater than that displayed by Aaron Copland and Virgil Thomson, who habitually ignored or denigrated nineteenth-century Americans when narrating the quest for a native style.

Bernstein's underlying polemic was made explicit in his second Young People's Concert, "What Makes Music American?" (February 1, 1958). This exegesis for youngsters, typically, was not a satellite enterprise, but an outgrowth of his subscription agenda. American music, Bernstein explained to a national television audience, poses a problem: compared to Poland, Italy, Ireland, Spain, Hungary, or Russia — countries whose music he briefly sampled—the United States lacks a common folk music. The first

> "Mature" American **contemporary music** Bernstein concluded, embraces a **multiplicity** of personality traits, its strength is a **"many-sidedness."**

"really serious" American music, he continued, began about seventy-five years ago. "At that time the few American composers we did have were imitating European composers, like Brahms and Liszt and Wagner. …We might call that the kindergarten period of American music." Bernstein here conducted a snatch of Chadwick's *Melpomene* Overture—"straight European stuff." The "grammar school" period was exemplified by MacDowell's *Indian* Suite—"I still can't say that it sounds very American to me!"—and Gilbert's *Dance in Place Congo*.

After World War I came "high school." By this time, "something new and very special had come into American music. … Jazz had been born and that changed everything. Because at last there was something like an American folk music that belonged to all Americans." Even serious composers couldn't keep jazz out of their ears. Bernstein here illustrated with bits of Copland and Gershwin. But Copland and Gershwin remained in high school: they "were still being American *on pur-*

pose." Only in the 1930s was the jazz influence integrated, so that Americans "just wrote music, and it came out American all by itself." This was "college," and its students included Roger Sessions. "Mature" American contemporary concert music, Bernstein concluded, embraces a multiplicity of personality traits. In fact, America's strength is its "many-sidedness." "We've taken it all in: French, Dutch, German, Scotch, Scandinavian, Italian, and all the rest, and learned it from one another, borrowed it, stolen it, cooked it all up in a melting pot. So what our composers are finally nourished on is a folk music that is probably the richest in the world, and all of it is American."

> Bernstein performed **American music** not merely to remedy neglect, but **to ask:** What is America?

It is easy enough to poke holes in Bernstein's evolutionary template and the concomitant repertoire choices shaping his 1958–59 survey. An earlier formulation—his Harvard senior thesis of 1939 ("The Absorption of Race Elements into American Music")—notably predated his discovery of Ives, who obviously did not belong in "kindergarten," "grammar school," or "high school," and so vitiated the entire narrative. For that matter, Gottschalk's *The Banjo* and *Night in the Tropics,* from the 1850s, already "sound American." So does much of Chadwick—by picking his *Melpomene* (which begins with a near-quote from Wagner's *Tristan* Prelude), Bernstein stacked the deck.

No matter: the Bernstein agenda here laid out, however skewed or tendentious, was a stirring declaration of intent. Every announcement of Bernstein's appointment had stressed his American origins, all previous Principal Conductors of the Philharmonic having been born abroad. In fact, with the possible exception of Seidl (who took American citizenship, championed MacDowell and Victor Herbert, and was called by friends an "Americamaniac"), no previous Principal Conductor of the Philharmonic had brandished so special a commitment to American repertoire. Bernstein's first season showed that his American birth mattered. Self-evidently, he performed American music not merely to remedy neglect, but to ask: What is America? Given his own bifurcation as an American musician—his chronic oscillation between Broadway and Carnegie Hall, jazz and symphony (Bernstein came relatively late to classical music)—Bernstein's search for America acquired personal urgency. That Bernstein was also a significant American *composer* mandated a second urgent topic: where was music heading in the mid-twentieth century? In the decade to come, Bernstein's music directorship would make these questions matter greatly to others, because they mattered greatly to him.

Under New Management

The changing of the guard changed the Philharmonic's office as well: as of fall 1956, Arthur Judson was gone; a necessary pre-condition to wholesale change. From 1961 to 1970 Carlos Moseley, who knew Bernstein from Tanglewood, was managing director—a soothing presence, amenable to Bernstein and to innovation.

The New York Times' Howard Taubman, in 1956, had complained that the Philharmonic regularly failed to engage "talented young Americans" as soloists. Bernstein told the Music Policy Committee he would change that, and he did. Of his twenty-one 1958–59 piano soloists, ten were born in North America; of twelve violinists and cellists, six were American-born. Then, in 1959–60, Bernstein undertook an electrifying programming initiative bigger in impact than anything attempted the season before. No less than Seidl in the glory days of American Wagnerism,

Greeting crowds with Philharmonic Managing Director Carlos Moseley (left) and Frank Milburn (right) on arrival in Tokyo, 1968.

Bernstein attained a messianic pitch of advocacy, scheduling Mahler's Symphonies 1, 2, 4, 5, and 9, plus the first movement of the Tenth; the *Kindertotenlieder*; an additional set of songs with orchestra; and *Das Lied von der Erde*. As chroniclers of this historic Mahler Festival have stressed, Bernstein was by no means the Philharmonic's first important Mahler conductor. That would have been Mahler himself. Mengelberg, Klemperer, Barbirolli, Mitropoulos, Leopold Stokowski, and Bruno Walter were also significant Mahler interpreters with the Philharmonic. What is not stressed is that during Bernstein's tenure, this diversity of Mahler perspectives was maintained. In fact, the Mahler festival of 1959–60 was shared, at Bernstein's suggestion, with Mitropoulos and Walter. Of one hundred forty-four subscription-series Mahler performances during Bernstein's directorship, fifty-nine were led by conductors other than Bernstein, including Barbirolli, Krips, Mitropoulos, Solti, Steinberg, and Walter.

With Igor Stravinsky while filming their television program The Creative Performer, *1960.*

To launch his Young People's Concert, "Who Is Gustav Mahler?", broadcast on February 7, 1960, Bernstein cited as a point of pride that, "There's one of his pieces on every [Philharmonic] program for at least two months." (Mahler was heard on every Philharmonic program from December 31, 1959 to February 21, 1960 and again on four concerts in April. For that matter, there were fifteen more Mahler performances during Bernstein's tenure than in the entire previous history of the Orchestra.) Mahler's uniqueness, Bernstein told his national television audience, was his ability to "recapture the pure emotions of childhood," oscillating between extremes of happiness and gloom. Mahler was at the same time Romantic and modern. He was both conductor and composer. He was rooted yet marginal. Torn between East and West, he was Jewish, he was Austrian, he absorbed Slavic and Chinese influences. Mahler, in effect, was an exuberant and depressive man-child, a twentieth century American eclectic.

For Bernstein's detractors, such self-referential zeal seemed an annoying sideshow. But over the course of his Philharmonic career, this signature Bernstein factor became a strength. Intensely personal self-engagement

guided Bernstein's Mahler advocacy, as it had catalyzed patriotic identification with his fellow New Englander Ives. And there would be several more such transactions to come.

In a concert featuring the Avant-Garde, 1964, Bernstein conducted Available Forms II, *for Orchestra Four Hands along with the work's composer, Earle Brown.*

The Future Symphony

Four years after ending his Philharmonic directorship, Bernstein delivered six Norton Lectures at Harvard. Their collective title, borrowed from Ives, was "The Unanswered Question," by which he meant: Whither music in our time? Exploring formidable answers offered by Schoenberg and Stravinsky, he longed for (or tendentiously uncovered) the Romantic yearnings of the music he most loved. Remarkably, he anointed Mahler, who died in 1911, the emblematic twentieth-century composer, whose laments for the death of tonality ("which for him meant the death of music itself") conveyed sorrow for a lost Romantic world of feeling.

The shifting emphases and topics of Bernstein's Philharmonic repertoire document a comparable, if less dire, trajectory. Sporadically, but tenaciously, Bernstein inquired into the fate of contemporary music. The 1960–61 season explored "Keys to the Twentieth Century"; 1963–64 incorporated five programs investigating "The Avant-Garde." But Bernstein was himself all too obviously looking for answers. That his head and heart balked at non-tonal music was a confession this confessional musician could not hide. His spoken introductions to various esoteric opuses

New York Philharmonic

PHILHARMONIC HALL · BROADWAY AT 65TH STREET · NEW YORK 23, N. Y.

LEONARD BERNSTEIN, *Music Director*

January 18, 1966

Miss Ruth Selman
315 East 68th Street
New York, N. Y.

Dear Miss Selman:

It is the duty of any Symphony Orchestra – particularly that of a cultural capital like New York – to keep its audiences abreast of main currents in the development of 20th century music. The truth is that the New York Philharmonic does not go far enough in this obligation, out of consideration for its large subscription audiences. If the Webern symphony, already some forty years old, already a classic, and a mere eight minutes in length, cannot be comfortably absorbed in a season of more conventional music, then I am at a loss for an answer.

Sincerely,

Leonard Bernstein

LB:hc

A reply to an unhappy Philharmonic subscriber.

(which may be sampled on the Philharmonic's *Bernstein Live* CD compendium) betrayed ambivalence. "Mr. Bernstein tried everything short of a Flit gun in his attempt to kill off the avant-garde," wrote Alan Rich in the *Herald Tribune*. "Mr. Bernstein practically passed out the ripe tomatoes." The world premiere of Stefan Wolpe's Symphony No. 1—an event eagerly anticipated by a coterie of believers—was assigned to another conductor, Stefan Bauer-Mengelberg; only two of its three movements were performed. Though both behind the scenes and on stage, Bernstein's supportive efforts (as recounted by Bauer-Mengelberg) were heroic, the entire episode did not sit well with the press or the public.

The contract renewal Bernstein had negotiated with the Philharmonic in 1960 permitted him to reduce his time commitment to the Orchestra. It also permitted a season-long sabbatical, which Bernstein took in 1964–65. His prime objective was to compose. A planned Broadway musical proved painfully abortive. By his own account, Bernstein also attempted "a lot of music, twelve-tone music and avant-garde music of various kinds," only to discard it. He acknowledged that *Chichester Psalms*, which he did not discard, was "old-fashioned and sweet." Writing in the *Times*, he mulled "the ancient cliché that the certainty of one's knowledge decreases in proportion to thought and experience," pondered "the present crisis in composition," asked if tonality were forever dead, and worried that orchestras would "become museums of the past." In 1966, he announced his resignation as Music Director, effective in 1969.

One positive product of the Bernstein sabbatical was a trip to Denmark in May 1965. In Copenhagen, he conducted the Royal Danish Orchestra in Carl Nielsen's

With Dmitri Shostakovich in Moscow, 1959.

Symphony No. 3. The performances were a triumph. And, though the Philharmonic was not the orchestra, his electrifying Copenhagen recording of the Nielsen Third, for Columbia Records, was one of the most important he ever made, forecasting his culminating mission in New York. Bernstein's remaining four Philharmonic seasons stressed the resilience of the symphonic genre after Mahler. Nearly every subscription program that he led included a twentieth-century symphony or concerto—and with few exceptions, all the works were tonal.

When in Spring 1958 Thomas Schippers had been asked by Bernstein to explore twentieth-century Scandinavian music during his two weeks in the fall of 1958, Schippers had replied to the Philharmonic, "Nielsen is awful! Lenny spoke well of the Fifth Symphony but it's not for me *ne sono certo!*" Bernstein wound up performing and recording Nielsen's Fifth with the Philharmonic in 1962. As anyone (such as this writer) who collected LPs during the sixties well remembers, Bernstein's recordings of the Nielsen Third and Fifth—the first Nielsen symphony recordings on an American label—permanently catapulted an obscure Scandinavian to world prominence.

A second beneficiary of Bernstein's post-sabbatical resolve was Dmitri Shostakovich—evidenced not so much by a couple of Shostakovich works Bernstein now added to his Philharmonic repertoire, but by a Young People's Concert, "Birthday Tribute to Shostakovich," broadcast on January 5, 1966. Bernstein began with an excerpt from the *Leningrad* Symphony to illustrate "a typical Shostakovich sound—broad, noble, proud, songful, rich with feeling." Then, expelling his own dalliance with serial music and the avant-garde, he said it all:

> In these days of musical experimentation, with new fads chasing each other in and out of the concert halls, a composer like Shostakovich can be easily put down. After all he's basically a traditional Russian composer, a true son of Tchaikovsky—and no matter how modern he ever gets, he never loses that tradition. So the music is always in some way old-fashioned—or at least what critics and musical intellectuals like to call old-fashioned. But they're forgetting the most important thing—he's a genius: a real authentic genius, and there aren't too many of those around any more.

But by far the twentieth-century symphonists who chiefly galvanized Bernstein were the two he associated with "key turning points" in renewing the genre: Mahler and Jean Sibelius, both heroic practitioners whose stylistic innovations girded a Romantic subjectivity susceptible to expressions of twentieth-century triumph and travail. Between 1965 and 1969, Bernstein and the Philharmonic performed every Mahler and Sibelius symphony.

Studying a score in his Carnegie Hall dressing room just prior to the performance, 1960.

Bernstein's advocacy of Nielsen and Shostakovich, Mahler and Sibelius was both timely and prescient. The snubs that Shostakovich and Sibelius had long endured from modernists—that their symphonies were provincial, bombastic, prolix—still re-echoed. But the Mahler, Ives, and Nielsen causes were more rapidly won, and augured a shift in taste that would ultimately redeem Shostakovich and Sibelius as twentieth-century masters, *pace* Schoenberg and Stravinsky. However: for the most part, no comparable shift buoyed the reputations of the Americans Bernstein continued to program in quantity. Bernstein's post-sabbatical survey of the twentieth-century symphony did not neglect Americans. But with a single exception, no American composer received anything like the consolidated attention Bernstein now paid to his favorite twentieth-century Europeans. Even Copland's music dropped precipitously from Bernstein's Philharmonic agenda. The exception, of course, was Ives: yet more performances of the Second Symphony, plus the Third Symphony, two big movements from the *Holiday* Symphony, a bevy of shorter works, and an all-Ives Young People's Concert in 1967. (Bernstein's post-1969 American repertoire as the Philharmonic's Laureate Conductor shrank to a sprinkling of fourteen composers over a period of two decades.)

> By 1970, Bernstein's programs document a shift from the **New World to Old.** As well, New York City seemed embattled by crime and white flight.

Retreating to the Past

It was merely predictable that Bernstein's swan song as the Philharmonic's first American Music Director was not an American program, but a huge Mahler work: the Symphony No. 3, which as of 1969 remained on the margins of the mainstream repertoire. Taken as a whole, Bernstein's post-sabbatical programs document a shift in emphasis from New World to Old, a loss of interest in radical ideas, a reconnection to tradition. Mahler, in 1907, had moved from Vienna to New York. Bernstein, his Philharmonic directorship behind him, now transferred his attention from New York to Vienna. He had not managed to follow *West Side Story* with a comparable music-theater breakthrough. His three symphonies had not led toward any American epiphany. The Kennedy White House, in which he had been a welcome and esteemed guest, was no more. American popular music, which he had adored for its vitality and inventiveness, had in his opinion lost its way. New York City seemed embattled by crime and white flight. Bernstein's ill-publicized dalliance with the Black Panthers further estranged him from his native land. Performing and recording Beethoven, Schumann, Brahms, and Mahler with the Vienna Philharmonic, shaping his interpretations with a new ripeness and breadth, rid of the acoustical challenges of Philharmonic Hall, Bernstein the conductor was lionized—in Vienna and New York both—as he had never been during his Philharmonic tenure.

As a musical pedagogue, Leonard Bernstein managed to be both leader and Everyman. His personal taste, in the long run, was more Romantic than modern, never arcane. His personal touch was ever fervent. His need to share was equally a need to know: publicly, he figured out—or tried to—where he stood and what he sought. His colleagues in Boston and Philadelphia, Chicago and Cleveland left no remotely comparable legacy of music exhumed, propagated, even popularized. His New York Philharmonic programs disclose and narrate an active quest: a veritable musical autobiography.

a brother's recollection

Charismatic Teacher, Consummate Performer

For my brother, life was all about forging relationships through music, both onstage and off, and his influence can be felt to this day among those who knew him closely, or only from afar.

It's no secret that Lenny loved people. Whether he was composing a Broadway show with collaborators, leading the New York Philharmonic or his beloved orchestras in Vienna, Boston, and Israel, or passing on his knowledge to young people, being a musician for Lenny was all about relationships. His earliest, formative ties as a musician were with two very different mentors; somehow, Lenny being Lenny, ers with intellectual discipline. Amazingly, Lenny was eventually able to emerge as a blend of those two great mentors and become, well, Leonard Bernstein.

While Koussevitzky was never called "Koussie" to his face and Reiner was certainly never "Fritzy" to *his* face, Lenny was almost always "Lenny" to one and all—even to his students and old-school foreign musicians. But both Koussevitzky and

While Koussetvitzky was never called "Koussie" to his face, Lenny was almost always "Lenny" to one and all.

he was able to find a way to take the best from both of them and create his own unique style. First, there was Serge Koussevitzky—Russian-Jewish, Dionysian, heart over head, conveying music to his players with a cocked eyebrow or that pulsating vein on his right temple. Theirs was a spiritual father-son relationship, born at Tanglewood and as strong as blood. Later at the Curtis Institute of Music, there was Fritz Reiner—German, Apollonian, head over heart, conveying music to his play-

Reiner instilled in their "Lenushka" and "Leonard" the absolute necessity of encouraging and teaching young talent, just as they had done for him and others. So many of today's successful musicians owe so much to Lenny as a result. (The emergence of Marin Alsop the first woman to head a major American orchestra—is just one example of his deep and abiding influence.) The instances of inspiration he so generously gave to orchestral musicians and soloists are legion. I grew weary

Greeting his adoring fans after a performance in South America, 1958.

of hearing them tell me that they never realized they could play as well as they did under Lenny's baton, even when he tested them strenuously. When I asked him in his later years why he had slowed certain tempos (in Mahler, especially), he said, "To see if I could sustain it, and if the orchestra could, too. To find a new dimension that maybe the composer reached for." That struck me as the amalgam of Reiner and Koussevitzky coming through in spades. When it worked in the concert hall, it was scary and sublime.

As generous as Lenny was to conducting students and musicians, he was equally so to his fellow composers—young or old, unknown or renowned. He programmed them as often as possible; works by Aaron Copland, Irving Fine, Lukas Foss, Harold Shapero, and David Diamond. His sense of competition with his fellow composers was keen, but mostly in fun—making light of each other's influences and "borrowings." One of the longer-lived bits was with Marc Blitzstein, a hero of Lenny's since his Harvard days. For years, they would sing together "Blitzstein and Bernstein" to the trochees of the second move-

At a rehearsal in Tokyo, 1961, with Assistant Conductor Seiji Ozawa.

ment of Beethoven's Seventh, to see which "-stein" would come out last and thus on top. It was a contest that was never decided; each would claim triumph according to how he sang the last bar.

Studying scores and programming interesting concerts—largely solitary activities—were a strain. Occasionally the strain became too much to bear, since one can't please everyone—musicians, soloists, orchestra board members, managers, audiences, critics, and even stagehands. In such moments of stress, comic relief was called for, as it often was in the Bernstein family. To ease the tension, we made up

phony potential programs. Here are a few of the better ones:

  Bach Piston Beethoven
  Fine and d'Indy
  Handel with Carr [Howard, an
    English composer, 1880–1960]

Well, believe it or not, it helped.

Lenny's largest musical struggle was balancing his love of conducting and his love of composing. Everyone has to make such choices—the successful trial attorney who yearns to leave the courtroom for his true love, farming; the CEO who wants to return to being an architect; the writer who really wants to fly light

aircraft (me, for instance)—but in Lenny's case the professional collision was magnified for all to see. He had an innate need to perform before an audience—whether at the dinner table telling a story to family and friends or lecturing on television, or, most happily, conducting—and just as innately, a need to go into solitary confinement, as it were, in his studio for all-night sessions eking out a creation while the rest of the world slept. These public and private personas were at war within him. When his composing went well, he gloried in its ultimate acceptance; he had showed his creative stuff and received his appropriate due, a kind of private satisfaction that few people can lay claim to. Then the satisfaction would wane; he would get edgy and begin to crave the enthralling ovations that great maestros bask in. He once told me that leading an orchestra was the closest thing to complete control and power. "It's like being an emperor, even more," he said. "You point a finger and the brasses explode, the drums and cymbals crash. Sometimes you just walk out on the stage and before you even step up on the podium, the house comes down—and you haven't even done anything yet."

As sick and frail as he was in his last weeks on earth, he would still be sorely tempted by inducements to conduct all over the world. The temptations would include special helicopters whisking him off to luxurious hotel suites after he arrived by Concorde or private jet. Barely able to breathe, he actually gave in to a couple of those seductions, despite all our protests and the obvious toll it took on him. The need for performance, for collaboration, for people, was that strong.

—Burton Bernstein

"A conductor's right hand." With Philharmonic Concertmaster John Corigliano, Sr., who was a member of the Orchestra from 1946 to 1966.

On the Podium: Intellect and Ecstasy

BY BILL MCGLAUGHLIN

Some years ago I was having dinner with Ensemble Wien Berlin, the extraordinary wind quintet made up of solo players from the Berlin and Vienna Philharmonics. With each course came cavalcades of stories and opinions and music-business gossip. Finally, Milan Turkovic, the great bassoonist said, "Bill, we think Leonard Bernstein is your greatest." When I quickly agreed, five Germans and Austrians said as one, "No. Not just as a conductor. As everything, including composer." I still agreed. But I knew what they meant.

Following his first concert as Music Director, Bernstein is congratulated by Philharmonic musicians, including Principal Trumpet William Vacchiano (to Bernstein's right), Concertmaster John Corigliano (second from right), and Principal Cello Lazlo Varga (with mustache).

Back in those days, Bernstein's fame and ubiquity as a conductor seemed to overshadow his other achievements. But things have changed; the years since Bernstein's death in 1990 have been kind to the composer, but perhaps not as kind to the conductor. What has changed is that like actors, singers, and dancers, conductors—even Leonard Bernstein—are mortal. In fact, I think conductors are more mortal. As valuable as recordings are, a conductor's reputation depends upon live performances. Once a conductor leaves us, how do we recapture his essence? In Bernstein's case, we are blessed with a record on film and television, and, of course, reviews.

It's an education to read reviews of Bernstein's concerts over the years. Critics couldn't ignore his tremendous talent and vitality, but the energy and sheer personal power he exuded seemed to have overwhelmed them. Commonly, one reads about his over-conducting; histrionic is a word that shows up with some frequency. Self-indulgence is noted, his taste is questioned, it's alleged that Bernstein's work has a single subject—himself. I think those boys and girls writing the reviews were looking at Leonard Bernstein from the wrong vantage point: he wasn't conducting the audience; he was conducting the musicians on the stage. Two-thirds of what a conductor does is completely out of the view of the audience. To bolster my audacious notion that it's very difficult to judge a conductor from the audience, let me call upon a witness. Orin O'Brien, a bassist who joined the New York Philharmonic in

1966, once told the radio host Robert Sherman that she worked as an usher at Carnegie Hall while she was studying at Juilliard, and "hardly ever missed a Philharmonic concert. From the audience I found it difficult to take some of Bernstein's gyrations and dancing around the podium," she recalled. But once she joined the Orchestra, "I thought, 'Gee whiz, I don't find him difficult to follow at all, he's extremely clear.' He had an unbelievable rhythm in his body language. Whenever you had an after-beat or something else that was tricky, he would give you the rhythm with the flick of an eyebrow, or a smile, or just a look. … We knew then that his movements weren't put on for the audience's benefit, but that he was simply living music that he believed in so deeply." Other musicians who played for Bernstein over the years confirm Ms. O'Brien's testimony over and over.

"Finding the Sound of the Composer"

So, if Bernstein wasn't bouncing and leaping and dancing to impress the audience, what was making him look like that on the podium? Simply, it was the music. Here's what he had to say: "It's a combination of study and experience. The conductor's ability to hear the score and to be able to imagine the composer's intention—that's the main ingredient in a successful conductor—putting himself in the place of the composer writing this piece and then re-transferring it." And this solitary process, conductor sitting with score in his lap, trying to find his way into a composer's soul, is what defined Bernstein. His greatest triumphs came from his returning to scores he'd studied deeply for decades, continually finding new insights and delights.

Ever the student. Bernstein noted new discoveries on his scores of Tchaikovsky's Sixth Symphony.

"I think Lenny was a student all his life," said New York Philharmonic cellist Evangeline Benedetti, whom Bernstein hired in 1967. "I'll never forget his coming in with the Tchaikovsky Sixth Symphony, thrilled like a kid with a new toy, because he'd discovered that the whole first movement was based on *appoggiaturas*, and he changed our interpretation to emphasize that."

More important, Bernstein was also a teacher—perhaps the greatest and most influential teacher of music in the twentieth century. "He was a great educator, Lenny, which is why everybody enjoyed his children's concerts," Julius Baker, principal flute from 1965 to 1983, said in a Philarmonic interview. "When I'd leave for rehearsal I'd tell my wife, 'Okay, I'm going for my music lesson,' and when I came home, Ruth would ask, 'So, what did you learn today?' "

Bernstein's teaching began with the score, and was only complete, in his mind, when he got the results he wanted from the orchestra. The challenge, he said, is to "find the sound of the composer in my head and then ... to get whatever orchestra you're leading to deliver that. The markings in my scores are very detailed. They're geared to that end—transferring the sound in my head to these instrumentalists on the stage and having them give it back to the listener. Then, that's a complete operation, and only then is the operation a success."

In Search of Lenny's Markings

Bernstein placed great importance in his markings—those notations in his conducting scores that he added to the composers' own. I wanted to see Bernstein's markings for myself, and there was only one place to go: the New York Philharmonic Archives, where Lenny's scores now reside.

I'm sitting in the Archives at a decent-sized desk in a quiet room (now that the man with the vacuum cleaner has departed), with a box full of Mahler scores beside me. Not just any Mahler scores, but the scores used by the man who had succeeded Mahler as Music Director of the Philharmonic a half-century after Mahler went back to Europe. The Sixth Symphony is on the top of the heap, so I'll start there. Two scores, actually. The newer score in the familiar baby-blue binding of the Mahler Gesellschaft is a modern (1962) revision that bears relatively few markings, almost all in red pencil. (I'm learning that Bernstein used red pencil to communicate to this Orchestra's librarians, who would, in turn, transfer Lenny's markings to each musician's part.) So, what did he mark? Mostly dynamic indications that reinforced Mahler's own marks, trying to bring a gesture into sharper focus, just as Mahler had revised his own scores after he'd heard a work from the podium. Some of the markings indicate refinements of balance and texture.

> "Volcanic auftakten, gasping luftpausen, titanic accents ... **cadences that bless** like the moment when an excruciating pain suddenly ceases."

There's another Mahler Sixth from Universal, this one without marks; neither of the two scores feels like the one Bernstein used when he learned the work. So I inquire, and am handed a carefully printed, digitized version of close to three hundred sheets. (The original, I am informed, is such an icon and in such demand that it has been scanned for preservation purposes.) Aha! A page with notes in Bernstein's hand that sounds rather familiar ... yes, some of this shows up in his writings on

Mahler: Opera symphonist
(#6 most operatic yet, perhaps because
purely instrumental; yet final resembles (including choral
#2 (recitative, trauma,...)) Basic elements of German
music (also It. opera, music (also It. opera,
known to their friends
ultimate power; result:
neurotic intensity, irony, extreme
sentimentalism, despair (that it
can't go even further) apocalyptic
radiance, shuddering silence,
Volcanic... auftakten,
gasping luftpause, fitina

accents achieved by every
means (tonic + tonic); rituale
stretched to motivelessness, dynamics over-
marches like a heart attack de) to a point
fashioned of 4-bar phrases punctuated
in brass + fine, cadences
That bless; like the moment
when an excruciating pain
suddenly ceases;

Operatic Mahler:
variously so; Lieder
origin, dramatic
structure, Certain...
raising preludes, interludes,
magnitude, intensity (+reality)
Theatre; Climaxes, etc.
Parsifal (#6), Aida (#2)
(Traviata (#4),
Tristan ''brall

Also, Mahler not here: the
commentary on all 9 symphs.
(footnote re #10)

{ Mozart—
Beeth.—Brahms,
Liszt—Wagner }

Mahler: "volcanic auftakten, gasping luftpausen, titanic accents .... ritards stretched to near motionlessness, marches like a heart attack." As a conductor, I have actually quoted those lines of Bernstein to orchestras to spur them on, and here they are, penciled into his Mahler Sixth score. In fact, there's another line that I don't see here, one of my favorites: "His chorales are like all Christendom gone mad." Bernstein must have added that later.

His notes are in a careful, rather graceful hand, blue pencil trailing down the page at an oblique angle. Nothing is scrawled or written in haste. I'm surprised; I always thought of him as working at white heat. But the passion will come later, when he's "re-transferring" his understanding to the performers and the audience. Yes, this is the score he used to learn Mahler's Sixth. Lots of blue pencil. Lots! Dynamics circled, tents showing the phrase length—the first page shows a two-measure grouping and then three, accents are marked in: you can almost hear Bernstein begging the strings not to phrase off and lose the last note of a figure. The sudden explosion in the strings at measure thirteen is forcefully marked—*FFF!*, Bernstein adding an exclamation point to Mahler's dynamic. And so it goes, on through the score—every one of Mahler's dynamics is repeated in Bernstein's hand as if in writing them over himself, he was taking possession of the score.

Look at this passage in the *Finale*, where Mahler invokes the sound of the full orchestra playing very softly, just four measures after a terrific climax: you see Bernstein seeking clarity in the low strings and brass. Next to the *pp* marking Bernstein adds *ma marc. molto*. Softly, yes, but bring out this figure; it's not just soft, it's IMPORTANT. Meanwhile, to the solo trumpeter sustaining a high A *pp*, Bernstein implores *dolcissimo*—"Sweetly, please. Start that long crescendo with your most engagingly warm sound, you'll have your moment." Paging through this score is like watching Bernstein think.

The passion leaps off the page. Bernstein takes conducting directions, written in his score of the Mahler Sixth Symphony, into rehearsal.

"Sex With One Hundred People"

Okay, we've examined the markings and heard how Lenny communicated with the musicians; now it's time to see the man in action—on DVD. Bernstein was one of the first conductors to come of age in the television era. We are fortunate that he loved the medium and it loved him. I have twenty discs to look at. Where to start? I decide on "The Love of Three Orchestras" (wouldn't Prokofiev have loved that?). Wow! This is almost too much to bear: Bernstein conducting the *Adagietto* of Mahler's Fifth with the Vienna Philharmonic. This was the piece he chose to play with the New York Philharmonic at Bobby Kennedy's funeral. Bernstein's voice enters in the middle of the second phrase: "There is a kind of closeness that can develop with the members of an orchestra in which you and a body are breathing together, lifting and sinking together. Am I making this sound too lurid? Too sexual? … It is sort of sexual—(long pause)—but it's with one hundred people."

The musicians felt his intensity, too. John Cerminaro, who played in the Philharmonic's horn section from 1969 to 1979, remembered rehearsals with Bernstein: "Many times he would rehearse something really big—a Mahler symphony—and there was so much going on, so much intensity, such nit-picking, that it almost created a crisis in everybody's life. You couldn't just play a solo according to the legal letter of the notes: he wanted something special on an emotional level. He wanted you to give; he wanted you to sweat with him. By the time the concert came, everybody was high strung, and it would be a great moment."

The three orchestras of the DVD's title are the Israel Philharmonic, the Vienna Philharmonic, and the New York Philharmonic. From 1943, when he made his now-legendary New York Philharmonic debut, through eleven seasons as Music Director—and another twenty years as Music Director Laureate from 1970 to his death in 1990—he conducted the New York Philharmonic in 1,247 concerts, a total that is light years beyond that of any other conductor.

A Born Conductor

Bernstein was a born conductor, but he was one of the last to realize it. As a student at Harvard, he'd been a pianist and a composer. His playing of Aaron Copland's Piano Variations endeared him to Copland who counseled him, "Lenny, calm down, get enough sleep, practice and write music." Then came a friendship with Dimitri Mitropoulos. "Mitropoulos had put the idea in my head that I must be a conductor," Bernstein once said. "I never had this ambition, or vision of myself—it seemed far too remote, and glamorous a thing." But it wouldn't be remote, not the way he embraced the orchestra. Here's Evangeline Benedetti again: "With Lenny as a major figure in the world, there was a certain awe about working with him … but there was also a very personal connection. You somehow felt that you were playing just for Lenny at that moment. As a conductor … he had the ability to inspire us individually as well as collectively. I felt that he wanted each person to really do his utmost, and for all of us to put in our personalities as well as being part of the group. I've not experienced that kind of oneness on a collective emotional level with any other conductor."

The years leading up to Bernstein's becoming Music Director of the Philharmonic would have filled any one else's plate for a life time: conducting all over the world (at La Scala, for heaven's sake, with Maria Callas), and adventures in show biz—*On the Town, Candide, West Side Story*, a score for *On the Waterfront*.

But then came the invitation of a lifetime, to be Music Director of the New York Philharmonic. "I didn't throw anything away," Bernstein says on "Love for Three Orchestras." "I just added this family to my existence. I thought I could now learn to know the great works of the orchestral literature, know them in the best way I could—something special, individual." Bernstein threw himself into his position with total commitment. He was very proud of developing not a single New York Philharmonic style, but a versatility for which the Orchestra became famous: "The New York Philharmonic could change on the dime. Other orchestras are mired in their own sound. One conductor wants a sound that bespeaks himself, another an X-ray picture of the orchestra."

Let's look at what he means, beginning with the New York Philharmonic in Japan in 1979, playing Schumann's Symphony No.1. Bernstein is concentrating. He doesn't look overjoyed or destroyed by passion. It's strangely businesslike. I'm starting to get it: this Schumann sounds classical, and I am reminded that Bernstein was a great Haydn conductor—"the best we have," in the judgment of the great Haydn scholar H.C. Robbins Landon. Demolishing the heresy that Schumann was a poor orchestrator was one of Bernstein's lifelong passions. In the *Largo*, I observe Bernstein slightly suppressing the string choir in favor of the winds and horns.

Rehearsing the New York Philharmonic, c. 1965.

Unlike Mahler (who published major re-orchestrations of Schumann) and others, Bernstein doesn't re-orchestrate Schumann; he brings out the color that's already there. But that takes the ear of a composer/orchestrator … and the imagination.

Touching the Music

Bernstein needs to touch the music. This leads to a great deal of subdividing of the rhythm, bringing out the smaller notes between the big beats. Conducting teachers generally condemn this practice on the theory that too much information can be a hindrance to the players. Try doing this mindlessly and you'll hear the players muttering, "We're playing already. Leave us alone." Somehow, when Bernstein conducts all these little pulses, it doesn't get in the way. That's because he doesn't want to control all those little gestures, he just needs to touch the music.

That desire to touch the music is more than a metaphor. Leonard Davis, who played viola in the Philharmonic from 1949 to 1991, recalled Bernstein once "telling my wife and me that he had just communicated with Tchaikovsky. We thought he was kidding, but now I don't think he was. I asked him if he ever got a busy signal trying to get through, and he said, 'It happens most of the time, but when I do reach him, I end up with first-hand information.' He needed to come as close as he could to the spirit of a composer, and then he did everything with that kind of intense conviction."

With that in mind, I watch Bernstein conducting Tchaikovsky's *Pathétique* at the Sydney Opera House in 1979. I have the sound of his controversial 1986 recording firmly in mind, with unprecedentedly slow tempi that stretched the work to close to an hour. This earlier performance on DVD is something else. I jump to the *Allegro*. It's very fast, almost wild. Hell, it's just one step away from completely out of control. He can't get enough out of the orchestra, especially from the trombones. No, wait. That's not right. He's already unleashed a Niagara of sound. There couldn't really be more sound. But he wants something more. And he'll get it somehow—grasping the stick with both hands, shaking it as if he's wrestling with some enormous force. Two final hammerblows. Bernstein exhausted but exhilarated, milking the second climax. I love it. He's got us convinced that we need it. From that point on, he's the consoling father—reassuring us— helping us deal with loss. He's strong. He's seen it all. He's caring for us with each phrase.

We come to the *Allegro con grazia*. It's a shame we've lost the original meaning of the word "gay." Nothing else really describes Bernstein's pleasure in this movement, beginning with his delight in Tchaikovsky's 5/4 rhythm. His markings in the score are a mixture of the analytical and whimsical ("simultaneously {2/3, 3/2}=ambiguity=charm"), but once he's on the podium he's simply the rhythm man. Lovely body language, a slight graceful swaying, side-to-side. This is dance music.

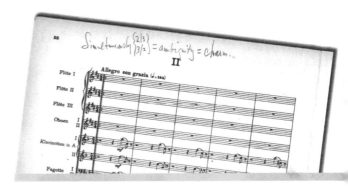

Bernstein's comments on the second movement of Tchaikovsky's Sixth Symphony.

And finally we reach the last movement, the *Adagio lamentoso* that concludes this suicide symphony. He just loves this deliciously sad stuff. Nothing else brings such a look of joy—joy and suffering, but not sadness. This is transcendence. Throbbing. Unlike the close of the first movement, where he was consoling us, by now this really hurts him. I'm convinced. This is real and it's between Bernstein and Tchaikovsky and the orchestra. The audience and the camera just happen to be there.

Every Performance a Show

Every orchestra and conductor has to struggle against routine. The familiarity that can lend great depth to a reading of a masterpiece can also lead to a lackluster performance in which all of the elements seem to be in place but the performance fails to move the audience. Bernstein's remarkable creativity surmounted routine. "Every performance was a show," Newton Mansfield, a violinist who joined the Orchestra in 1961, once told Robert Sherman. "His sense of showmanship was so acute that he treated everything pretty much like a play: it had its moments of tension and moments of relaxation, and symmetry within the emotional scope, and he was absolutely unafraid to go ahead and do anything that he wanted. Taste—good or bad—was not an issue. The thing was to be convincing, and if you're convinced yourself, you can convince a hell of a lot of other people."

Finally, let's turn to Bernstein conducting the Philharmonic on its historic tour to the Soviet Union in 1959, a singular moment in Cold War history which culminated in Moscow with a performance of Shostakovich's Seventh Symphony, attended by the composer. It's worth remembering that Stokowski and Toscanini had fought for the right to give the first American performance of this piece during the war, when the Soviet Union was our ally against the Facist forces.

In the first movement, broad gestures from Bernstein call forth the extended string unison. It's common for conductors to "mirror" their gestures—right hand opens to the right and the left hand mirrors that movement to the left. Textbooks warn against this, but every great conductor does it—often one hand is not enough. But this? Both hands swinging across his body? It's like swinging a broadsword, but this is past broad; it's almost brutal.

After lyrical music for flute and oboe and solo violin (gorgeously played by John

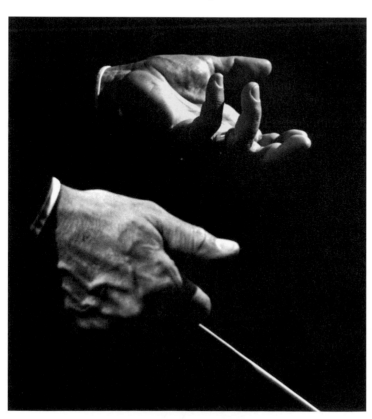

Wummer, Harold Gomberg, and Concertmaster John Corigliano, Sr.) one of Shostakovich's most unusual creations appears: a snare drum calls forth an odd little tune from the strings, a sort of march, perhaps a snatch of *The Merry Widow*. Here is a challenge for a conductor, especially one who lives music as viscerally as Bernstein. This little tune goes on and on—twelve repetitions, grinding away, becoming monstrous. Shostakovich referred to this section as "the invasion music." This has none of the charm of Ravel's repetitions in *Bolero*; this is anti-music. Bernstein looks cool as a cucumber, his gestures are small, the Orchestra is contained. He calmly marks out the foursquare rhythm. There must be no hint of what is to come. Bernstein's score, which I had consulted earlier in the Archives, is revealing. On a page from a hotel note pad—The Mayfair Regent in Chicago (added during Bernstein's 1988 recording with the CSO?)—in blue pencil, in that same careful handwriting, are these words running down the page:

remorseless
immutable
inscrutable
impenetrable
impervious
unapproachable
mindless/faceless
robotic
ineluctable

Running out of space, he adds two more at the top:

inexorable
imperturbable

The march goes on. The creature grows. Bernstein struggles to remain cool. A repeated counter-line crashes down through the orchestral fabric. Bernstein stays cool. He's got this thing running on autopilot. Robotic. Inexorable. Remorseless. But he's struggling within himself. This is the man who wants to touch the music. A couple of times he can't help himself—he shakes his fists against the air, miming the relentless snares. The tempo climbs. The Orchestra is playing at full tilt. And now, finally, he's deeply into it, singing the parts along, miming the violin bowing, climbing that great unison scale along with the Orchestra, finding—what? Release? Transcendence?

The horns sound a funereal fanfare and then … the miracle: the opening music, given originally in quick tempo and stark unison, returns, much slower, har-monized, singing sweetly—healing. Bernstein, calm. He's consoling us. The camera swings away to the audience, finding the face of young man fighting to hold back tears. So are we all. The tempo gathers, we hear an echo of the invasion music fol-lowed by one of Shostakovich's searing unisons. Again, those funereal horns. Angelic music from the strings. Then, once more, the robotic snare and the last echo of the trumpet. Three pizzicati from the strings. Bernstein simply lets his hands fall to his side with the final *pizz.* It's over.

I return to the words of Philharmonic cellist Evangeline Benedetti: "Lenny kept growing and changing through the years … he seemed to get deeper and deeper into the works we were playing, his concentration was less on Lenny him-self, and more about what this thing of music was all about. Everything he did seemed real, it came from someplace very deep within him."

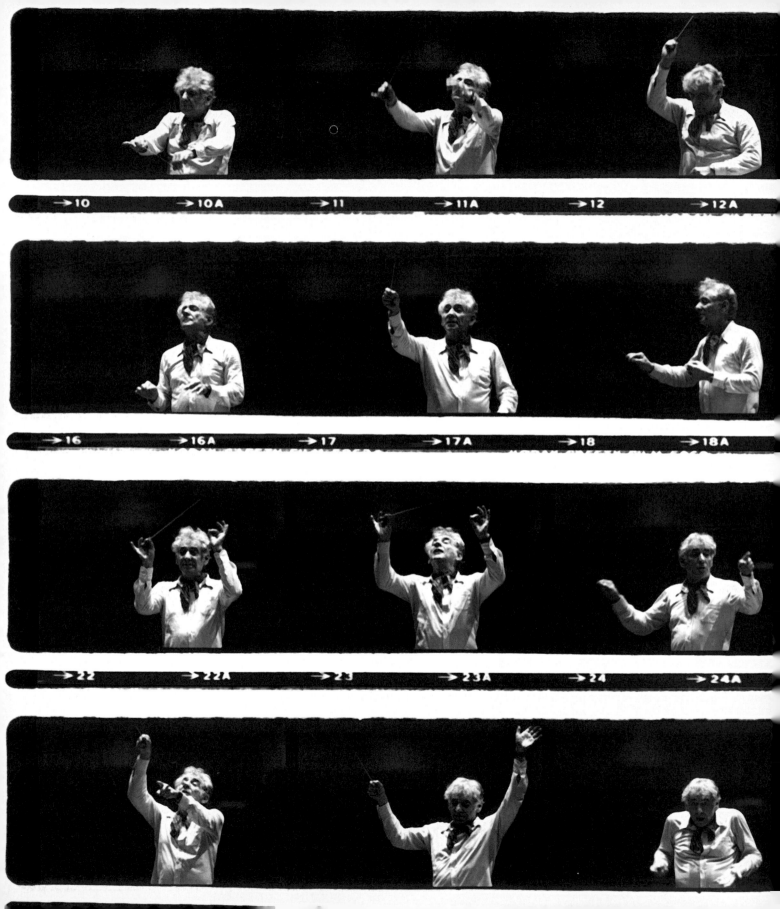

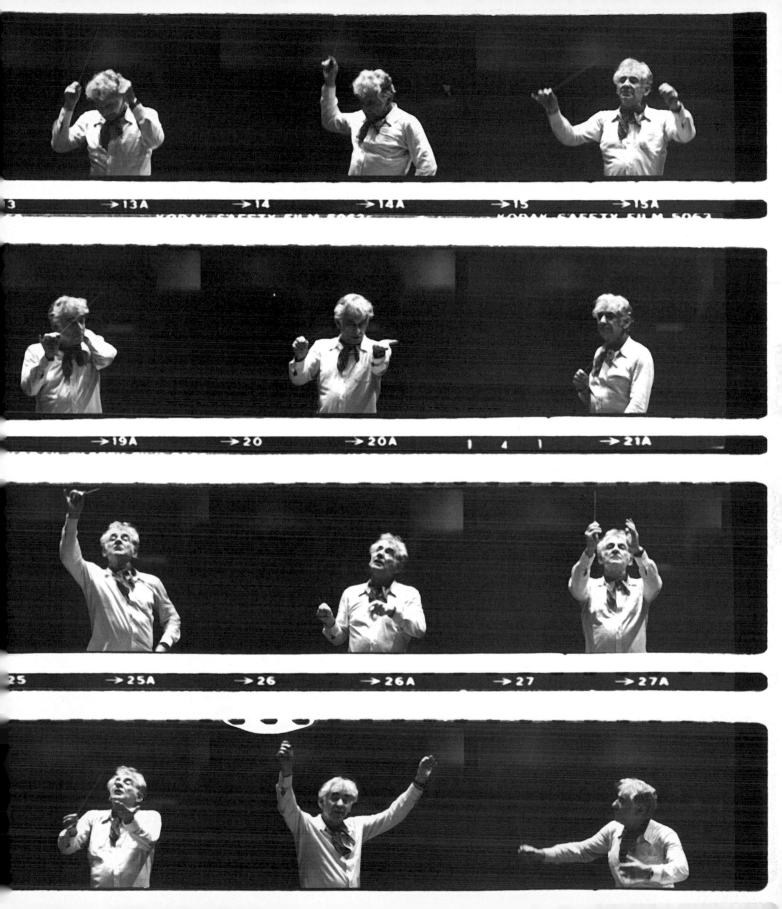

SYMPHONIE N̄o. 1.

1. Satz.

Gustav Mahler.

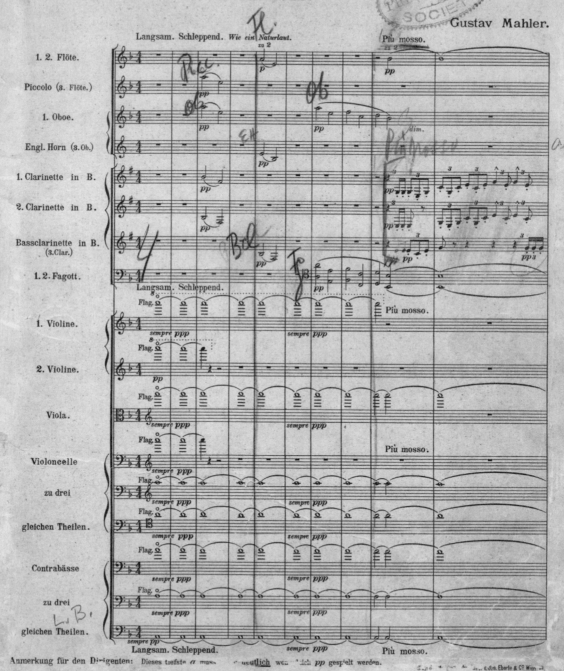

Anmerkung für den Dirigenten: Dieses tiefste a muss ... eutlich ... lich *pp* gespielt werden.

Bernstein and Mahler: Channeling a Prophet

BY JAMES M. KELLER

On February 7, 1960, music lovers of an up-and-coming generation seated themselves in front of television sets across the United States to catch the latest of Leonard Bernstein's Young People's Concerts with the New York Philharmonic, and for the first time in that series' history they were treated to a program that spotlighted a single composer: Gustav Mahler. With figures like Beethoven or Brahms hovering in the wings, the choice of Mahler for such an honor was surely provocative in 1960, when few concertgoers would have thought to include him on the A-list of great composers.

Mahler's copy of his First Symphony, used by the composer the last time he conducted the work in New York, 1909. The score remained in the Philharmonic's Library after his death and was used by Bruno Walter in 1933 and Bernstein in 1959. The markings on this page are Bernstein's and his initials are in pencil at the bottom left corner.

It was an act of devotion and bravura by Bernstein, who in one fell swoop was harnessing together the prestige of the New York Philharmonic and the technological reach of television broadcasting to reposition Mahler in the pantheon of composers. The event itself was a small part of a large initiative, the New York Philharmonic's Mahler Festival of 1960. But if the concerts of that festival made the case for Mahler to mature concertgoers, the Young People's broadcast proposed the argument where it might achieve an especially long-lasting effect. In that broadcast Bernstein introduced Mahler to young and receptive viewers whose musical tastes were very much in formation—and those viewers would reward him by continuing to associate the names of Mahler and Bernstein as inseparable through succeeding decades.

> "We're playing an **awful lot of Mahler** these days right here at the Philharmonic ... and the reason is that this year is his **hundredth birthday**."

"Now, I'll bet there isn't a person in this whole Carnegie Hall who knows what that music is," Bernstein declared to his young viewers after conducting the New York Philharmonic in the opening of Mahler's Fourth Symphony. "You see, Mahler isn't one of those big popular names like Beethoven or Gershwin or Ravel, but he's sure famous among music lovers. In fact we're playing an awful lot of Mahler these days right here at the Philharmonic; there's one of his pieces on every program for at least two months. And the reason is that this year is his hundredth birthday."

The Double Men

By the time the hour was through, Bernstein had walked his young listeners through further excerpts from the Fourth Symphony, Second Symphony, *Des Knaben Wunderhorn* and *Das Lied von der Erde*. It was hardly childish fare by any reckoning, but Bernstein insisted that he had no qualms about presenting it because "you already know more about Mahler than most people do, and you'll understand also all the doublenesses, those fights in him, all those things we've talked about today." One of "those things" was how Mahler struggled to balance the competing demands of composing and conducting. "They say that anyway a conductor's head is too full of everyone else's music, so how can he write original stuff of his own?" Bernstein observed, immediately dismissing the argument. "But still I admit it's a problem to be both a conductor and a composer; there never seems to be enough time and energy to be both things. I ought to know because I have the same problem myself, and that's one of the reasons why I'm so sympathetic to Mahler: I understand his problem. It's like being two different men locked up in the same body; one man is a conductor and the other a composer, and they're both one fellow called Mahler (or Bernstein). It's like being a double man."

Bernstein's identification with Mahler was by that time well advanced, as was his intimate familiarity with the composer's music. Bernstein's own relationship to his Judaism was apparently no less complicated than Mahler's had been, and there is no overlooking the extent to which this shared legacy helped fuel his identification with Mahler. He was fond of quoting Mahler's famous statement (or overstatement): "I am thrice homeless, as a native of Bohemia in Austria, as an Austrian among Germans, and as a Jew throughout all the world. Everywhere an intruder, never welcomed." Bernstein was fond of amending Mahler, too. In *The Little Drummer Boy*, a Mahler documentary he made in 1984, the music of "Der Tambourg'sell" segues into a close-up of Bernstein as a "talking head," riffing fancifully in the first person: "When they ask me who I was I tell them I was a little German-Czech-Moravian-Jewish-Polish-Austrian boy named Gustav Mahler." Much of what follows displays a similar merg-

A television listing for the Young People's Concert that posed the question: "Who Is Gustav Mahler?" By program's end, a new and receptive generation nationwide would know the answer.

CLOSE-UP 1:00 ② ③ YOUNG PEOPLE'S CONCERTS

THE MUSIC OF MAHLER

Gustav Mahler:
Head by Rodin

SPECIAL A new season of occasional "Young People's Concerts" begins, with Leonard Bernstein conducting the New York Philharmonic and addressing youngsters at Carnegie Hall. "Who Is Gustav Mahler?" is the title of the program. Bernstein explains that Mahler was both a composer and a conductor, born 100 years ago in Bohemia. He too conducted the New York Philharmonic, from 1908 until his death in 1911. Mahler was a link between the romantic and modern composers and his music reflected Oriental influences and was often operatic in nature.

The Philharmonic plays brief excerpts from Mahler's First and Second Symphonies, the complete last movement of the Fourth Symphony, and portions of "The Song of the Earth" and "The Boy's Magic Horn." Vocal soloists are soprano Reri Grist, contralto Helen Raab and tenor William Lewis. (60 min.)

A-2

TV GUIDE

Wearing a favorite sweatshirt while rehearsing the Philharmonic in Philharmonic Hall.

ing of personas, which can come across as unsettling. And yet there is no doubting Bernstein's sincerity, any more than one would care to doubt the sincerity of his famously unbuttoned, highly idiosyncratic interpretations of Mahler's music. Although he encountered serious criticism for what came to be viewed as an extreme approach to Mahler, Bernstein defended his interpretations as both informed and authentic. He would explain in his 1971 film *Four Ways to Say Farewell*, a lecture-performance about the Ninth Symphony, with the Vienna Philharmonic:

> I have tried in the past in performances of this and other Mahler symphonies to underplay early climaxes, to save, also for my own sanity and for the sake of the orchestra's, so they don't give their all and have nothing left. It's impossible with Mahler. You have to give everything you have emotionally to bar 39 and eight bars later even more. … All Mahler symphonies, all Mahler works, for that matter, deal in extremes: extremes of dynamics, of tempo, of emotional meaning. When it is there, it is extremely there. When it's thick and rich, it's thicker and richer than anything in *Götterdämmerung*. When it is suffering it is suffering to a point that no music has ever suffered before.

The notations he inscribed (I know not when) on the score of that symphony that resides in the New York Philharmonic Archives evoke precisely the emphasis on extremes—and on his beloved dualities—that informed his Mahler interpretations from the outset. At the top of the third movement, for example, his markings include "Nasty/hilarious," "spastic/sophisticated," "sour/'pious.' "

A Mahler Missionary

Bernstein's identification with Mahler, the man, was born of intimate familiarity with the composer's scores. His formative years as a musician had placed him in the orbits of numerous figures who qualified as Mahler champions, including Artur Rodzinski, a forceful Mahler advocate whose Philharmonic performances of the Second Symphony Bernstein had followed as the assistant conductor and understudy in December 1943; Bruno Walter, who had served as the composer's amanuensis from 1901–11 and whose eleventh-hour cancellation afforded Bernstein his high-profile Philharmonic conducting debut, which was broadcast, in November 1943; Fritz Reiner, Bernstein's conducting professor at the Curtis Institute, whose credits included the English premiere of *Kindertotenlieder*, in 1924; Serge Koussevitzky, who had led the American premiere of the Ninth Symphony, in 1931, and served as Bernstein's mentor at the outset of his conducting career; and Dimitri Mitropoulos, who made the first-ever studio recording of the First Symphony, in 1940 with the Minneapolis Symphony Orchestra, and was Bernstein's predecessor as the Philharmonic's Music Director, serving together with him as co-conductor for the 1957–58 season.

> Bernstein's **identification with Mahler**, the man, was born of **intimate familiarity** with the composer's scores.

Bernstein first conducted Mahler's music at the season-opening concert of the New York City Symphony Orchestra at City Center, on September 22, 1947, the first of a pair of performances he led as that group's music director. His not-very-modest selection for the event was the *Resurrection* Symphony—still an "occasion" whenever it is programmed, and certainly one in 1947. The critic Irving Kolodin, writing the next day in the *New York Sun*, welcomed the piece as "the most bumptious, empty noise ever contrived." From the outset, then, Bernstein found himself playing both offense and defense in the Mahler arena, conducting the composer's works in the spirit of a devout and energetic acolyte, often in the face of incomprehension or downright hostility. *(continued on page 181)*

a brother's recollection

Mahler's Muse Tempts Another

An encounter with the infamous Alma Mahler affirmed Lenny's interpretations of the composer's music, and reinforced his own deeply held religious convictions.

Alma Mahler, attending Bernstein's rehearsal with the Philharmonic at Carnegie Hall, 1959.

Alma Mahler, the famously seductive Viennese beauty who was mistress to several artists and wife to three outstanding men of culture, settled in America during the Second World War after barely escaping from Europe with her third husband, the novelist Franz Werfel. Her reputation as a companion and mate of great men had preceded her: there was, first, Gustav Mahler. After his death in 1911 she took up with the painter Oskar Kokoschka, then married and divorced the Bauhaus architect Walter Gropius, and was, ultimately, widowed by Werfel in 1945—all in all, a distinguished marital history that even inspired a witty ditty by the satirist Tom Lehrer simply called "Alma."

As a conductor and composer who had long identified with Mahler, Lenny was, of course, both fascinated and amused by Alma's exploits and her influence on those extraordinary gentlemen. When Alma turned up in person one day at a Philharmonic rehearsal of a Mahler work, Lenny's fascination and amusement grew exponentially. I recall his description of their meeting, more or less in these words:

There was Alma herself, the Viennese courtesan of world fame, looking far younger than her eighty or so years, coming down to the edge of the stage during a break in the rehearsal. With half the Philharmonic staring, she looked up at me as I leaned over the stage to greet her and she flashed her puppy-dog eyes upward. She told me how wonderful my Mahler interpretation was and how much Gustav would have liked it. Then those lovely eyelashes fluttered and I got the definite sense that she wouldn't have at all minded making me her third Jewish husband, or at least lover, if only I could be persuaded to ditch Felicia and run off with her. I suddenly understood all her mysterious powers over artists.

(There is a photograph of this historic encounter taken by a *Life* photographer but it is unavailable, alas.)

That Lenny referred to himself as Alma's possibly prospective third Jewish conquest, after Mahler and

Upon his retirement as Music Director, the New York Philharmonic musicians presented Bernstein with a mezuzah *designed by Resia Schor, May 1969.*

Werfel, revealed a great deal about a question that nagged Lenny to his last days: Two of the most influential figures in his life and work, Serge Koussevitzky (a sort of spiritual father) and Gustav Mahler (a revered model as conductor and composer), were both Jewish by birth and manner, yet both converted for various reasons to Christianity—Koussevitzky to the Russian Orthodox Church and Mahler to a kind of Catholicism. Koussevitzky did his level best to persuade Lenny to follow his religious footsteps, but to no avail. He even went so far as to urge Lenny to at least change his last name to Burns, which might somehow make him more acceptable to the Boston Symphony Orchestra's powers-that-were as a possible successor to Koussevitzky. Again, no soap. As much as he admired and loved Koussevitzky and Mahler, Lenny was Jewish to the very end—only openly and proudly so, and unwilling to sacrifice his heritage for anything, professional or spiritual.

Selah.

—*Burton Bernstein*

Mahler: New York's Own

The New York Philharmonic Archives possesses a roster of Bernstein's Mahler performances compiled from its own records, documentation from numerous other orchestras, and the tour books of Helen Coates (Bernstein's one-time teacher and for many years his secretary). The list chronicles 342 performances of Mahler's symphonic works conducted by Bernstein in his hyperactive career. Because the list does not mention his 1947 City Center concerts we can be assured that it is not exhaustive, but it seems to come close to being complete. It charts what may be taken as the peregrinations of a missionary who was intent on spreading Mahler throughout the concertgoing world, from New York to Boston, Chicago, Los Angeles, San Francisco, Vancouver, Tokyo, Seoul, Sydney, Jerusalem, Rome, Milan, Lucerne, Salzburg, Vienna, Leipzig, Berlin, Munich, Amsterdam, Paris, London, Edinburgh, Stockholm, and dozens of points in between.

But New York far outnumbers any other city when it comes to Bernstein's Mahler performances, hosting 148 of the 342 concerts; and in a further forty-three performances Bernstein was conducting the New York Philharmonic in tour engagements. In other words, more than half of Bernstein's performances of symphonic works by Mahler took place in New York or in other cities with the New York Philharmonic. By way of comparison, he led thirty-five such performances in Israel (Jerusalem, Tel-Aviv, and several other locations) and thirty-three in Vienna—the two (distant) runners-up.

When Bernstein set about "claiming ownership" of Mahler—and, looking back from the distance of nearly a half-century that seems not to be an overstatement—he did so from his base in New York. This was possible, in part, because New York was by that time enjoying esteem as one of the unarguable cultural capitals of the post-war world. But there were other reasons that New York should have been the center of Bernstein's campaign. Mahler himself had been the New York Philharmonic's Principal Conductor from 1909 until his death in 1911, and his successors had included such preeminent Mahlerites as Willem Mengelberg and Walter, not to mention Rodzinski and Mitropoulos. New York's Mahler tradition had continued unbroken since the composer's time. In contrast, even such European Mahler hotbeds as Vienna and Amsterdam had lagged, in part because of the suppression of the Jewish composer's music during the years of Nazi domination and occupation.

Music lovers who came of age in the 1960s often assume that Bernstein all but rescued Mahler's scores from the dustbin, single-handedly restoring a corner of the repertoire that had fallen into desuetude. But by the time Bernstein's 1960 Mahler Festival got underway, Mahler's music had passed across the Philharmonic's music stands in no fewer than one hundred sixty-six different performances under the direction of fifteen different conductors—not counting Bernstein, who prior to the festival had led the Philharmonic in only the third movement of the First Symphony during a Young People's Concert in February 1959. By 1960 all of the major Mahler works had a place in the Philharmonic's repertoire, and much of his *oeuvre* had a long history with the Orchestra. The First Symphony was introduced to Philharmonic audiences by Mahler himself in 1909 and had returned in eleven seasons since. The Second was also introduced in 1908 (by Mahler); the Third in 1922 (the first of several Mahler works Mengelberg would introduce); the Fourth in 1904 (even before Mahler's Philharmonic tenure, by Walter Damrosch and the New York Symphony Society, which would merge with the Philharmonic in 1928); the Fifth in 1926 (by Mengelberg, not counting the first movement only—the "Trauermarsch"—conducted in 1911 by Josef Stransky as a memorial to Mahler); the Sixth in 1947 (by Mitropoulos); the Seventh in 1923 (by Mengelberg); the Eighth in 1950 (by Leopold Stokowski); the Ninth in 1945 (by Walter); *Das Lied von der Erde* in 1929 (by Mengelberg); *Kindertotenlieder* in 1910 (by Mahler); and *Lieder eines fahrenden Gesellen* in 1916 (by Walter Damrosch and the Symphony Society, following Mahler's conducting of an excerpt—plus a song from *Des Knaben Wunderhorn*—in 1910).

> Bernstein lost no time declaring his **commitment to Mahler** ... but he did so modestly; in a way that could not be construed as **overly possessive or greedy**.

Becoming the Mahler Conductor

The Mahler Festival that Bernstein organized for the winter of 1960—the centennial tribute that included the Young People's Concert about the composer—was nonetheless a major and unaccustomed undertaking, not least because it effectively introduced Bernstein to Philharmonic audiences as a Mahler conductor. The 1959–60 season was Bernstein's second at the helm of the New York Philharmonic; he was losing no time declaring his commitment to Mahler before his New York audience, but he did so modestly, in a way that could not be construed as overly possessive or greedy. In fact, the lion's share of the conducting went to Mitropoulos, who led the First, Fifth, and Ninth Symphonies, as well as Ernst Krenek's version of the slow movement of the Tenth. Walter returned to the Philharmonic at the age of eighty-four to preside over *Das Lied von der Erde*. As the

Third, Sixth, Seventh, and Eighth Symphonies were not programmed, Bernstein was left with a portion less ample than he could have claimed: the Second and Fourth Symphonies, *Kindertotenlieder*, and a song set comprising three items from the *Rückert-Lieder* and one from *Des Knaben Wunderhorn*. It is perhaps not a coincidence that Bernstein's repertoire on this occasion largely overlapped with the works Mahler himself had conducted during his years in New York, which were limited to the Symphonies No. 2 (with the New York Symphony Society) and—with the Philharmonic itself—Nos. 1 and 4, *Kindertotenlieder*, and a couple of songs (though not the same ones Bernstein selected).

Bernstein kept a demure presence even in the program books for the 1960 Mahler Festival. One might have expected to find an appreciative essay from the Music Director in all of the Festival programs; most, instead, contained relevant essays, reprinted or newly written, from such figures as Krenek, the music analyst

Bernstein affixed this bumper sticker to the first page of his score of the Mahler Sixth Symphony.

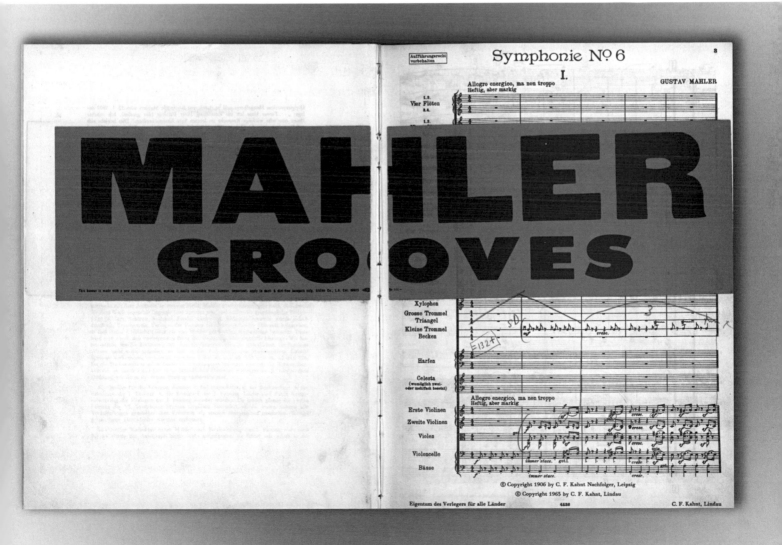

Donald Francis Tovey, the musicologist Dika Newlin, and the psychoanalyst Theodor Reik (musing on *Kindertotenlieder*), in addition to a 1910 interview with Mahler himself and a recent one with his widow, Alma Mahler Werfel, by then residing in New York.

The programs for the concerts in which Bernstein conducted the Fourth Symphony include a justificatory piece titled "Why a Mahler Festival?" by the Orchestra's program annotator Howard Shanet, doubtless voicing a viewpoint that Bernstein espoused, but not carrying Bernstein's byline. The only program contribution from Bernstein accompanies the Second Symphony. The essay, titled "The Double Mahler," is presented as "adapted from Mr. Bernstein's television script for his Young People's Concert," and, true to its title, it emphasizes the dualities to which Bernstein found himself so sympathetic in "this strange double man": "Mahler the conductor and Mahler the composer," "Mahler the sad grown-up and Mahler the innocent child," "Mahler the Jew and Mahler the Christian," and so on.

Robert F. Kennedy's funeral at St. Patrick's Cathedral, New York City. Bernstein led members of the Philharmonic in the Adagietto *from Mahler's Fifth Symphony, 1968.*

The Philharmonic's Mahler Festival was widely reported by the New York press, though nearly all of the coverage took the form of single-concert reviews rather than commentary about the festival as a whole. Reading through the files of relevant clippings one gets the impression that the critical community viewed the event as interesting but not really extraordinary; most reviewers applauded what they heard, and those who didn't almost always revealed that their reaction involved a distaste for Mahler rather than any grievous shortcomings in the performances. One critic who was eager to discuss the festival as a festival was Jack Diether, who on March 13, 1960, wrote perceptively in *The New York Times*: "If the 'Mahler Centennial Year' had occurred just ten or fifteen years ago, a nine-week Philharmonic festival would have been quite unthinkable here. Yet such a festival, under Leonard Bernstein and Dimitri Mitropoulos, has this season brought swelling cheers and cries for more. One reason is that this is simply one aspect of the growing concern of people with the fundamental problem of existence in our equivocal age, seemingly so close to both ultimate realization and ultimate annihilation." Diether's relating Mahler's music to the existential concerns of life in 1960 was concordant with Bernstein's own inclinations, and before long Bernstein would be voicing such an explicit connection himself.

What Mahler Foretold

In April 1967 Bernstein published a famous essay titled "Mahler: His Time has Come" in the record-review magazine *High Fidelity*. Here we find Bernstein revisiting the familiar themes of Mahlerian duality, now expressed in some of the most passionate prose he would ever commit to paper and working up to a sweeping historical pronouncement:

> This is what Mahler meant when he said, "My time will come." It is only after fifty, sixty, seventy years of world holocausts, of the simultaneous advance of democracy with our increasing inability to stop making war, of the simultaneous magnification of national pieties with the intensification of our active resistance to social equality—only after we have experienced all this through the smoking ovens of Auschwitz, the frantically bombed jungles of Vietnam, through Hungary, Suez, the Bay of Pigs, the farce-trial of Sinyavsky and Daniel, the refueling of the Nazi machine, the murder in Dallas, the arrogance of South Africa, the Hiss-Chambers travesty, the Trotskyite purges, Black Power, Red Guards, the Arab encirclement of Israel, the plague of McCarthyism, the Tweedledum armaments race—only after all this can we finally listen to Mahler's music and understand that it foretold all.

Many an eyebrow has been raised over this passage, which does strike a reader as possibly exceeding what Mahler had in mind when he said, "My time will come." Nonetheless, it would take a hard heart to deny the sincerity of Bernstein's rant, and he most assuredly felt himself entitled to it. It obviously did not strike him as inappropriate to justify Mahler's music from his own historical perspective even while all but ascribing that position to Mahler, who had departed this earth long before any of those events took place. By that time Bernstein, with the help of the New York Philharmonic, had effectively melded his identity with that of Gustav Mahler. He had grown comfortable in his role as avatar, and he had ensured that he and Mahler would remain connected in posterity.

But let us return to the New York Philharmonic's Mahler Festival: even in 1960 the idea of such a festival was not novel in New York. Several critics made note of an earlier Mahler festival, which had taken place in the city in 1942. The organizer and conductor for that tribute had been Erno Rapee, a Hungarian émigré not widely remembered today who spent much of his career conducting theater and broadcasting orchestras. Over the course of thirteen weeks, from January to April 1942, he had conducted the Radio City Music Hall Orchestra in a series of Sunday-afternoon radio concerts, on NBC's Blue Network, that included the Symphonies Nos. 1, 2, 3, 4, 5, 8, and 9, plus *Das Lied von der Erde*, in appreciation for which he was awarded the Mahler Medal of the Bruckner Society of America.

> Smoking ovens of **Auschwitz**... Frantically **bombed** jungles of Vietnam...**Murder** in Dallas... Plague of **McCarthyism**...

Even if it was not a wholly original idea, the 1960 festival was the moment when Bernstein staked his claim on Mahler territory, and he lost little time adding the remaining Mahler works to his repertoire at the Philharmonic: the Third Symphony in 1961; the First in 1962; the Eighth in 1963, having already included the work's first movement in the opening concert of Philharmonic (later Avery Fisher) Hall, on September 23, 1962; the Fifth in 1963; the Seventh, Eighth, and Ninth in a Mahler mini-festival (this time an all-Bernstein one) in the late autumn of 1965; *Das Lied von der Erde* in 1967 (he had already essayed it in 1965 with the Vienna Philharmonic); and the Sixth Symphony that same year (his three April 1967 concerts, plus an additional broadcast, would remain his only New York Philharmonic performances of that work).

Taking Mahler Public

But concert-hall performances heard by a relatively small number of people cannot account alone for the enduring association between Bernstein and Mahler in the minds of music-lovers. While he was forging this connection on the stage he was also ensuring a role for Mahler outside the concert hall by rendering the composer's

music at public events of overwhelming national significance. It was a major statement to play part of the Eighth Symphony at the opening of Philharmonic Hall; but fourteen months later, on November 24, 1963, Bernstein introduced the entire United States to the Second Symphony when he conducted the Philharmonic in a national telecast, from the CBS Studios in New York, as a tribute to President John F. Kennedy, who had been assassinated two days before. Notwithstanding the New York Philharmonic's 1911 performance of the Fifth Symphony's "Trauermarsch" as an official tribute on Mahler's passing, the composer's music had not gone on to assume a funerary function. Bernstein accordingly found himself justifying his choice, in a speech he delivered at a United Jewish Appeal benefit at Madison Square Garden on November 25:

With his long-time record producer, John McClure, who produced the first complete cycle of Mahler symphonies released on Columbia (later CBS Records).

Last night the New York Philharmonic and I performed Mahler's Second Symphony—"The Resurrection"—in tribute to the memory of our beloved late President. There were those who asked: Why the "Resurrection" Symphony, with its visionary concept of hope and triumph over worldly pain, instead of a Requiem, or the customary Funeral March from the "Eroica"? Why indeed? We played the Mahler symphony not only in terms of resurrection for the soul of one we love, but also for the resurrection of hope in all of us who mourn him. In spite of our shock, our shame, and our despair at the diminution of man that follows from this death, we must somehow gather strength for the increase of man, strength to go on striving for those goals he cherished. In mourning him, we must be worthy of him.

Bernstein would go on to press other Mahler movements into similar use. In November 1965 he dedicated four performances of the Ninth Symphony, including a national broadcast, to the memory of J.F.K. On June 8, 1968, Bernstein led the Philharmonic in the *Adagietto* from the Fifth Symphony in St. Patrick's Cathedral, at the funeral of Robert F. Kennedy. Through such high-profile performances Bernstein helped inject Mahler into some of the most deeply shared emotional experiences in American history, and set the stage for a tradition that would continue. The next year,

Pierre Boulez led the *Adagietto* on March 28, 1969 in memory of President Dwight D. Eisenhower (who had died earlier that day), and on October 16, 1990, Leonard Slatkin conducted the same piece as a memorial to Bernstein himself, just two days after his passing.

Mahler for Posterity

At the same time that Bernstein was taking Mahler's music beyond the concert hall and into the American consciousness at major commemorative events, he was also recording Mahler's music for posterity using the latest recording technology. He had signed his first contract with Columbia Records in 1950; when his contract was up for renewal in 1959 he struck a bargain that gave him free rein in choosing repertoire. Mahler would be Bernstein's chief priority, and the Fourth Symphony, *Kindertotenlieder*, and excerpts from the *Rückert-Lieder* had already been committed to tape (in studio sessions at the St. George Hotel in Brooklyn Heights) in February 1960, while the Mahler Festival was in progress. The Third Symphony followed in 1961 and the Second in late September 1963, both recorded at the Manhattan Center. After that Bernstein's Mahler recordings became a showcase not only for the New York Philharmonic but also for the Orchestra's new home at Lincoln Center. In May 1967 Bernstein's Mahler project reached its completion with his recording of the Sixth Symphony (it having been decided that he would record the Eighth Symphony with the London Symphony rather than record the New York Philharmonic's performance because of protracted uncertainties occasioned by choral-union negotiations in New York). Later that year CBS Records (it had changed its name from Columbia the year before) issued Bernstein's recordings of the Mahler symphonies—the first-ever integral recording of all nine works—as a sumptuous set of fourteen long-playing records, plus a "bonus record" of interviews and reminiscences, encased in a black leather box.

The public perception of Bernstein as an unrivaled champion of Mahler was helped not only by the number and comprehensiveness of recordings he made but also by improvements in recording technology itself. By the time Bernstein's boxed

Bernstein conducted Mahler's Ninth Symphony in memory of President Kennedy, 1965.

set appeared, many Mahler recordings had been made, stretching back into the era of the 78-rpm record. Diether's *New York Times* article, which was principally devoted to recordings, noted: "In 1935 there was only one complete Mahler symphony listed in the record catalogues (the Second, a Victor recording on eleven shellac disks). By 1953, the fifth year of the long-playing record, all of his ten symphonies and all his published songs were available—a quite remarkable achievement. With the aid of the LP they at last began to come into their own."

The recording of the Second Symphony to which Diether was referring was made in 1935 by Eugene Ormandy and the Minneapolis Symphony Orchestra. It was the first complete Mahler symphony recording produced in America. Whether he was aware of an earlier recording of that symphony by Oskar Fried and the Berlin State Opera Orchestra (for Deutsche Grammophon c. 1923) or the recording of Mahler's Fourth with Hidemaro Konoye and the Tokyo New Symphony Orchestra (for Parlophone in 1930) I cannot say; but his statement probably stands as generally correct, as neither was likely listed at that time in catalogues serving the American market.

> An advertisement attached to the LP package proclaimed that Bernstein "has a kind of **clairvoyance where Mahler** is concerned."

We tend not to notice limitations in technology until improvements come along, and music lovers in the 78-rpm era, who had to piece together snippets of a Mahler symphony in their imaginations, were doubtless more grateful than resentful. Nonetheless, it's hard to think of a composer whose symphonies would have been less suited to the constraints of 78-rpm platters, which needed to be changed every four or five minutes. When LPs replaced them in the early 1950s music could suddenly spin out for an uninterrupted twenty-five minutes, a span that could accommodate all but a few Mahler movements. Nearly as important was a drastic improvement in audio quality. By the mid-1960s high-fidelity was very high indeed, and the stereophonic LPs of that time could convey the extremes of dynamics and of timbrel contrast that stood at the heart of Mahler—or at least at the heart of Bernstein's Mahler interpretations, which unquestionably dealt with extremes.

Testing Interpretative Limits

Bernstein's late-in-life re-recordings of Mahler's works with the Vienna Philharmonic would clarify the extent to which he would continue to test interpretive limits after leaving the music directorship of the New York Philharmonic. And yet, when he revisited these works in Vienna and Amsterdam he was mostly fine-tuning what was essentially in place when he guided the New York Philharmonic through them some years earlier. Already with the release of the New York Philharmonic "complete-symphonies" set in 1967 Bernstein's public musical identification with Mahler had been rendered permanent. A sticker attached to the LP package for marketing purposes proclaimed that Bernstein "has a kind of clairvoyance where Mahler is concerned," a blurb from none other than Irving Kolodin, by then at *Saturday Review* and considerably reconciled to Mahler since his expression of indignity two decades earlier. In very little time, Bernstein's personal identification with Mahler had become received opinion in the public realm, and in the process Mahler's music had itself been catapulted to a position of esteem it had never enjoyed previously and from which it has not retreated since.

Listening to the playback at a recording session with his producer and engineers, c. 1962.

An American Voice

BY JOHN ADAMS

first heard the name Leonard Bernstein some time in the late fifties, when I was not yet a teenager. It was in a conversation between my parents about an open rehearsal they'd attended at Tanglewood some fifteen years earlier. My mother had been enthralled by this young conductor's evident charisma, his good looks, his innate musicality, and his uninhibited podium gyrations. My father, skeptical Yankee that he was (he could never stomach even FDR) had remained a doubter, suspicious of showmanship and perhaps a little alarmed at the thought of a local Massachusetts boy with a pompadour at the helm of New England's most revered cultural institution.

Yeee-ha! Bernstein lets loose with the most American of cowboy salutations to the great delight of his Las Vegas welcoming committee, which included the Las Vegas High School Rhythmettes, 1960.

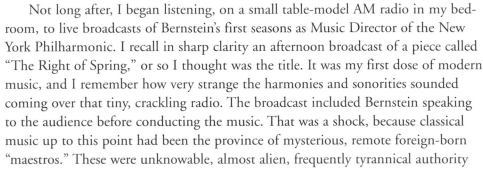

Not long after, I began listening, on a small table-model AM radio in my bedroom, to live broadcasts of Bernstein's first seasons as Music Director of the New York Philharmonic. I recall in sharp clarity an afternoon broadcast of a piece called "The Right of Spring," or so I thought was the title. It was my first dose of modern music, and I remember how very strange the harmonies and sonorities sounded coming over that tiny, crackling radio. The broadcast included Bernstein speaking to the audience before conducting the music. That was a shock, because classical music up to this point had been the province of mysterious, remote foreign-born "maestros." These were unknowable, almost alien, frequently tyrannical authority figures, crystallized in the public's mind by iconic images of Toscanini, Stokowski, or Fritz Reiner on record jackets and program books. These forbidding "maestros" certainly never would chat with their audience, least of all in the relaxed, familiar style of this young, handsome, and brainy upstart. It was a shock and a delight, then, to turn on the radio and hear the voice of an American speaking in the common vernacular, but with vivid images of the music of such daring and radical composers as Igor Stravinsky and Charles Ives. And then I saw on a magazine cover the face that went with this charming voice—Bernstein's face—and I thought "this guy looks more like James Dean than he looks like Toscanini."

My parents were adamantly opposed to having a television, so I went to a friend's house to watch my first Young People's Concert. That was a revelation. I was riveted to the television screen as "Lenny" talked about everything from Beethoven's Fifth to Stravinsky to jazz. I took every opportunity to see as many of these telecasts as I possibly could. For me they were a vindication. Growing up in rural New Hampshire and having a passionate interest in classical music, I'd had to weather much ridicule and contempt from other boys who thought this was the stuff of sissies. Bernstein put the lie to all that; he was like a movie star, only better. Good looking and fully at ease in the glare of the television lights, he was also persuasive and articulate about the music that I loved, and he had a way of making listening to Beethoven or Stravinsky exciting and even cool.

An American Icon

Lenny had the perfect pedigree for an American cultural icon, having been highly educated in European classics of music and literature while at the same time being thoroughly at home with American popular culture. He'd already written some of the finest show tunes in the history of Broadway; he knew his jazz and could even sit down at a moment's notice and improvise on a bop tune; he was able to cite a Beatles' song in a discussion of musical form; and, a serious composer of concert music himself, he was a crusader for establishing a new American symphonic repertoire. By the time Philharmonic Hall opened in 1962, his was quite possibly the most glamorous profile in the country outside of those of the Kennedys and Elizabeth Taylor. He had appropriated the archetypical mystique and persona of the "famous conductor" and Americanized it, countering the classic image of the beady-eyed, long-haired, and omniscient conductor with an image of a regular guy, hip but sophisticated, convivial but capable of great seriousness. Like the urban America he used as a backdrop for his best stage works, he was all nervous energy, enthusiasm, and constant industry, able to do Beethoven one minute and then turn around and converse with kids or sit

In an impromptu jazz performance at a 1959 Moscow party given for the Philharmonic by the Soviet Minister of Culture, Bernstein, joined by drummer Morris Lang and bassist Robert Gladstone, was prompted by what he called "a last-minute inspiration—I haven't played jazz for years."

in on a jam session the next. I loved it, and even though at an early age I was already able to detect something a bit hasty and rough about his performances, I thought I'd found the model for what the future of classical music in America would be.

High and Low Culture

We Americans want our cultural leaders to be simultaneously high- and low-brow. Since the days of Mark Twain, and even before, we have conflated "intellectual" with "elite." Unless you are a college professor, comfortably resigned to a small circle of like-minded scholars, you must hide your loftier sentiments and conceal your hunger for the depth that great art provides. Everyone must adore Elvis. Bernstein's great gift was that he could operate with total ease and naturalness in both worlds, that of high art and that of American "popular" culture. No one since has quite been able to straddle the two worlds with such ease, although many have tried.

When I ponder the dizzying whirl of activity that characterizes Bernstein's years with the New York Philharmonic, I am struck by the astonishing powers of imagina-

Wherever he went, Americans embraced Bernstein as one of their own. During the Philharmonic's 1963 U.S. tour, young fans turned out in droves to greet the Orchestra at the airport.

tion he brought to the post. The Young People's Concerts not only made him a nationally recognized media star, they also launched a whole generation's enthrallment with good music, and I count myself as one of his successes. Bernstein was not a strict disciplinarian like Szell or Reiner, who would laboriously hone an orchestra over time into a laser-sharp, finely tuned ensemble with hair-trigger sensibilities. Instead he used his bully pulpit to educate and to advocate. We remember him most for his missionary zeal on behalf of the music of his own countrymen and of course in his devotion to the music of Mahler, whose work he elevated to a much wider public consciousness. It boggles

With W.H. Auden, whose poem "The Age of Anxiety" inspired Bernstein's Symphony No. 2, which was premiered in 1949 by the Boston Symphony Orchestra.

the mind to realize that as recently as 1960 Mahler was a rarity on orchestra programs in the United States. Bruno Walter had been Mahler's apostle to the New World, making famous recordings of five of the nine complete symphonies, most of them with the New York Philharmonic. But the larger of Mahler's symphonies—the Third, Sixth, Seventh, Eighth, and Ninth—almost never appeared on the programs of American orchestras until Bernstein took them up and made them standard fare. Through him Mahler came to the forefront of our awareness and finally reached his rightful status as one of the greatest composers of all time. This triumph was already accomplished before Bernstein left New York in the 1970s to focus his activities in Vienna and elsewhere in Europe.

Bernstein also brought Charles Ives' music out of its decades of obscurity and made of Ives, if not the proverbial household name, at least the acknowledged "grandfather" of American classical music. Bernstein's recording of the Second Symphony was a memorable event for all of us composers who were searching for a lost patrimony. (This lifting of Ives out of obscurity and into iconic status was much aided by Columbia Records, whose corny Americana imagery accompanied every new release.) Ives, formerly the province of a small band of new-music cognoscenti, was suddenly proclaimed, by Bernstein at a 1958 Philharmonic Preview concert, "our Washington, Jefferson, and Lincoln of music."

Paradoxically, the Ives that Bernstein was drawn to was the conservative Dvořák-tinged folksong symphonist of the Second Symphony. Bernstein left it to others, particularly his protégé Michael Tilson Thomas, to discover and champion the truly radical and experimental music of Ives' maturity. I doubt it was timidity

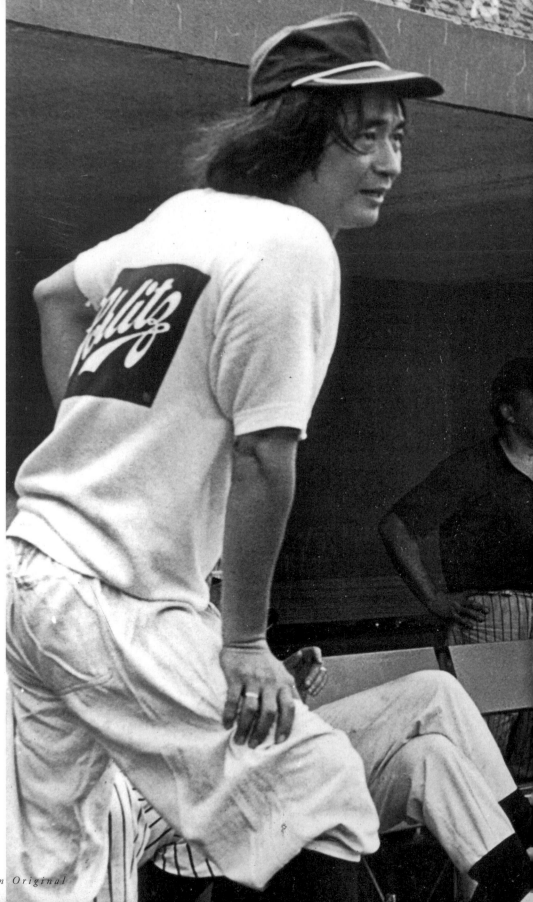

The first American-born and trained Music Director was also the first to "manage" his musicians in the Great American Pastime of baseball. In 1970, the Philharmonic Penguins played in Japan with a lineup that included Assistant Conductor Seiji Ozawa, far left, Stephen Freeman, bass clarinet (sitting on bench), and Sol Greitzer, viola (with cigarette).

on Bernstein's part not to tackle the really gnarly later Ives pieces. I suspect more that he simply had a natural aversion to music that was hypercomplex or aggressively dissonant.

Likewise, Bernstein had brief encounters with Milton Babbitt, the Yoda of American academic serialism, and with another not easily accessible master, Elliott Carter. Bernstein conducted Babbitt's punishingly difficult *Relata II* for orchestra on four concerts in January of 1969. He never programmed that piece or any other Babbitt music thereafter. He did the music of John Cage once on subscription concerts in 1964. That piece was *Atlas Eclipticalis*, a work in which the pitches, durations, and dynamics are all determined by placing a map of the stars on music staff paper. It asks the conductor not to conduct but rather to be a human stopwatch. Is there a long-lost film of Lenny's performance of *Atlas Eclipticalis*? Probably not, but it would be fun to see it if it exists and see how the normally hyper-expressive Bernstein dealt with momentarily having to become an automaton.

In 1970, Bernstein gave the world premiere of the one and only Carter piece he ever conducted during his long tenure with the Orchestra, the dense and rhythmically multi-layered Concerto for Orchestra, which had been commissioned by the Philharmonic. Carter's music, with its pungent dissonances, irregular rhythmic groupings, and constantly dislocating pulsations, seems to summon up the fault line between Lenny's more native-born populist proclivities and the then-current European high modernism (a style that fit the sensibilities

of his successor, Pierre Boulez, to a T).

Clearly Bernstein's curiosity and open-mindedness would prod him to try something at least once. A little-known fact: The world premiere of Olivier Messiaen's mammoth *Turangalîla-Symphonie*, one of the few undisputed additions to the orchestral canon from the latter part of the twentieth century, was given in 1949 by the Boston Symphony Orchestra, conducted by a thirty-one-year-old Leonard Bernstein.

When it came to atonality and rhythmically disjunctive music, Bernstein could not overcome a deep-seated antipathy, an almost gut reaction against it. And his programming reflected that. Aaron Copland's music appears on Philharmonic concerts two hun-

> When it came to **atonality**, Bernstein could not overcome a **deep-seated antipathy** . . . an almost gut reaction against it.

dred forty-three times. Roy Harris and William Schuman, two other American "populists" whose music in the intervening years has suffered a decline in interest, were also frequent choices for Bernstein programs (Harris for eighty-four performances and Schuman for eighty-one). But Roger Sessions, an equally respected member of the same thirties generation, but a more "difficult" composer of densely argued expression, barely made a showing on Philharmonic concerts.

Battling Atonality

After his retirement as Music Director, Bernstein, with the help of his readings of Noam Chomsky's theories of structural linguistics, would use his Norton Lectures at Harvard to try and explain his feelings about the crisis in contemporary music, and why his intuition told him that tonality and pulsation were essential to the musical experience.

For all his native intelligence and astonishing mental powers, Bernstein was fundamentally a musician for whom Eros was a prime mover. Bernstein doubtless couldn't find the erotic potential in the music of Schoenberg or Carter, and, the music leaving him cold and untouched, he could not bring himself to go near it again, not even as a collegial gesture of support for a fellow composer.

You could see Eros not only in the way his small, compact, and lithe body moved in sync with what he was conducting, but also in the very nature of his own music, which, not in the least troubled by modesty, he programmed with the Philharmonic no fewer than one hundred seventy-five times—second only to

By 1966, when the Metropolitan Opera opened at Lincoln Center, high art in America was personified by three leaders: Bernstein at the Philharmonic, George Balanchine at the New York City Ballet, and Rudolph Bing at the Met. Bernstein was the only one who was American-born.

Copland among American composers. Bernstein the composer is at his best when the music is choreographic and suffused with sensuality. *West Side Story* is, to my mind, by far and away his masterpiece. None of the "serious" symphonic works can come near it for spontaneity, verve, sheer sexual energy, and the power to move the listener emotionally and physically. Bernstein's weightier, more philosophical symphonies seem barely able to support their own emotion, and come alive only when they burst out into dance or some kind of rhythmically impelled physical expression. As a composer, Bernstein did not move comfortably back and forth over the continuum between solemnity and joy. In *The Age of Anxiety*, only the fleet, balletic evanescence of the "Masque" movement transports you into the realm of pure, uncluttered pleasure.

> With **composers** he could relate to, especially Aaron Copland, Bernstein was enthusiastic in his **advocacy**.

With composers he could relate to, and especially with his esteemed Aaron Copland, Bernstein was generous and enthusiastic in his advocacy. By the time Bernstein ascended to the music directorship of the Philharmonic, Copland was already well established as America's most honored "classical" composer, but Bernstein made him even more legendary. His recordings of *Rodeo*, *Billy the Kid*, the Piano Concerto, *El Salón México*, and *Appalachian Spring* sparkle with an inner rhythmic life, striking a perfect balance among the signature elements of Copland's style. He'd begun conducting Copland very early in his career, championing, among other works, the big, grandiose Third Symphony, and he was on the podium again in September of 1962 to introduce, via a widely viewed national telecast, that composer's stridently dissonant, piss-n-vinegar twelve-tone essay, *Connotations for Orchestra*. I well recall watching, on a black-and-white television screen, the gala opening of what was then Philharmonic Hall, seeing Bernstein as he greeted Jackie Kennedy, and then, minutes later, as he shocked the country by drawing forth the crunching dissonances of Copland's new score. One wonders what private thoughts passed through Bernstein's mind as he performed this music, written in an idiom so alien to his own sensibilities.

The last time I saw Bernstein was toward the end of his life, when he was on tour with the Los Angeles Philharmonic, performing an all-American program. This program was by that time something out of the ordinary for him, as he'd more and more become absorbed with the European masters and, with the exception of his own pieces, rarely if ever took on the challenge of learning a newly created piece by a living composer. Bernstein's program that evening was a compilation of what must have been sentimental favorites: William Schuman's *American Festival Overture*, Barber's *Adagio for Strings*, Copland's *Appalachian Spring* and, if my memory is right, his own Symphonic Dances from *West Side Story*. It was a thrill to see him walk out onto the stage of Davies Hall in San Francisco, but he looked tired. The packed house demanded an encore. I don't recall if he consented—perhaps he responded with the *Candide* Overture—but I remember that after the third or fourth curtain call he looked at his wristwatch and gestured "bedtime" with folded hands cushioning his tilted head. He was tired, cosmically tired, and well he might have been, having burned bright like a supernova for so many years and given so much to us all.

afterword

BY BURTON BERNSTEIN

At a crowded private funeral service in Lenny's immense apartment on Central Park West—two days after his death on October 14, 1990, and a few hours before he was interred at Green-Wood Cemetery in Brooklyn—I delivered the following tribute to him. I wrote it almost immediately after I learned of his death, as a kind of therapy.

my brother, Lenny, who was always larger than life, turned out to be smaller than death. Amazingly—just like that—he is no more. It seems impossible.

Those of us who were closest to him, who knew him best and longest, who loved him most, we—such lucky ones we are!—we somehow assumed that he would go on forever, like time itself, that he was somehow immortal, not just perishable matter like the rest of us.

There would, we felt, always be our Lenny doing what he did so passionately, so brilliantly, so charmingly, so originally, so lovingly, and, yes, sometimes so excessively—always so full of life and so much larger than life.

All the world knows what he did:

Teaching people—his favorite occupation, really. Descended from rabbis, he was a rabbi at heart, a master teacher. Just listening to Lenny was an education. (I know this better than most because I was taught by Lenny from just about my first day on this earth.) There was nothing he'd rather do than stimulate new thoughts for, especially, young minds.

Making history. He was the living precedent for American music—the first American to be taken seriously on the concert stage. I think it can be said that he made it possible for any talented American kid to follow in his footsteps.

Experimenting with the new, even though he was a hopeless traditionalist. He welcomed the avant-garde but he cherished the pristine, lovely tune—the simple song.

Revivifying the old—which I believe was his greatest gift as a conductor. How often have we heard, as if for the first time, an *echt* Lenny rendition of, say,

In an unusual game of Down Under football with Philharmonic musicians while on tour in Australia in 1974, Lenny evades a "tackle" by his son, Alexander, who accompanied the tour.

Tchaikovsky's Fifth or Brahms' First, and marveled at all the nuances we had missed over the years? How often have we seen and listened to him draw, through sheer love and musicianly example, unforgettable performances from orchestras—performances the musicians would later admit that they never knew they had in them? His very last concert—conducting Beethoven's Seventh at Tanglewood—was only the most recent case in point.

Preaching love and peace. Naïvely, he wanted the whole world to love itself into one big happy family, and he took it as a personal affront when the world refused to comply. He maintained unflinching optimism and religious trust in the ultimate improvability of man, despite all the hard evidence to the contrary. Lenny was in love with love.

Helping young talent and his less-celebrated, less-lucky contemporaries, some of whom responded to his kindnesses with rank envy and disloyalty, which, typically, Lenny was quick to ignore or forgive.

And for those of us who were his nearest and dearest, there will always be the special memories:

His love of games and, particularly, his infuriating success in trouncing us at anagrams—the game of games, at least to him. And then there were tennis and squash and skiing and swimming and sailing and touch football—the last featuring the annual Thanksgiving classic, called the Nose Bowl, in the backyard of his house in Fairfield, Connecticut.

His grand generosity with his worldly goods and with his loving spirit. No one in Lenny's company was ever left wanting. And a compliment from Lenny was like no other compliment; it was total, absolute, and thoroughly thrilling for the fortunate recipient. (Of course, he could also be occasionally tactless. Shirley once said that if you happened to have a pimple on the end of your nose, Lenny would lose no time in pointing it out to you—and perhaps the entire world. He was an *enfant terrible* to the end.)

His happiness at others' happiness. He really did share in others' joy, and also in their grief.

His "obliging at the pianoforte," as he put it—at Thanksgiving, Christmas, birthdays, Passover, whatever, whenever, great occasion or not.

His humor, which so often went with the "obliging." A great joke was a great performance for Lenny. He could laugh—and make us all laugh—in a dozen languages, including our very own private family language called Rybernian.

Language: To Lenny, words were mysterious, astonishing creatures—to be scrutinized and analyzed like cells under a microscope. Words were the equals of musical notes for him, and he loved them with equal fervor. One of the last conversa-

Passport photo, 1958

tions we had together was about handling words. "I'm a pretty good editor," he said simply—and proudly.

All those things that were Lenny are no more, and that terrible fact is unbelievable and unbearable. For my part, I miss him more than I can ever say. He was my brother, my best friend, and a sort of father, too. Whatever I am, for better or worse, I owe to Lenny. And a lot of other kith and kin can say the same. He is irreplaceable for me and mine—and, I suspect, for you and yours, too.

And yet, of course, the great, obvious cliché that springs to mind is quite true: Lenny is immortal, after all. The memories of him will be there, along with the recordings and the revivals and the writings, for generations upon generations. Just as long as people care a damn about something finer in life than power and money and their imagined superiority over others there will always be Lenny around to educate, entertain, edify, move, and inspire—to change us all in some wonderful, subtle way.

In that sense, Lenny is larger than mere death, too.

—October 16, 1990

chronology

A Selective Bernstein Timeline

1918
Born August 25 to Jennie (née Resnick) and Samuel Joseph Bernstein, Lawrence, Massachusetts.

1923
October 3, birth of sister, Shirley Anne.

1931
Bar Mitzvah, Temple Mishkan Tefila, Boston.

1932
January 31, birth of brother, Burton.

1934
May 14, first appearance as concert pianist in Grieg's Piano Concerto (Mvt. I), Boston Public Schools Symphony Orchestra.

1935
Enters Harvard.

1937
January, meets Dimitri Mitropoulos at Harvard reception and is invited by conductor to sit in on his Boston Symphony Orchestra rehearsals.

Summer, works as music counselor at Camp Onota, Mass., meets Adolph Green.

November 14, meets Aaron Copland at a dance performance in NYC. At Copland's birthday party that evening, meets Paul Bowles and Virgil Thomson.

1939
April 21, first appearance as a conductor, leading his own incidental score to *The Birds*, at Harvard.

June 22, graduates Harvard, cum laude in music, with senior thesis entitled "The Absorption of Race Elements into American Music."

1941
May 3, receives diploma in conducting from Curtis Institute of Music, Philadelphia.

1942
Summer, works as assistant to Serge Koussevitzky at Tanglewood.

1942–43
Works at Harms-Witmark, Inc., New York publishers, using pseudonym of Lenny Amber. First full year in NYC.

1943
August 24, premiere of *I Hate Music*, Jennie Tourel, mezzo-soprano, and Bernstein, Lenox, Mass.

August 25, Invited by Artur Rodzinski to be Assistant Conductor of the New York Philharmonic.

November 14, debut with New York Philharmonic, substituting for Bruno Walter, concert from Carnegie Hall is broadcast nationwide.

FBI begins compiling Bernstein file, eventually reaches nearly 700 pages.

1944
January 28, leads premiere of Symphony No. 1: *Jeremiah*, Pittsburgh Symphony, with Jennie Tourel.

April 18, leads premiere of his and Jerome Robbins' ballet *Fancy Free*, NYC.

December 28, premiere of *On the Town*, Adelphi Theatre, NYC.

1945
May 11, premiere of *Hashkiveinu*, Park Avenue Synagogue, NYC.

October 8, begins three-year directorship of the New York City Symphony.

1946
August 6, conducts American premiere of Britten's *Peter Grimes*, Berkshire Music Center.

1947
November 2, article "The Negro in Music" in *The New York Times* calls for affirmative action in orchestras.

1948
May 10, leads orchestra of 16 concentration camp survivors, the Judiszen Reprezentanc Orkester fun der Szeerit-Hapleitah, Landsberg, Germany.

October 2-28, leads concerts of Israel Philharmonic Orchestra in Israel during the War of Independence.

Signs manifesto, with 50 artists and celebrities, decrying House Un-American Activities hearings.

1949
March, signs letter of welcome to Dmitri Shostakovich, who represents the Soviet Union at the Cultural and Scientific Conference for World Peace, NYC.

April 8, premiere of *The Age of Anxiety*, Symphony No. 2, Boston Symphony Orchestra, Koussevitzky, conductor, Bernstein as piano soloist.

December 2, leads premiere Messiaen's *Turangalila* Symphony, Boston Symphony Orchestra.

December 2, film premiere of *On the Town*, MGM.

1950
First recording with NYP, conducting *The Age of Anxiety*, Lukas Foss, piano.

1951
February 22, leads world premiere of Charles Ives' Symphony No. 2, with NYP.

September 9, marries Chilean-born actress Felicia Montealegre Cohn.

1952
June 12, leads premiere of *Trouble in Tahiti*, Brandeis University Festival of the Creative Arts.

September 8, birth of daughter, Jamie Anne Maria.

1953
January 19, premiere of *Wonderful Town*, Winter Garden Theatre, NYC.

U.S. passport application refused due to suspected Communist ties.

1954
July 28, premiere of *On the Waterfront*, Columbia Pictures, film score by Bernstein.

September 12, premiere of *Serenade* with Isaac Stern and Bernstein, Venice.

November 14, first *Omnibus* telecast, on the sketches of Beethoven's Fifth Symphony.

1955
July 7, birth of son, Alexander Serge Leonard.

1956
April 2, signs first long-term contract with Columbia Records (later CBS).

October 15, named one of two Principal Conductors of the NYP along with Dimitri Mitropoulos.

December 1, premiere of *Candide*, Martin Beck Theater, NYC.

1957
January 2, directs his first concert as Co-Principal Conductor of NYP.

January 26, leads premiere of *Candide* Overture (concert version), NYP.

September 26, premiere of *West Side Story*, Winter Garden Theatre, NYC.

November 19, named Music Director of NYP (the first American born and trained conductor to be so designated), effective 1958–59 season.

1958
January 18, begins series of televised NYP Young People's Concerts on CBS. Young People's Concerts continue until 1972, with Bernstein leading 53 different programs.

April–June, leads NYP in 28 concerts on Latin American tour, shared with Dimitri Mitropoulos. Encounters Vice President Richard Nixon, who is also on a goodwill tour of South America.

October 2, begins eleven-year period as Music Director of NYP.

November 30, starts new television series: *Leonard Bernstein and The New York Philharmonic*, geared toward adults. Series continues until 1962, with 15 programs.

1959
May 14, Leads NYP at groundbreaking ceremony for Lincoln Center, with President Dwight D. Eisenhower turning the first shovel of dirt.

August–September, leads NYP tour of 17 European and Near East countries, conducting 36 of 50 concerts, including two weeks in the U.S.S.R., where Bernstein represents the "typical" American at the American National Exhibition.

October 25, U.S. television broadcast of Moscow concert (performed September 11) attended by dissident author Boris Pasternak and composer Dmitri Shostakovich.

November, publication of first book, *The Joy of Music*, Simon & Schuster.

Seymour Lipkin, Stefan Bauer-Mengelberg, Kenneth Schermerhorn appointed LB's Assistant Conductors at NYP for 1959–60 season.

1960
January, leads concerts for NYP Mahler Centennial, sharing conducting duties with Dimitri Mitropoulos and Bruno Walter.

March–April, leads NYP in survey of "Twentieth-Century Problems in Music," part of Pergolesi Commemoration. Programs explore "The Search for Style" and "The Search for God."

August–September, NYP tour of the U.S., including Hawaii, and tour to West Berlin, when LB meets Seiji Ozawa.

Gregory Millar, Elyakum Shapira, Russell Stanger appointed LB's Assistant Conductors at NYP, 1960–61 season.

1961
January 19, premieres his *Fanfare* at Inaugural Gala for President John F. Kennedy, Washington, D.C.

February 13, "A Valentine to Leonard Bernstein" NYP program features the premiere of Symphonic Dances from *West Side Story*, Lukas Foss, conductor.

April–May, first NYP tour of Japan and visits to Alaska, Canada, and Southern U.S., 20 concerts.

September–November, conducts NYP in a series of concerts, "The Gallic Approach."

October 18, film premiere of *West Side Story*, United Artists.

John Canarina, Seiji Ozawa, Maurice Peress appointed LB's Assistant Conductors at NYP for 1961–62 season.

1962
February 28, birth of daughter, Nina Maria Felicia.

September 23, leads NYP in Philharmonic Hall (later renamed Avery Fisher Hall) to open Lincoln Center. Nationally televised program includes world premiere of Copland's *Connotations for Orchestra* and Mahler's Eighth Symphony (Mvt. 1).

Serge Fournier, Yuri Krasnopolsky, Zoltan Rozsnyai appointed LB's Assistant Conductors at NYP for 1962–63 season.

Appoints violinist Sanford Allen to NYP as first full-time black musician.

1963

August–September, U.S. tour with NYP, conducting 17 concerts in 13 cities.

November 24, leads JFK memorial concert on CBS, Mahler's Symphony No. 2: *Resurrection*, with NYP. First time a complete Mahler symphony is performed on television.

December 10, leads premiere of Symphony No. 3: *Kaddish*, dedicated to JFK, with the Israel Philharmonic Orchestra in Tel Aviv, Hannah Rovina, Jennie Tourel as soloists.

Claudio Abbado, Pedro Calderon, Zdenek Kosler appointed LB's Assistant Conductors at the NYP for 1963–64 season.

1964

January–February, five-week avant-garde series with NYP. Bernstein conducts seven works, including U.S. premiere of Ligeti's *Atmosphères*.

March 6, U.S. operatic debut at Metropolitan Opera House, Verdi's *Falstaff*, Franco Zefferilli, director, NYC.

Seiji Ozawa appointed LB's Assistant Conductor at NYP, 1964–65 season.

Bernstein begins sabbatical from NYP to work on composing.

1965

March 24, flies to Montgomery, Alabama to participate in "Stars for Freedom" rally during the civil rights march from Selma.

March 30, leads Jerome Robbins' new choreography for Stravinsky's *Les Noces*, American Ballet Theatre, NYC.

July 15, leads premiere of his *Chichester Psalms*, NYP, written during a six-month sabbatical from the Orchestra.

James DePreist, Edo de Waart, Jacques Houtmann appointed LB's Assistant Conductors at NYP for 1965–66 season.

1966

November, *The Infinite Variety of Music* published by Simon & Schuster.

Sylvia Caduff, Juan Pablo Izquierdo, Alain Lombard appointed LB's Assistant Conductors at NYP for 1966–67 season.

Appoints first woman as regular member of NYP, Orin O'Brien, double bassist.

1967

April, essay "Mahler: His Time Has Come" appears in *High Fidelity* magazine.

July 9, conducts Israel Philharmonic Orchestra on Mt. Scopus after the Six-Day War, filmed as *Journey to Jerusalem*.

August–September, leads NYP on 25-concert tour of Israel and Europe.

CBS Records releases boxed set of LB's Mahler recordings, the first complete nine-symphony set.

Paul Capolongo, Helen Quach, Alois Springer appointed LB's Assistant Conductors at NYP for 1967–68 season.

1968

April 13, leads first of five performances of Strauss' *Der Rosenkavalier*, Vienna State Opera, Otto Schenk, director.

June 8, leads members of NYP in Mahler's *Adagietto* from Symphony No. 5, at Robert F. Kennedy funeral, St. Patrick's Cathedral, NYC.

Boris Brott, Gaetano Delogu, Francois Huybrechts, Farhad Mechkat appointed LB's Assistant Conductors at NYP for 1968–69 season.

1969

April 30, death of Samuel J. Bernstein.

May 17, leads last concert as Music Director of NYP, after having conducted 939 concerts (831 as Music Director), more than any other conductor in the Orchestra's history. Tenure includes 36 world premieres, 14 U.S. premieres, 15 NYC premieres, plus 40 works never before performed by the NYP. Receives title of Laureate Conductor.

September 29, testifies in discrimination suit filed against NYP. NYC Human Rights Commission dismisses action, finding no pattern of discrimination in hiring of new members.

1970

January 14, fundraising event at Bernstein home for the Black Panthers Legal Defense Fund draws intense criticism from media and public.

July, becomes Advisor to Tanglewood through 1974, with Seiji Ozawa and Gunther Schuller as Artistic Directors.

August–September, NYP tour of Japan, conducting duties shared with Seiji Ozawa, 11 concerts.

1971

January 19, signs contract with Unitel for filming of Mahler and Brahms, performed primarily with the Vienna Philharmonic. Almost 200 films are created over the next 20 years.

September 8, inaugurates the John F. Kennedy Center for the Performing Arts, Washington, D.C., with premiere of *Mass,* A Theater Piece. Commission initiated by Jacqueline Kennedy Onassis.

December 15, conducts his 1,000th concert with the NYP, a milestone never before achieved.

1972

March 28, premiere of Meditations I & II for Violoncello and Piano, NYC, Bernstein and Stephen Kates.

1973

January 19, leads Concert for Peace at National Cathedral, Washington, with members of National Symphony Orchestra, in protest against President Nixon, on the eve of Nixon's second term in office.

October 9, delivers first of six lectures entitled "The Unanswered Question," as the Charles Eliot Norton Professor of Poetry at Harvard University.

1974
May 16, leads premiere of his and Jerome Robbins' ballet *Dybbuk*, NYC Ballet.

August–September, leads NYP tour along with Pierre Boulez to New Zealand, Australia and Japan, 18 concerts.

1976
May 4, premiere of *1600 Pennsylvania Avenue*, Mark Hellinger Theater, NYC, run of only seven performances.

May–July, leads NYP on United States Bicentennial tour of Europe, along with André Kostelanetz and William Warfield, 32 concerts, all works by American composers.

November 24, leads Juilliard students as part of United New York rally in Times Square, responding to federal government refusal to aid the city's fiscal crisis.

1977
January 19, conducts two of his songs at inaugural event for President Jimmy Carter, Kennedy Center, Washington, D.C.

1978
June 16, death of Felicia Montealegre Bernstein.

1979
June–July, leads NYP on U.S. transcontinental tour and tour to Hawaii, Japan and Korea, 17 concerts.

1980
October 11, premiere of *A Musical Toast,* NYP, Zubin Mehta, conductor, as a memorial tribute to André Kostelanetz.

December 7, receives Kennedy Center Honor for Lifetime of Contributions to American Culture through the Performing Arts, Washington, D.C.

1981
June 12, conducts the Santa Cecilia Orchestra at the Vatican, honoring Pope John Paul II.

1982
Publishes his fifth book, *Findings*, Simon & Schuster.

October 13, opera-house version of *Candide* opens at New York City Opera, Lincoln Center.

1983
June 17, premiere of *A Quiet Place* (first version), Houston Grand Opera, John DeMain, conductor.

August 25, Leonard Bernstein Day, Lawrence, Mass., dedicated to nuclear disarmament.

December 31, speaks at The Cathedral of St John the Divine, NYC, addressing anti-nuclear and peace causes.

1985
July–August, with European Community Youth Orchestra, tours in a "Journey for Peace" that includes Hiroshima (40th anniversary).

September 26, opening of *Bernstein: The Television Work* at the Museum of Broadcasting, NYC.

1986
August 4, leads NYP on Great Lawn, Central Park, NYC, in his *Serenade* with Glenn Dicterow, violinist.

August, leads NYP tour of the United States, 6 concerts. Upon return, records Tchaikovsky Sixth Symphony for Deutsche Grammophon.

December 7, performs at benefit, "A Classical Evening for AIDS," at New York's Public Theater, with Isaac Stern and others.

December 15, leads premiere of *Opening Prayer*, NYP, at re-opening of Carnegie Hall, following the hall's renovations.

1988
May 9, premiere of *Arias and Barcarolles*, Equitable Center Auditorium, NYC.

November 14, leads NYP in all-Bernstein concert, marking the 45th anniversary of his debut with the Orchestra.

Establishes Felicia Montealegre Fund to support Amnesty International.

1989
October 19–31, last concerts with NYP, two programs of four concerts each, one all Copland works, the other all Tchaikovsky.

November 15, refuses National Medal of Arts from President George H.W. Bush as a protest against revoked NEA grant for a NYC exhibit on AIDS.

December 23, 25, leads international orchestra (including eight NYP musicians) in Beethoven Symphony No. 9, for Berlin Freedom Concert celebrating fall of Berlin Wall, first at the Philharmonie (formerly West Berlin) and then at Schauspielhaus (formerly East Berlin).

1990
March 11, conducts Vienna Philharmonic Orchestra at Carnegie Hall. Last New York concert.

August 19, leads last concert, Britten's *Three Sea Interludes* and Beethoven's Symphony No. 7, Boston Symphony Orchestra, Tanglewood.

October 9, announces retirement from public performances due to failing health.

October 14, the death of Leonard Bernstein, 6:15 p.m. at his home, 1 West 72nd Street, NYC. Cardiac arrest brought on by mesothelioma.

October 16, private funeral at Bernstein home followed by internment at Green-Wood Cemetery, Brooklyn, NY.

November 14, "A Concert Remembering Lenny," Carnegie Hall.

December 13, "Remembering Lenny: A Theater Tribute," Majestic Theater, NYC.

December 31, "Remembering Leonard Bernstein: The 1990 New Year's Eve Concert for Peace," Cathedral of St. John the Divine, NYC.

contributors

John Adams is one of America's most admired and respected composers, with works including the operas *Nixon in China*, *The Death of Klinghoffer*, and *Doctor Atomic*. In 2002, he composed *On the Transmigration of Souls* for the New York Philharmonic, in commemoration of the first anniversary of the World Trade Center attacks. The work received the 2003 Pulitzer Prize for Music and the Nonesuch recording won a rare "triple crown" at the Grammys, including "Best Classical Recording," "Best Orchestral Performance," and "Best Classical Contemporary Composition."

Paul S. Boyer is a U.S. cultural and intellectual historian. He is currently the Merle Curti Professor of History Emeritus at the University of Wisconsin-Madison, where he was the director of the Institute for Research in the Humanities from 1993 until 2001. He is Editor in Chief of *The Oxford Companion to United States History* and is the author of many books, including *By the Bomb's Early Light: American Thought and Culture at the Dawn of the Atomic Age*.

Joseph Horowitz's eight books include *Classical Music in America: A History* (named one of the best books of 2005 by The Economist) and—most recently— *Artists in Exile: How Refugees from Twentieth Century War and Revolution Transformed the American Performing Arts*. He is Artistic Director of the Post-Classical Ensemble in Washington, D.C., and was formerly Executive Director of the Brooklyn Philharmonic.

James Keller is Program Annotator of the New York Philharmonic and the San Francisco Symphony. Formerly a writer-editor on staff at *The New Yorker*, he has contributed articles to such publications as *Le Monde de la Musique*, *BBC Music Magazine*, *Opera News*, and *The New York Times*, as well as to several books, including the *Encyclopedia of New York City*, *George Crumb and the Alchemy of Sound*, and *Nouveaux regards sur Vincent d'Indy*.

Bill McGlaughlin is widely known for his work in broadcasting, as host of the Peabody Award-winning *St. Paul Sunday* and *Exploring Music*, as well as programs from Wolf Trap and the Library of Congress. After playing trombone with the Philadelphia Orchestra and Pittsburgh Symphony, he spent twenty-five years as an orchestral conductor, with posts ranging from the Saint Paul Chamber Orchestra to twelve seasons as Music Director of the Kansas City Symphony. McGlaughlin is also active as a composer.

Carol J. Oja is William Powell Mason Professor of Music at Harvard University and part of its History of American Civilization program. She is the author of *Making Music Modern: New York in the 1920s* and *Colin McPhee: Composer in Two Worlds*, as well as co-editor of *Aaron Copland and His World* and editor of *American Music Recordings: A Discography of U.S. Composers*. She is currently completing a book entitled *Bernstein and Broadway*.

Tim Page won the Pulitzer Prize for Distinguished Criticism in 1997 for his writings about music for the *Washington Post*. Before joining the *Post*, he was the music critic for *Newsday* and *New York Newsday* (1987–95) and a regular contributor to *The New York Times* (1982–87). He is the author of many books, including *Dawn Powell: A Biography*; *William Kapell: An Illustrated Life History of the American Pianist*; and *Tim Page on Music*. He is currently a professor of music and journalism at the University of Southern California.

Alan Rich turned to music after first studying medicine at Harvard, becoming a music critic for publications including *The New York Times*, *New York Herald Tribune*, *New York* magazine, *Newsweek*, *California* magazine, and the *Los Angeles Herald-Examiner*. Rich has also written a number of books including *So I've Heard: Notes of a Migratory Music Critic*, published in 2006.

Jonathan Rosenberg teaches 20th-century U.S. history at Hunter College and the City University of New York Graduate Center. After receiving an undergraduate degree in music from Juilliard, he earned his M.A. and Ph.D in American history at Harvard University. Rosenberg is the author of *How Far the Promised Land?: World Affairs and the American Civil Rights Movement from the First World War to Vietnam* and is currently working on a book entitled *From the New World: International Politics and the Culture of Classical Music in Modern America*.

photo credits

Introduction
Pages vi, viii, xi, xii, xiii,
NY Philharmonic Archives;
Page x, Library of Congress;
Page xv, Don Hunstein, Sussann
Strauss; Page xvii, Bert Bial, NY
Philharmonic Archives.

Foreword
Pages 2, 3, 5, 6, 9,
NY Philharmonic Archives;
Page 4, Heinz H. Weissenstein/
Whitestone Photo,
NY Philharmonic Archives;
Page 8, Henry Tregillas, NY
Philharmonic Archives.

Helluva Town
Pages 10, 12, 27, Lincoln Center
for the Performing Arts, Inc.;
Page 13, Photofest;
Pages 14, 17, 18, 19, 22, 23, 28,
29, NY Philharmonic Archives;
Page 15, Roger Wood, Corbis;
Page 20, Frank Driggs
Collection; Pages 24-25,
Arnold Newman, Getty Images;
Page 30, Metropolitan Opera
Archives; Page 31, New York
Daily News; Page 33, Linda
Kopczyk, New York *Daily News*.

Leonard Bernstein: Humanitarian and Social Activist
Page 34, Frank Dandridge,
Getty Images; Page 37, Carl T.
Gossett, Jr., *New York Times*
Pictures/Redux Photos; Pages 38,
44, Bert Bial, NY Philharmonic
Archives; Pages 40-41, Library of
Congress; Page 43, Ruth Orkin;
Page 46, Ron Barnell, Orin
O'Brien; Page 49, Neal Boenzi,
New York Times Pictures/Redux
Photos; Page 50, *New York Times*
Pictures/Redux Photos; Page 53,
Mel Finkelstein, New York *Daily*
News; Page 55, Carl Fischer
(*New York* magazine cover);
Page 57, NY Philharmonic
Archives.

Bernstein's Musicals
Page 58, Roger Phillips, Getty
Images; Pages 60, 67, 68, 81, 82,
Photofest; Page 61, Ford
Presents, NY Philharmonic
Archives; Page 62, *New York*
Times Pictures/Redux Photos;
Page 64, Billy Rose Theatre
Division, New York Public
Library for the Performing Arts,
Astor, Lenox and Tilden
Foundations; Page 71, Leonard
Bernstein Collection in the
Music Division of the Library of
Congress; Pages 72-73, Martha
Swope; Page 74, Theatre and
Music Collection, Museum of
the City of New York;
Page 75, Lincoln Center
for the Performing Arts, Inc.;
Page 77, Library of Congress;
Page 78, Paul Fusco/Magnum,
Library of Congress; Page 79,
Burton Bernstein.

Leonard Bernstein and Television
Page 84, Bert Bial,
NY Philharmonic Archives;
Pages 86, 89, 91, 94, 95, 96, 99,
100, 101, NY Philharmonic
Archives; Pages 87, 88, CBS;
Page 93, Roy Stevens, NY
Philharmonic Archives.

Leonard Bernstein's Separate Peace with Berlin
Pages 103, 104, 105, 107, 108,
111, 112, 114, 115, NY
Philharmonic Archives.

An Idealist Abroad
Pages 116, 122, 126,
Don Hunstein/Sony,
NY Philharmonic Archives;
Pages 118, 119, 123, 125, 128,
130, NY Philharmonic Archives;
Page 120, Peter Anderson/Sony,
NY Philharmonic Archives; Page
129, Bert Bial, NY Philharmonic
Archives; Page 133, Leonard
Bernstein Score Collection,
NY Philharmonic Archives.

As Music Director
Pages 134, 136, 137, 140, 143,
144, 146, 147, 153, 154,
NY Philharmonic Archives;
Page 138, Leonard Bernstein
Score Collection,
NY Philharmonic Archives;
Page 139, Bakalar-Cosmo
Photographers, NY Philharmonic
Archives; Page 145, Bert Bial,
NY Philharmonic Archives;
Page 148, Jack Stager, NY
Philharmonic Archives;
Page 151, Don Hunstein/Sony,
NY Philharmonic Archives;
Page 155, Heinz H. Weissenstein/
Whitestone Photo, NY
Philharmonic Archives.

On the Podium
Page 156, Walter Strate,
NY Philharmonic Archives;
Pages 158, 165, 166,
NY Philharmonic Archives;
Pages 159, 161, 163, 167,
Leonard Bernstein Score
Collection, NY Philharmonic
Archives; Page 162, William
Gottlieb, Jr.; Page 168, Boris
Goldenberg, NY Philharmonic
Archives; Pages 170-171, Martha
Swope, NY Philharmonic
Archives.

Bernstein and Mahler
Pages 172, 189, NY Philharmonic
Archives; Pages 176, 188, 191,
Don Hunstein/Sony, NY
Philharmonic Archives;
Page 178, Alfred Eisenstaedt,
Getty Images; Page 179, Bert
Bial, NY Philharmonic Archives;
Page 180, Eugene Cook,
NY Philharmonic Archives;
Page 183, Leonard Bernstein
Score Collection, NY
Philharmonic Archives;
Page 184, Edward Hauser,
New York Times Pictures/Redux
Photos; Page 187, Arty
Pomerantz, *New York Post*.

An American Voice
Pages 192, 194, 196,
NY Philharmonic Archives;
Page 195, E.I. Yavno,
NY Philharmonic Archives;
Page 197, Ben Greenhaus,
NY Philharmonic Archives;
Pages 198-99, 200, Bert Bial,
NY Philharmonic Archives;
Page 201, Christian Steiner,
NY Philharmonic Archives;
Page 202, Michael Rougier,
Getty Images; Page 205, Camera
Hawaii, NY Philharmonic
Archives.

Afterword
Pages 206, 208, 209,
NY Philharmonic Archives.

acknowledgements

One of the most meaningful constants in my life at the Philharmonic has been the friendship and wholehearted support I've received from the Bernstein family, both immediate and extended; Jamie, Alex, and Nina, as well as Marie Carter, Jack Gottlieb, and Charlie Harmon have all been essential to this book. Although I've met Burton on a couple of occasions over the years, this is the first time I've had the good fortune to collaborate with him on a large project. It's been an honor as well as great fun to hear so many wonderful stories, work with him on the articles and, a particular treat, to share in so many horrendous jokes.

Some of the contributors to the book I have known for years and others I have yet to meet in person, but they all were enthusiastic about the book's approach and their thoughtful exploration of their topics surpassed my expectations of what we might learn. From that other major Bernstein collection located at the Library of Congress, Mark Eden Horowitz was an indispensable, accommodating resource along with his colleague Cynthia Wayne. My colleagues here on the Lincoln Center campus, Judith Johnson, John Pennino, Robert Taylor and Jeremy Megrew were especially helpful. Frank Milburn, the Philharmonic's former Artistic Administrator whose encyclopedic memory makes life so much easier, read every word. The project wouldn't have seen the light of day if Arthur Klebanoff of Scott Meredith Literary Agency hadn't persevered and made the connection with all of the lovely people at HarperCollins Publishers.

It was a real joy to have such an insightful editing partner in Madeline Rogers and the whole editing team of Rebecca Winzenried, Ann Stedman, and Nan Wakefield was tireless, laser-eyed, and chipper about all the detailed tasks required. Richard Wandel, who has been a colleague for over 10 years, was a lifesaver time and time again.

And for Bill, who is the best intellectual partner anyone could have, I'm particularly lucky because he married me; and coming home every evening and being able to discuss and argue the revelations of my day has made this a much better book.

An important author of this book is the designer, Carole Erger-Fass. For 25 years, Carole has been my artistic partner, the one who has taken old crumbly scores or scraps of paper and found a way to present them beautifully and compellingly. She's the one who designed all of the packaging for our award-winning historic CD sets, and who created the graphics for our Avery Fisher Hall exhibits. Once, she even agreed to preserve a marzipan cake for me (a long, but very good story). She has never said no to any of my harebrained requests and she has never appeared to grow tired of my asking for "it" just a bit differently. So for my pal Carole, who always makes me look good, this book is yours.

An Archivist couldn't ask for a better champion than the Philharmonic's Chairman, Paul Guenther, whose absolute love of history has made him a great sounding board and resource. Philharmonic President and Executive Director Zarin Mehta's unwavering belief in the significance of this book—the first of its kind for the Philharmonic—was essential to the project. For almost 25 years, the musicians of the New York Philharmonic have generously welcomed me into the clan—sharing their music, memories, experiences, and gossip—making my "job" the best in the world.

—B.B.H.

index

Photographs indicated in bold.

A

Abbott, George, 60, 66, 76
"Absorption of Race Elements into American Music, The" (Bernstein thesis), 36–37, 142
Adams, Edith (Edie), 66–67, **67**
Adams, John: xv; on Bernstein's influence, 193–97, 200, 203–5; *On the Transmigration of Souls*, xvi
Aeolian Hall, 91
Alexander Nevsky (Eisenstein film), 21
Allen, Reginald, **25**
Allen, Sanford, 46, 47
Allen, Woody, 32
Alsop, Marin, 70, 152
Alva, Luigi, **30**
Amara, Lucine, **24**
American Bicentennial, x
American Civil Liberties Union (ACLU), 49
American Music: xiv, xvii; Bernstein's general survey of, 140–43
Ames, Amyas, 55
Amnesty International, 51
Anderson, Marian, 36, **43**, 47
ANTA (American National Theater and Academy), 118, 124
anti-Vietnam War protests: 50–51, **53**; "Another Mother for Peace," **50**; Broadway for Peace, 50
Armstrong, Louis, **20**
Artists and Writers Restaurant (Bleeck's), 30
Ashby, Jerome, **xvii**
Atkinson, Brooks, 45, 74
atonal music: xv, 23, **145**, 145–47, 200, 203; press and, 146–47
Auden, W. H. (*Age of Anxiety*), **197**
avant-garde music: 23, **145**, 145–47, 200, 203; press and, 146–47
Avol Laboratories, 92

B

Babbitt, Milton (*Relata II*), 200
Bach, J. S., xiii, 90, 107, 136

Bagar, Bob, 21
Baker, Julius, 159
Balanchine, George, **202**
Barber, Samuel: 28, 121, 141; *Adagio for Strings*, 205; *Anthony and Cleopatra*, 28
Barbirolli, John, 97, 138, 144
Barton, Dave, 12
Bauer-Mengelberg, Stefan, 146–47
Beethoven, Ludwig van: 52, 97, 136, 138, 151; Bernstein on, 131–32; *Bernstein/Beethoven*, 101
Beethoven, Ludwig van (works): First Piano Concerto in C Major, 106, **108**, 112, 113, 114, 131; Fifth Symphony, xiii, 87–88; Seventh Symphony, 128, 129, 140, 153–54, 208; Ninth Symphony, 100; Ninth Symphony in Berlin (1989), 52, 101, 132–33
Becker, John, **139**, 141
Beglarian, Grant, 141
Belafonte, Harry, **34**
Benedetti, Evangeline, 47, 159, 164, 169
Berg, Alban: 32, 138; *Lulu*, 32
Berlin Festival: New York Philharmonic tour (1960), 102–15, 131–32
Berlin State Opera Orchestra, 190
Berlin Wall (1989), Beethoven's Ninth Symphony at, 52, 101, 132–33, **133**
Bernstein, Alexander (son), **xv**, 95, **206**
Bernstein, Burton (brother): xiv, xv, **5**, **79, 103**; on Alma Mahler, 178–79; on brother as teacher and performer, 152–55; on brother's activism, 54–57; on brother's debut, 3–9; on brother's funeral, 207–9; on brother's televison appearances, 82–95; brother's wit and humor, 76–79; on New York City, 16–19; on the 1960 New York Philharmonic tour of Berlin,

102–15
Bernstein, Felicia Montealegre (wife): **xv**, 9, 18, 49, **50**, 51, 54; acting career, 93; in Istanbul, **131**; letter to the *New York Times*, **55**; and Pasternak, **116**, 128–29
Bernstein, Jennie (mother), 3–4, **4**, 76
Bernstein, Jamie (daughter), **xv**, 39, **89**, 95
Bernstein, Karen (Burton's daughter), 95
Bernstein, Leonard: appearance, 194; celebrity of, xv, 4, 5, 7–9, 16–18, 49, 164; childhood and education, 7, 36–37, 177; as cultural ambassador, 121–23; funeral and obituaries, 52, 207–9; idealism of, 117–18, 131–132, 132–33; Jewishness, 36, 95, 106–7, 109, 113–14, 132, 179, **179**; and Alma Mahler, 178–79, 184; mentors, 152, 164, 179; as pianist, 4, 50, 92, 121, 131, 164, **195**; press and reviews, 4, 5, 7, 23, 28, 31, 42, 44, 52, 54–56, 63, 65, 74–75, 80, 83, 97, 98, 121, 126-27, 158, 191; showmanship, 167–69; superstitions, 18–19; as a teacher, 93, 95, 98, 152–55, 159–60, 174–77, 194; temperament and personality, 9, 104–5, 122, 208; wit and humor, 76–78, 208
Bernstein, Leonard (as composer): xiii, 4, 150, 164; Carol J. Oja on, 59–75, 80-83; *Candide*, 42, 44, 69–70, 70, 74, 76, 164; *Chichester Psalms*, 147; First Symphony (*Jeremiah*), 76, 150; influence of, 193–97, 200, 203–5; influences on, 78–79; *Mass*, 60, 76, 78, 80–82, **81**; *On the Town*, x, 13, **13**, 60, 60–65, **64**, 65, 76, 164; *On the Waterfront* (film score), 164, politics in, 65, 68–70, 70, 74, press and reviews, 60, 63, 65; *A Quiet Place*, 32, 60, 78, reviews, 28, 31, 32, 42,

44, 81, 82; *1600 Pennsylvania Avenue*, x, 32, 57, 60, 78, **82**, 82–83; Second Symphony (*Age of Anxiety*), 150, 204; song cycle, 4; Symphonic Dances from *West Side Story*, 205; Third Symphony (*Kaddish*), 31, 150; *Trouble in Tahiti* (opera), **62**, 65–66; *West Side Story*, x, xvi, **15**, 42, 44–45, **58**, 60, **72–73**, 74, 74–75, 76, 80, 90, 150, 204; *Wonderful Town*, 66–67, **67**, 68–69, 76
Bernstein, Leonard (as conductor): 4, 9, 18–19, **170–71**, **180**, **205**, **209**; as an American, xiv, 91, 142, 193–97, 200, 203–5; and avant-garde/atonal music, xv, 23, **145**, 145–47, 200, 203; Beethoven's Ninth Symphony (Berlin, 1989), 52, 132-33, **133**; and Blitzstein, 14, 36, **37**, 50, 65, 153–54; and Copland, 36, 37, **38**, 39, 97, 99, 110, 121,150, 164, 203; *The Cradle Will Rock* (Blitzstein), 14, 36, 65; development as, 164–66; fans, **196**; Festival for the Creative Arts, (Brandeis University), **37**, 42; high and low culture, 196–97; and Ives, 97, 100, 127, 140, 145, 150, 197, 200; lecturing to the audience, 127, 128, 131–32; Lewisohn Stadium (City College), 15, **20**, 21, **43**; Los Angeles Philharmonic, 204–5; and Mahler, xiv, 28, 32, 149 50, 151, 160, **161**, 163, **163**, 163–64, **172**, 173–77, 181–91, 197; Metropolitan Opera debut, 30, **30**; New York City Department of Sanitation Band, 16, **17**, 18; New York City Symphony, 14, 37; on the podium, 152–55, 157–69, **170–71**; reviews, 23, 50, 121, 158; Royal Danish Orchestra, 149; score markings, xiv, **138**, **159**, 160, **161**, 163, **163**,

168–69, 177; scores, study of, **159**, 159–60; Times Square rally, 32, **33**; and the Vienna Philharmonic, 101, 151, 163–64, 176–77, 197

Bernstein, Leonard (as conductor: New York Philharmonic): debut, ix, 3–5, 63; general survey of American Music, 140–43; Joseph Horowitz on, 135–51; integration of, 45–48; as Laureate Conductor, 150, 164; as Music Director, ix, 4, 7, 45, 51, 80, 90–91, 135–36, 139–51, 165; programming, **134**, 143–44, 153; subscriber, letter to, **146**; Young People's Concerts, **8**, 47–48, 87, **87**, **88**, **89**, 91, **95**, 97–98, 98–101, 141–42, 144–45, 150, 174, 182, 194, 197

Bernstein, Leonard (recordings): 140, 149, 151; on DVD, 163–64; Columbia (CBS/Sony/BMG) Records, 188, 189–90, 197; Copland, 204; Ives, 197, 200; Mahler, 188, 189–90, 190–91; New York Philharmonic, 140, 149, 189–90; Vienna Philharmonic, 151, 163–64, 176, 190–91, 197

Bernstein, Leonard (touring): **128**; Berlin tour (1960), xiii, 102–15, 118, 131–32, 132–33; and Cold War diplomacy, 117–33; City Hall welcome (1959), 18, **28**; Japan (1979), 165; Japan (1961), **154**; Journey for Peace world tour, 51; Latin America, xiii, **118**, 118, **119**, 119-24, **122**, **153**; Latin America, return from (1958), 16, **18**; Jonathan Rosenberg on, 117–33; Soviet Union and Eastern Europe (1959), xiii, xvi, **116**, 118, 124–29, 168

Bernstein, Leonard (as humanitarian and social activist): xii, 35–52, 54–57, 208; anti-Vietnam War protests, xii, 50–51, **53**; Black Panther episode, xiii, xvi, 9, 31, 35–36, 51, 54–56,151; civil rights, **34**, 36–37, 37–39, 45–46, 48–51, 65, 83; and Communism, xiv, 36, 39, 42, 57; disarmament, 51; environmental awareness, 51; FBI file on, xiv, 39, **40–41**, 42; and feminism/women's rights, **46**, 47, **62**, 152; passport problems, 39

Bernstein, Leonard (televison, radio and film appearances): xiii, xiv, 85; *Avol Presents,* 92; *Bernstein/Beethoven,* 101; Burton Bernstein on, 92–95; Brahms, 101; CBS *Omnibus,* xiii, **84**, 87, 87–88, 88, 90, 95; *The Creative Performer,* **144**; *The Drama of Carmen,* **96**; *Four Ways to Say Farewell* (film), 176; *Information Please* (radio show), 92–93; *The Little Drummer Boy* (Mahler documentary), 175; Moscow broadcast (1959), **99**; Moscow interview, **91**; Tim Page on, 85–91, 97–101; tribute to John F. Kennedy, 188, **189**; *Young People's Concerts,* **8**, 47–48, 87, **87**, **88**, **89**, 91, **95**, 97–98, 98–101, 141–42, 144–45, 150, 174, 182, 194, 197

Bernstein, Leonard (writings and lectures): "The Absorption of Race Elements into American Music" (thesis), 36–37, 142; Charles Eliot Norton Lectures (Harvard University), 100, 203; John Hopkins University comment address (1980), 51; *The Joy of Music,* 76, 90; "Mahler: His Time has Come," 185–86; "The Negro in Music" (article), 37, **45**, 48

Bernstein, Michael (Burton's son), 95

Bernstein, Nina (daughter), **xv**, 95

Bernstein, Samuel J. (father): 3–4, **4**, 5, 7, **9**, 76, 95; *Avol Presents,* 92

Bernstein, Shirley (sister), 3, **64**, 76, 78, 208

Biancolli, Louis, 21

Bing, Rudolf, **25, 202**

Bizet, Georges (*Carmen*), **97**

Black Panther episode, xiii, xvi, 9, 31, 35–36, 51, 54–56, 151

Blitzstein, Marc: 14, 36, **37**, 65, 153; *The Airborne Symphony,* 50; *The Cradle Will Rock,* 14, 36, 65

Boston Symphony Orchestra, 138, 179, 203

Boulanger, Nadia, 47

Boulez, Pierre, 26, 200, **201**, 203

Boyer, Paul: xii; on Bernstein as an activist, 35–52

Brahms, Johannes: 138; Bernstein and, 101, 151; *Ein Deutsches Requiem,* xvi

Brandeis University: **37**, 42, 50–51; *Trouble in Tahiti* (Bernstein), **62**, 65–66

Breslin, Jimmy, 31

Breuning, Alfred, 104, 110

Brooklyn Academy of Music, 32

Broun, Heywood, 68

Brown, Earle, **145**

Brubeck, Dave, 75

Buchwald, Art, 126-27

Buckley, William F., 52

Buketoff, Igor, 97

C

Caesar, Sid, 92

Cage, John: 22–23, *Atlas Eclipticalis,* **200**

Caldwell, Sarah, 32

Callas, Maria, 28, 164

Calloway, Cab, 66

Candide (Bernstein): 42, 44, **68**, 69–70, 70, 74, 164; "Auto-da-fé," 69; "The Best of All Possible Worlds," 69; "Glitter and Be Gay," 70; "It Must Be So," 70; "Make Our Garden Grow," 70; overture, 74, 110, 205; political subtext, 69; reviews, 70; revivals, 70

Canvin, Rue, 31

Carabella, John, **xvii**

Carnegie Hall: 90, 99, 174; Leonard Bernstein's debut, ix, 3–5, 63; Isaac Stern's rescue of, 28

Carnegie Hall AIDS benefit, 52

Carnegie Recital Hall, 26

Carsen, Robert, 70

Carson, Margaret, 42

Carter, Elliot: 200, 203; Concerto for Orchestra, 200

Cartridge Music, 22–23

Caruso, Mariano, **30**

Catholic Standard, 81

CBS *Omnibus:* xiii, **84**, 87, 88, 90, 95; Bach program, 90; Beethoven's Fifth Symphony, 87–88; Ford Foundation and, 88. *See also Joy of Music, The*

Celebre, John, 16

Cerminaro, John, 164

Chadwick, George (*Melpomene* Overture), 141, 142

Chaplin, Charlie, 39

Charles Eliot Norton Lectures (Harvard University), 100, 145, 203

Chavez, Carlos, 121

Chenoweth, Kristin, 70

Chichester Psalms (Bernstein), 147

Chomsky, Noam, 100, 203

civil rights: 45; Marian Anderson, 36; Bernstein and, **34**, 36–37, 37–38, 45–46, 48–51; Black Panther episode, 9, 31, 35–36, 51, 54–56, 151; Selma-to-Montgomery freedom marchers, **34**, 49

Cleveland Orchestra, 47

Coates, Helen, 66, 181

Coca, Imogene, 92

Cocteau, Jean (*Blood of the Poet*), 21

Columbia (CBS/Sony/BMG) Records, 45, 188, 189–90, 197

Colzani, Anselmo, **30**

Comden, Betty, x, 18, 50, **60**, 60, **61**, 66, **67**, 76, 77

communism (in America), 36, 39, 42.

See also Popular Front movement

Congress of Racial Equality (CORE), 49

Constitution Hall, 36

contemporary music: xiv, 23, **145**, 145–47, 200, 203; press and, 146–47

Cook, Barbara, 69

Cooke, Alistair, 88

Copland, Aaron: 36, 37, **38**, 39, 99, 121, 141, 142, 150, 153, 164, 203; *Appalachian Spring,* 204, 205; *Billy the Kid,* 204; *Connotations for Orchestra,* 204; *El Salón México,* 110, 204; *Piano Variations,* 164; recordings, 204; *Rodeo,* 204; *The Second Hurricane* (opera), 97

Corigliano, John, Sr., **155**, **158**, 168, **200**

Creative Performer, The (TV program), **144**

Crist, Judith, 31

Crosby, Bing, 62

Cultural and Scientific Conference for World Peace, 39

Curtis, Charlotte, 54

Curtis Institute of Music, 3, 152, 177

D

Daily Worker, 80

Damrosch, Walter, 182

Davis, Leonard, 166

Davis, J. Arthur, 48, **49**

De Angelis, Joseph, 46

De Intinis, Ranier, **xvii**
De Koven (Seymour), 22
De Mille, Agnes, 62
DePreist, James, 47, 98
Diamond, David, 153
Diether, Jack, 185, 190
disarmament, 51
Dixon, Dean, 37
Donnell Library Center, 26
Doulie, Sylvia, **72-23**
Downes, Olin, 21
Draper, Paul, 65
Dylan, Bob ("Blowin' in the Wind"),
  80

E

Earth Day, 51
Eastern Europe: New York
  Philharmonic tour of (1959), **117**,
  118, 124–29, 168
Einstein, Albert, 39
Eisenhower, Dwight D., 42, 51, 117,
  124
Eisler, Hanns, 39
Elias, Rosalind, **30**
Elie, Rudolph, 12
Eliot, T. S. ("The Love Song of J.
  Alfred Prufrock") 92–93
Emerson, Ralph Waldo (*The American
  Scholar*), 91
Emmy Awards: for the *Young People's
  Concerts*, 99
Engel, Lehman, 69
Englander, Roger, 98
English Tea Room (NYC), 12
Ensemble Wien Berlin, 157
Ericson, Ray, 26
Esquire magazine, 102–15

F

Facenda, Aubrey, **xvii**
Fadiman, Clifton, 92–93
Fall, Bernard B. (*Viet-Nam Witness*), 50
FBI and Bernstein, xiv, 39, **40–41**, 49,
  55
Federal Theater Project, 36
Felicia Montealegre Fund, 51
Felker, Clay, 26
Ferrier, Kathleen, 21–22
Festival for the Creative Arts (Brandeis
  University), **37**, 42
Fine, Irving, 141, 153
First Symphony (*Jeremiah*) (Bernstein),
  76, 150

Fishberg, Jack, 103–4
Foote, Arthur, 141
Ford, Gerald: *Daily News* front page,
  x, **31**, 32; and New York City, 32;
  Times Square rally, **33**
Ford Foundation, 88
Ford Motor Company, 102, 105, 131
Foss, Lukas, **140**, 141, 153
Foster, Stephen, 62
Four Ways to Say Farewell (film),
  176–77
Franck, César, 90
Freedman, Gerald, **72-73**
Freedom of Information Act, 39
Freidan, Betty (*The Feminine
  Mystique*), 47
Fried, Oskar, 190
Fryer, Robert, **67**

G

Gaburo, Kenneth, 141
Galjour, Warren, 67
Ganz, Rudolph, 97
Gaynes, George, 67
Gellhorn, Martha, 45, 77
Gershwin, George: 15, 36, 62, 121,
  141, 142; *Porgy and Bess*, 37, 66;
  Rhapsody in Blue, 37, 80
Ghostley, Alice, 66
Giannini, Dusolina, 15
Gilbert, Henry, *Dance in Place Congo*,
  141
Gilbert, Alan, 5
Ginsberg, Allen (*Howl*), 51, 52
Gladstone, Robert, **195**
Glaser, Milton, 26
Gomberg, Harold, 168
Gottschalk, Louis Moreau, 140, *The
  Banjo,* 142; *Night in the Tropics*,
  142
Gould, Glen, 47, 101
Graham, Martha, **24**
Graham, William, 113
Gramophone Shop (NYC), 21
Great Hall of the Tchaikovsky
  Conservatory (Moscow), 127–28
Greek amphitheatre *Herodus Atticus*
  (Athens), **125**
Green, Adolph, x, 18, 50, 57, **60**, 60,
  61, 66, **67**, 76, 77, 92–93
Greitzer, Sol, **199**
Griffiths, Robert E., **72-73**
Gropius, Walter, 178
Grosser Sendesaal des Senders Freies

Berlin, **108**, 109–10
Gruson, Sidney, 110–11
Guarnieri, Carmago, 121
Guggenheimer, Minnie, 15, 21
Guthrie, Tyrone, 69
Guttierez, Horacio, 98

H

Haggin, B. H., 21, 31
Hamlisch, Marvin, (*A Chorus Line), 83*
Handel, George Frideric (*Giulio
  Cesare*), 28
Harrell, Lynn, 98
Harrington, Michael (*The Other
  America*), 44
Harris, Julie, **25**
Harris, Roy, 121, 141, 203; Third
  Symphony, 110
Harvard University: 3, 36; Charles
  Eliot Norton Lectures, 100, 203
Haws, Barbara: on Bernstein, Burton,
  xv-xvi; on contributors, x-xv; on
  NYC, ix-x; on NYP Archives, xvi;
  on orchestra's relevance, xvi
Haydn, Joseph, 165
Heifetz, Jascha, 62
Hellman, Lillian, 69
Herbert, Victor, 142
High Fidelity (magazine), 185–86
Hindemith, Paul, 97
Holmes, Oliver Wendell, 52
Holst, Gustav (*The Planets*), 99
Home of the Brave (film), 44
Hoover, J. Edgar, xiv, 55
Horowitz, Joseph: xiv; on Bernstein as
  New York Philharmonic Music
  Director, 135–36, 138–51
Horowitz, Vladimir, 48
House Un-American Activities
  Committee (HUAC), 39, 69
Hughes, Allen, 26
Hughes, Langston, 39
Humphrey, Hubert, 50

I

Information Please (radio show), 92–93
International Rescue Committee, 49
Israel Philharmonic, 164
Ives, Charles: 97, 100, 127, 141, 145,
  150, 194; *Holiday* Symphony, 150;
  recordings, 140, 197; Second
  Symphony, **138**, 140, 150, 197,
  Bernstein's markings, **138;**
  Third Symphony, 150;

The Unanswered Question, 127

J

James, Henry (*The Wings of The Dove*),
  93
jazz: "The Absorption of Race
  Elements into American Music"
  (Bernstein thesis), 36–37, 142;
  Bernstein and, 48–49, 75, 91,
  142–43, 195; influence of, 36–37,
  141–42
Jewish Defense League, 55
Johns Hopkins University, 51
Johnson, Harriett, 21
Johnson, Lyndon B., 31, 49
Joy of Music, The (Bernstein), 76, 90.
  See also CBS *Omnibus*
Judd, George E., Jr., **25**, 103, 131,
  131
Judson, Arthur, 138, 139, 143
Juilliard student orchestra, 32, **33**

K

Kander, John/Ebb, Fred (*Chicago*), 83
Kandinsky, Wassily, 21
Karr, Gary, 98
Kastendieck, Miles, 21
Kates, Stephen, 98
Keiser, David, **111**, 122, 136, 138–
  39, **194**
Keller, James M.: xiv; on Bernstein and
  Mahler, 173–77, 181–91
Kennedy, John F.: 28, 80, 83; Bern-
  stein's tribute to, xiv, 188, **189**
Kennedy, Robert F.: 31, 48, 50;
  funeral, 163, **184**
Kennedy Center (Washington, D.C.),
  80, **81**
Kerr, Walter, 42, 44, 74
Kert, Larry, 74
Kim, Young Uck, 98
King, Martin Luther, Jr., 31, 35, 45,
  48, 55, 83
Klee, Paul, 21
Klemperer, Otto, 9, 144
Kokoschka, Oskar, 178
Kolodin, Irving, 15, 191
Konoye, Hidemaro, 190
Koussevitzky, Sergei, 4, 7, 18, 152,
  177, 179
Kraft Television Theater, 93
Kramer, Hilton, 52
Krenek, Ernst, 183
Krips, Josef, 144

L

La Côte Basque restaurant, 22
La Scala (Milan), 70, 164
La Touche, John, 69
LaGuardia, Fiorello, **13**, 14
Landon, H.C. Robbins, 165
Lang, Morris, **195**
Lang, Paul Henry, 26
Las Vegas High School Rhythmettes, **192**
Laurents, Arthur, x, 44, **72–73**, 74, 75, 79
Lawes, Hubert, 48
Lawrence, Carol, 38, 45
Le Pavilion restaurant, 22
Lehrer, Tom ("Alma"), 178
Lehwalder, Heidi, 98
Leinsdorf, Erich, 48
Lennon, John: 51, 97; "Imagine," 51; Lennon/McCartney ("And I Love Her"), 97
Lerner, Alan Jay: 70, 77–78, 82; Lerner/Loewe, Frederick, 78, *Brigadoon,* 62, *My Fair Lady,* 70, 77-78
Levine, James, 52
Lewisohn Stadium (City College): 15, 21, **21**; Marian Anderson at, **43**, 47
Liberty Music, 21
Lieberson, Goddard, 18, 77
Lincoln Center for the Performing Arts: **24–25**, **202**; Philharmonic Hall (Avery Fisher Hall), 28–29, 99, 186, 188, 189, 204
Lincoln Memorial, Marian Anderson at, 36
Lindsay, John, **29**, 31
Liszt, Franz (*Faust* Symphony), 99
Little Drummer Boy, The (Mahler documentary), 175
Lloyd Webber, Andrew (*Jesus Christ Superstar*), 82
London Symphony Orchestra, 189
Los Angeles Music Center, 29
Los Angeles Philharmonic, 204–5
"Love of Three Orchestras, The" (DVD), 163
Luca, Sergiu, 98
Lutosławski, Witold, 26

M

Maazel, Lorin, xvi, 5
McCarthy, Joseph, xii, 18, 39, 69
McCarthy, Eugene, 50

McClure, John, **188**
MacDermot, Galt (*Hair*), 31
MacDowell, Edward, 141, 142; *Indian Suite*, 141
McGlaughlin, Bill: xiv; on Bernstein's conducting, 157–69
Mackay, Clarence, 136
McKenney, Ruth (*My Sister Eileen*), 68
Madison, Earl, 48, **49**
Mahler, Alma: xvi, **178**, 184; Burton Bernstein on, 178–79
Mahler, Gustav: 8, 28, 32, **136**, 144; Bernstein and, xiv, 91, 144–45, 149–50, 151, 160, **161**, 163, **163**, 163–64, **172**, 173–77, 181–91, 197; Bernstein's identification with, 176–77, 177, 181; as conductor, 136, 138, 182; *Das Lied von der Erde*, 22, 144, 174, 182, 182, 186; *Four Ways to Say Farewell* (film), 176–77; *Kindertotenlieder*, 144, 177, 182, 183, 184, recordings, 189; *Des Knaben Wunderhorn*, 182, 183; *Lieder eines fahren den Gesellen,* 182; Nazism and, 181; *The Little Drummer Boy* (documentary), 175; and the New York Philharmonic, 136, 138, 144–45, 181–82, 182–85; press and reviews, 177, 185, 191; recordings, 177, **188**, 189–90, 190–91; Rückert-Lieder, 183, 189
Mahler, Gustav (symphonies): Erno Rapee and, 186; First Symphony, 144, **172**, 177, 182, 182, 183, 186, 189, 190; Second (*Resurrection*) Symphony, xiv, 28, 144, 174, 177, 182, 183, 184, 189, 190; Third Symphony, 32, 144, 150, 182, 186, 189; Fourth Symphony, 144, 174, 182, 183, 184, 186, recordings of, 189, 190; Fifth Symphony, 144, 163–64, 182, 182, 186, 188–89, and Robert Kennedy's funeral, 163, **184**, 188, as tribute to Mahler's death, 188; Sixth Symphony, 160, **161**, 163, **163**, 182, **183**, 186; Seventh Symphony, 182, 186; Eighth Symphony, 182, 186, 188; Ninth Symphony, 144, 182, 186; Bernstein on, 176–77; Bernstein's score markings, 177; as John F. Kennedy tribute, 188, **189**; Tenth

Symphony (1st movement), 144
Mahler festival (New York Philharmonic 1959–60), 144, 174, 182–85
Mahler Gesellschaft, 160
Mahler Medal of the Bruckner Society of America, 186
Mailer, Norman, 31, 52
Mamma Leone's restaurant, 22
Manhattan Center, 189
Mann, Thomas, 39
Mansfield, Newton, 167
Markova, Alicia, **24**
Mass (Bernstein): 60, 76, 78, 80–82; controversy concerning, 81, 82; PBS broadcast, 81; premiere, **81**; reviews, 81, 82
Masur, Kurt, xvi
Medvedev, Alexsandr, 127
Mendelssohn, Felix, 121, 136
Mengelberg, Willem, 136, 138, 144, 181, 182
Menotti, Gian Carlo: 66, *Amahl and the Night Visitors,* 83; *The Consul,* 66, 67
Merrill, Robert, **32**
Messaien, Olivier (*Turangalila-Symphonie*), 203
Metropolitan Opera: 12, 28; and African-Americans, 45; and Marian Anderson, 47; and Maria Callas, 28; *Falstaff* program and rehearsal, **30**; telecasts, 87; standing room, 12–13
Midori, 51
Milburn, Frank, **143**
Miller, Arthur, 39
Miller Brothers restaurant, discrimination at, 46
Mindlin, Mike, 77
Minneapolis Symphony Orchestra, 177, 190
Minow, Newton N., 88
Minton, Bruce, 68
Mitropoulos, Dimitri, 4, 16, **18**, 28, **57**, 119, 121, **137**, 138, 139, 164, 177, 181, 182, 197
Moore, Charles, 102
Moorman, Charlotte, 26
Moreno, Rita, 80
Moseley, Carlos, 48, **49**, 143, **143**
Mozart, Wolfgang Amadeus (Sinfonia Concertante, K. 364), 12
Murrow, Edward R., 88, 90

Museum of Modern Art, 21, 22–23
Music Policy Committee (New York Philharmonic), 136, 138–39, 143
Musicians Against Nuclear Arms, 51
Mussorgsky, Modest, 97

N

NAACP, 48–49
Nass, Richard, 104–5
Nation (magazine), 21, 46, 50
National Committee Against Discrimination in Housing, 48
National Committee for a Sane Nuclear Policy, 49
National Conference of Christians and Jews, 49
National Negro Congress, 39
NBC Symphony Orchestra, 86
New Faces of 1952 (revue), 66
New York (magazine): 31, 54–56; Bernstein cover, **55**
New York City: x, xiii, xvii, **10**; blackouts and strikes, 29; Gerald Ford and, x, **31**, 32; Lincoln Center for the Performing Arts, **24–25**, 8–29; 1964 World's Fair, **23**; Alan Rich on, 11–15, 21–32; tenements, **75**; Time Square rally, 32, **33**; Upper West Side, 74–75; youth gang crime, 74–75
New York City Center of Music and Drama, 14–15
New York City Department of Sanitation Band, 16, **17**, 18
New York City Human Rights Commission, xiii, 48
New York City Opera, 15, 28
New York City Symphony, 14, 37
New York *Daily News:* 4; Gerald Ford front page, x, **31**, 32
New York *Herald-Tribune*, 12, 21, 23, 26, 31, 74, 146
New York *Journal-American,* 21
New York *People's Voice* newspaper, 65
New York Philharmonic: xvi; and American soloists, 143; and Marian Anderson, **43**, 47; avant-garde music, 23, **145**, 145–47, 200, 202–3; and Copland, 203, 204; discrimination charges against, 48, **49**; general survey of American Music, 140–43; and guest conductors, 138; history of, 136–40; integration of, 45–48; at Lincoln

Center, 28–29, 99; and Mahler, 90–91, 138, 149–50, 181–82, 182–85; Mahler as conductor, 136, 138, 182; Mahler festival (1959–60), 144, 174, 182–85; Music Policy Committee, 136, 139, 143; press and reviews, 136, 138–39, 143, 185; programing, **134**, 136, 138–40, 143–44, 153; recording and DVDs, 140, 149, 164; and Wagnerism, 136, 138, 144

New York Philharmonic (and Leonard Bernstein): *Candide* revival (2004), 70; debut, 3–5, 63; as Laureate Conductor, 150, 164; as Music Director, 4, 7, 45, 51, 80, 90–91, 135–36, 139–51, 165; performing Bernstein's musical compositions, 203–4; programming, **134**, 136, 138–40, 143–44, 153; recording and DVDs, 149, 164

New York Philharmonic (touring): 102; Berlin 1960, xiii, xiv, 102–15, 118, 131–32, 132–33; City Hall welcome (1959), **28**; and Cold War diplomacy, 117–33; Latin America, **118**, 118, **119**, 119-24, **122**; Latin America, return from (1958), 16, **18**; Jonathan Rosenberg on, 117–33; Soviet Union and Eastern Europe (1959), xiii, **117**, 118, 124–29, 168

New York Philharmonic Archives, xiv, xvi, 160

New York Philharmonic Young People's Concerts with Leonard Bernstein: **8**, 47–48, 87, 91, 97–98, 98–101; and American composers, 141–42; awards, 99; influence of, 194, 197; and Ives, 150; and Mahler, 144–45, 174, **175**, 182, 184; need for sunglasses, **87**; programming, 97, 99; rehearsal, **89**; on the radio, 97; reviews, 97, 98; script, **95**

New York Symphony Society, 182, 183

New York Times: 21, 26, 37, 39, 42, **45**, 47, 48, 54, 66, 74, 75, 81, 147, 185, 190; Howard Taubman on the New York Philharmonic, 136, 138–39; Felicia Bernstein's letter to, **55**; on Young People's Concerts, 97

New York Urban League, 37, 45–46

New Yorker (magazine): 16; "Talk of the Town," 16, 18

Newlin, Dika, 184

Nichols, Mike, 77

Nielsen, Carl: 149–50; Third Symphony, 149; Fifth Symphony, 149

1964 World's Fair (NYC), **23**

Nixon, Richard M., x, 16, 18, **123,** 123-24

O

O'Brien, Orin, **46**, 47, 158–59

Oja, Carol J.: xiii; on Bernstein's musicals, 59–75, 80-83

Olivera, Elmar, 98

Olivier, Laurence, 13

On the Town (Bernstein): x, 13, 60, 60–65, 65, 164; album cover, **13**; "Carnegie Hall Pavane," 63; "I Get Carried Away," **61**, 63; cast, **64**; integration of, 65; "New York, New York," 65; press & reviews, 60, 63, 65; "Rosie the Riveter," 63

On the Waterfront (Bernstein film score), 164

Onassis, Jacqueline Kennedy, **27**, 28, 80, 204

Ono, Yoko, 26

Ormandy, Eugene, 4, 190

Osato, Sono, **13**

Ozawa, Seiji, 110, **154**, **198**

P

Page, Tim: xiii; on Bernstein's televison appearances, 85–91, 97–101

Paik, Nam June, 26

Parker, Dorothy, 69

Parmenter, Ross, 26

de Pasquale, Robert, 104

Pasternak, Boris: **117**, 128–29; *Dr. Zhivago*, 117, 128

Pearl's Chinese restaurant, 22

Pelletier, Wilfred, 97

Philadelphia Orchestra, 138, 139

Physicians for Social Responsibility, 51

Picasso, Pablo, 21, 39

Piston, Walter, 141

Pixley, Dorothy, **24**

PM (newspaper), 63

Pons, Lily, 13

Popular Front movement, 36, 39

press: 47; and avant-garde music, 145–46; and Bernstein, 4, 5, 7, 23, 28, 31; Bernstein, reviews of, 23, 28, 31, 32, 42, 44, 50; Black Panther episode, 9, 31, 35–36, 51, 54–56, 151; music critics, 21, 26, 28; and the NY musical establishment, 26, 28; and race, 37, **45**, 47; sexism in, 47

Price, Leontyne, 66

Price, Lonny, 70

Prince, Harold, **72–73**, 74

Puccini, Giacomo (*Tosca*), 15

Pudovkin, Vsevolod, 21

Q

Quiet Place, A (Bernstein), 32, 60, 78

R

Rachmaninoff, Sergi, 90

Radio City Music Hall Orchestra, 186

Ran, Shulamit (Capriccio for Piano and Orchestra), 98

Rapee, Erno, 186

Raskin, Judith, **30**

Ravel, Maurice (Piano Concerto in G), 121

recording collecting, 22

recording session (St. George Hotel, Brooklyn Heights), 189

Red Channels, 42

Reik, Theodor, 184

Reiner, Fritz, 4, 152, 177, 194

Resnik, Regina, **30**

Rich, Alan: xi; and avant-garde music, 145; and Bernstein, 13–14, 32; on New York City, 11–15, 21–32; *So I've Heard*, 31

Riegger, Wallingford, **139**, 141

Rififi (West Berlin nightclub), 110, **112**

Rivera, Chita, 38

Riverside Church (NYC), 51, **53**

Robbins, Jerome, x, 44, **60**, 60, 66, **72–73**, 74, 75, 76, 79

Robert Saudek and Associates, 103

Robinson, Jackie, 5, 7, 47

rock'n'roll, Bernstein and, 91

Rockefeller, John D., III, **27**

Rodzinski, Artur, 4, 138, 177, 181

Rodgers, Richard/Hammerstein, Oscar: *Carousel*, 62; *Oklahoma!*, 62, 63

Rome, Harold/Auerbach, Arnold (*Call Me Mister)*, 13

Roosevelt, Eleanor, 42

Roosevelt, Franklin D., xii, 36

Rorem, Ned, 66, 141

Rosenberg, Jonathan: xiii; on Bernstein's NYP tours, 117–33

Rounseville, Robert, 69

Royal Danish Orchestra, 149

Rózsa, Miklós, 3

Ruggles, Carl, **139**, 141

Russell, Rosalind, 66, **67**

Russo, William, 141

S

Saddler, Donald, 66

St. Patrick's Cathedral: Robert Kennedy's funeral, **184**, 188

Salzman, Eric, 26

Saudek, Robert, 95, 103

Schelling, Ernest, 91, 97

Schiff, David, 82

Schiøtz, Aksel, 21

Schippers, Thomas, 149

Schoenberg, Arnold, 138, 145, 150, 203

Schonberg, Harold C., 21, 26, 28, 52, 81, 97

Schor, Resia, 179

Schuman, William: **24**, 121, 140, 203, 205; *American Festival* 140, 205

Schumann, Robert: 3, 151, 165; *Manfred Overture*, 3; First Symphony, 165

Schwartz, Stephen/Tebelak, John-Michael (*Godspell*), 82

Scott, Norman, **30**

Second Symphony (*Age of Anxiety*) (Bernstein), 197, 204

Seidl, Anton, **136**, 136, 138, 142, 144

Senate Permanent Subcommittee on Investigations, 69

Sessions, Roger, 141, 142, 203

Shakespeare, William (*Romeo and Juliet*), 74, 75, 79

Shanet, Howard, 184

Shapero, Harold, 153

Sharaff, Irene, 69

Shaw, George Bernard (*Pygmalion*), 70, 77–78

Sheehy, Gail, 31

Sherman, Robert, 159

Shostakovich, Dmitri: 97, **147**; Bernstein and, 149–50, 127–28, 129, **129**; Fifth Symphony, 128, 129; Seventh (*Leningrad*) Symphony, 127–28, 149, 168–69

Sibelius, Jean, 97, 149–50
Siccama, Ellen, 18, 54
Sigma Alpha Iota awards for the Young
People's Concerts, 99
Sills, Beverly, 28
Simon, Henry, 63
1600 Pennsylvania Avenue (Bernstein): 32, 57, 60, 78, **82**, 82–83; "Duet for One," 83; political subtext, 83; "Take Care of This House," 83
Smith, Oliver, 60, 74
Solti, George, 144
Sondheim, Stephen: x, 44, **72–73**, 74; *Pacific Overtures*, 83
Sophocles (*Oedipus Rex*), 13
Soria, Dorle, 15
Soulé, Henri, 22
Sousa, John Phillip (*The Stars and Stripes Forever*), 16, **17**, 18
Soviet Union: New York Philharmonic tour of (1959), xiii, **117**, 118, 124–29,168
Special International Program for Cultural Presentations, 118
Stapleton, Maureen, 65
Star-Spangled Banner, **33**
Steinberg, William, 144
Steinem, Gloria, 26 , 31
Stern, Isaac, 28, 49, 52
Stevenson, Adlai, 42
Stokowski, Leopold, 14, 62, 139, 144, 182, 194
Stransky, Josef, 136, 182
Strauss, Richard: 87; *Also Sprach Zarathustra*, 99; *Elektra*, 87
Stravinsky, Igor: 90, 97, 110, **144**, 145, 150, 194; "Infernal Dance" from *The Firebird*, 110
Streisand, Barbra, 50
Styne, Jule (*Gentlemen Prefer Blondes*), 62
Studio One, 93
Sweets restaurant, 31
Sydney Opera House, 167
Symphonic Dances from *West Side Story* (Bernstein), 205
Szell, George, 47, 197

T

Tanglewood, 193, 208
Taubman, Howard: 26, 28; on the New York Philharmonic, 138–39, 143

Taylor, Laurette, 13
Tchaikovsky, Pyotr Ilyich: 90, 97, 110; Fifth Symphony, 110; Sixth (*Pathétique*) Symphony, 159, 166, 167, **167**
televison (and classical music): xiii, xiv, 86–87; Bernstein and, 85–91, 92–95, 97–101; CBS *Omnibus*, **84**, 87, 87–88, 88, 90, 95; Metropolitan Opera telecasts, 87; NBC Symphony Orchestra, 86; Toscanini and, 86; *Young People's Concerts*, **8**, 47–48, 87, **86**, **89**, 91, **95**, 97–98, 98–101, 141–42
Temple Mishkan Tefila (Roxbury, MA), 36
Théâtre du Châtelet (Paris), 70
Third Symphony (*Kaddish*) (Bernstein), 31
Thomas, Theodore, 91, 136, 138
Thomas Alva Edison awards for the Young People's Concerts, 99
Thomas, Michael Tilson, 99–100, 197
Thompson, Randall, 141
Thomson, Virgil: 21, 26, 28, 66, 86, 141; Thomson/Stein, Gertrude (*Four Saints in Three Acts*), 66
Tokyo New Symphony Orchestra, 190
Toscanini, Arturo, xvi, 4, 86, **136**, 136, 138, 194
Tourel, Jennie, 4
Tovey, Donald Francis, 184
Town Hall, 4
Tristano, Lennie, 75
Trouble in Tahiti (Bernstein opera), **62**, 65–66
Truman, Harry S., 39
Tucci, Gabriella, **30**
Tudor, David, 22
Turkovic, Milan, 157
Twain, Mark, 196

U

"Unanswered Question, The" (Bernstein), 100, 145
United Nations Children's Emergency Fund, 49

V

Vacchiano, William, **158**
VanDruten, John (*I Remember Mama*), 13
Varèse, Edgard, 26, 141
Varga, Lazlo, **158**

Velis, Andrea, **30**
Verdi, Giuseppe (*Falstaff*): 29; Metropolitan Opera, program, **30**, rehearsal, **30**
Veterans of the Abraham Lincoln Brigade, 39
Vienna Philharmonic: 101, 151, 163–64, 176, 190; Bernstein's Mahler recordings, 190–97
Vietnam War protests: xii, 50–51, **53**; Another Mother for Peace, **50**; Broadway for Peace, 50
Voltaire (*Candide*), 74
von Karajan, Herbert: xvi, **57**; Nazis, involvement with, 56

W

de Waart, Edo, 98
Wagner, Richard: xvi, 3, 12, 136, 138, 144; *Die Meistersinger*, 3, 12,
Wagner, Robert F., **19**
Wall Street, x
Wallace, Henry, 39
Walter, Bruno, 3, 4, 22, 144, 177, · 181, 197
Warfield, William, 66
Watergate scandal, 83, **83**
Watts, André, **44**, 47, 98
Weber, Carl Maria von, 136
Webern, Anton von, 97, 138, 146
Weill, Kurt/Blitzstein, Marc (*The Three Penny Opera*), 37
Werfel, Franz, 178
West Berlin Music, Drama, and Arts Festival, xvi, 102
West Side Story (Bernstein): x, xvi, 42, 44–45,60, **74**, 74–75, 76, 80, 90, 150, 204; "Cool," 75; "Dance at the Gym," 75; "Gee, Officer Krupke," 75; handwritten score, **71**; "Mambo," 75-79; "One Hand, One Heart," 75, 80; out-of-town tryout, **58**; political subtext, 74–75; production team, **72–73**; reviews, 74; setting, **78–79**; "Something's Coming," **71**; Symphonic Dances from *West Side Story*, 205; "Tonight," 75
West Side Story (film): opening, **15**
White, Donald, 47
Whitehead, Robert, **25**
Wilbur, Richard, 69
Williams, Tennessee: 65; *The Glass Menagerie*, 13; *27 Wagons Full of*

Cotton, 65
Willson, Meredith (*The Music Man*), 75, 80
Wolfe, Tom: 26, 31; Black Panther episode, 9, 31, 32, 35–36, 51, 52, 54–56
Wolpe, Stefan: 146–47; First Symphony, 146–47
Wonderful Town: 66–67, **67**, 68–69, 76; "Christopher Street," 69; "Conversation Piece," 67; "Self-Expression," 69; political subtext, 69; press, 66; "What a Waste," 67, 69
women's rights; Bernstein and, **46**, 47
Wood, Natalie, 80
World Peace Conference (1949), 51
Wummer, John, 168

X

Xenakis, Yannis, 26

Y

Young People's Concerts. *See New York Philharmonic Young People's Concerts with Leonard Bernstein*

Z

Zeffirelli, Franco, 30
Zirato, Bruno, 4, 138, 139

2/09

DATE DUE

OCT 11 2008	FEB 17 2009
NOV – 4 2008	FEB 25 2009
NOV 12 2008	
	MAR 11 2009
DEC 16 2008	
	MAY 17 2010
FEB 02 2009	

BRODART, CO.   Cat. No. 23-221